OXFORD MEDICAL PUBLICATIONS

Eating disorders

THE FACTS

ALSO PUBLISHED BY OXFORD UNIVERSITY PRESS

Eating Disorders

THE FACTS

Third Edition

SUZANNE ABRAHAM
Department of Obstetrics and Gynaecology
University of Sydney

and

DEREK LLEWELLYN-JONES
Consultant Emeritus, St Margaret's Hospital, Sydney.
Lately, Department of Obstetrics and Gynaecology
University of Sydney

Oxford   New York   Tokyo
OXFORD UNIVERSITY PRESS
1992

Oxford University Press, Walton Street, Oxford OX2 6DP

Oxford New York Toronto
Delhi Bombay Calcutta Madras Karachi
Petaling Jaya Singapore Hong Kong Tokyo
Nairobi Dar es Salaam Cape Town
Melbourne Auckland
and associated companies in
Berlin Ibadan

Oxford is a trade mark of Oxford University Press

Published in the United States
by Oxford University Press, New York

A catalogue record for this book is available from the British Library

Library of Congress Cataloging in Publication Data
Abraham, Suzanne.
Eating disorders : the facts / Suzanne Abraham and Derek Llewellyn-Jones. — 3rd ed.
p. cm. — (Oxford medical publications)
Includes bibliographical references and index.
1. Eating disorders.   I. Llewellyn-Jones, Derek.   II. Title.   III. Series.
RC552.E18A27   1992   616.85′26—dc20   91-47619
ISBN 0 19 262199 8
ISBN 0 19 262198 X (pbk)

Typeset by Downdell Ltd, Oxford
Printed and bound in Great Britain
by Biddles Ltd
Guildford and King's Lynn

Preface and Acknowledgements

Although we have written this book jointly, most of the clinical aspects reported are based on Suzanne Abraham's work in an Eating Disorder Unit. When we write *our* patients, we really mean *her* patients. Derek Llewellyn-Jones's main involvement has been in the sections relating to obstetrical and gynaecological issues and in the chapter on obesity.

The third edition of *Eating disorders – the facts* could not have been written if we had not had discussions with our colleagues and friends. They include Dr Janice Russell, Dr Michael Mira, Dr Wendy King, Dr George Ramsey Stewart, Ms Helen Storey, Sister Gloria de Martin Butler, and the staff of the Eating Disorders Unit at the Northside Clinic, Greenwich, New South Wales.

Most of all we thank our patients. Without them there would be no book. We would particularly thank those patients who permitted us to use their letters or tape recordings (appropriately modified for reasons of privacy) for the case histories and quotations.

We should also like to thank Edward McLachlan for drawing the illustrations on pp. 64, 103, and 142.

Note

Because of the problems of gender in the English language, we have had to decide whether to use 'he' or 'she' when referring to people. We feel that to use 'person' in each instance is distracting. As we treat more women than men, and as more women than men develop eating disorders, we have chosen to use she rather than he in all instances. The reader should not deduce that we have any sexist bias.

In this book a 'binge' refers to an episode of compulsive overeating, not a drinking bout. We have used the term as our patients describe their eating behaviour as 'bingeing' or binge-eating.

In many countries the metric system of weights and measures is replacing the older 'imperial' system. We have chosen to express weights as follows: kilograms, pounds, and stones and pounds. We have expressed heights in metres and in feet and inches. This should help readers who find difficulty with the metric system.

Sydney   S.A.
January 1992   D.L-J.

Contents

The nosology of insanity, the etiology, the symptomatology, pathology, diagnosis, prognosis, the care—how nicely the textbooks classified everything! How accurately they defined the idiot, the cretin, the imbecile, the epileptic, the hysteric, hypochondriac, and neurasthenic. Instead of admitting that little was known about what went on in the human brain, either healthy or sick, the professors stacked up Latin names.

from *The Estate*
Isaac Bashevis Singer

1

Adolescent eating behaviour

If I was going to get a job when I left school, I felt I had to be half a stone lighter. All my friends were dieting but my mother disapproved. She said it was puppy fat which would disappear. I knew it wouldn't, so I had to pretend I was not hungry because I wanted to be slim.

For most of recorded history a woman was seen as desirable when her body was plump due to the deposition of fat on her breasts, hips, thighs, and abdomen. It was fashionable to be fat. The cultural belief that to be fat was to be attractive was due to the uncertainty of food supplies in pre-industrial and early industrial societies, to the irregular occurrence of famines, and to the effects of pandemics which eliminated large numbers of farm labourers. A curvaceous female body indicated that the husband (or father) was prudent, efficient, and affluent. It also indicated that the woman had sufficient energy stored in the form of food in her larder to protect her family and in the form of fat on her body to protect herself in times of scarcity.

In the past 75 years, with abundant food supplies and good food distribution in many of the developed nations of the Western world, almost for the first time in history slimness has begun to become fashionable. This is documented in fashion magazines, in records of the 'vital statistics' of women winning beauty contests, and in books about diet which now appear at least every year. For the past three decades the public perception has been that a woman is attractive, desirable, and successful when she is slim. A study of the vital statistics of *Playboy* centre-folds and of competitors in the finals and the winners of the Miss America Pageant Contest over the past 25 years shows that, although the preferred breast size has varied, and there has been a slight increase in the height of the women, their weights have decreased and are below the average of American women of similar age and height.

Over the same period, articles on 'new and exciting' diets (often nutritionally inadequate and occasionally dangerous) have appeared at regular intervals in women's magazines, and the number is increasing. The publication of 'new and revolutionary' diet books is also increasing.

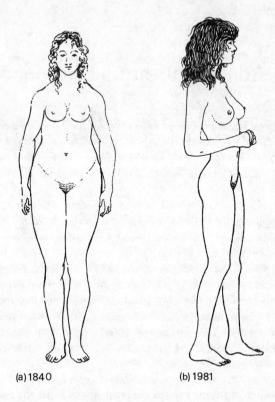

(a) 1840   (b) 1981

Fig. 1. The changing fashion in women's figures. The first illustration is taken from an obstetrical textbook printed in England in 1840, the second from a textbook produced in 1981.

Most people living in the developed nations also receive a constant stream of impressions from television commercials which use young, attractive, and lissom women to advertise products as diverse as soft drinks, security investments, cars, cigarettes, computers, fast foods, floor polishers etc.

The messages from the media stress how desirable it is for women to be young and to be or to become thin. These messages particularly influence teenage women at a period when they are undergoing emotional stress as they seek to achieve independence from their parents, to compete with their peers, and to find their identity. Adolescence is a time of concern about body image. Achieving the ideal body image is thought to ensure success and happiness.

In late childhood hormonal changes trigger an increase in height in girls and boys. The increase, or growth spurt, occurs at an earlier age in girls than boys and is achieved by the child increasing the amount of food he or she eats. In girls the onset of the growth spurt precedes the onset of menstruation and overlaps its establishment at an average age of 12½ years. There is a wide time range in the onset and duration of the growth spurt and the peak may be reached by girls as early as age 10 or as late as age 15 years. The growth spurt is accompanied by marked changes in the bodily appearance of the two sexes, which in turn are dependent on the sex hormones which are now being produced in the girl's ovaries or the boy's testicles. Both sexes show an increase in muscle bulk but this is much more marked in males. Girls have a particularly large spurt in hip growth and, in contrast to boys, do not lose fat during the growth spurt. In fact, girls have a general tendency to increase their body fat, particularly on the upper legs, as they cease to gain height. Fat is also deposited beneath the skin, in the breasts and over the hips. Obviously the amount of fat deposited is related to the energy absorbed from the food the girl eats and is influenced by the hormonal changes which are occurring at this time. Energy intake from food is limited by the person's appetite. During early adolescence, unknown factors stimulate the teenager to eat more, with the consequence that the energy intake for females reaches a maximum during the age range of 11 to 14, at a time when her energy needs are great. From about the age of 14, a teenage girl's energy needs fall, but if she continues to eat the same amount as she has been eating she will absorb an excess of energy which will be converted into fat, and she will become fat. She has to control her food intake, in order to control her weight (Figs. 2 and 3).

This is the adolescent female's dilemma. She may wish to remain thin or to become thin, because cultural norms expect her to be thin, or she may reject those norms, either because of conflict within herself or within her family, or because she enjoys and finds emotional release in eating. If she chooses to become and remain thin, she has to learn new eating habits, because she will inevitably become fat if she continues eating the quantity of food she has become used to eating. Her perception of her body is important to her psychological well-being. She may see her body as large and overweight compared with those of fashionable and popular media personalities. It is significant that, in contrast to older women, adolescent girls perceive their bodies part by part, noting par-

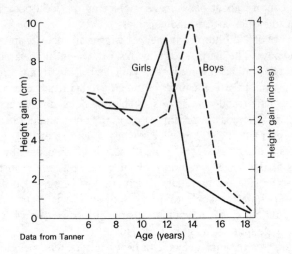

Fig. 2. The 'spurt' in growth at puberty.

ticularly the size and shape of their breasts and the size of their thighs, bottom, hips, and abdomen. The thighs are particularly vulnerable to an overperception of size—the girl perceiving her thighs as larger and uglier than they usually are.

The overperception of body size is found amongst teenage girls in many countries. In a Swedish study of the entire female population of a small town, 26 per cent of 14-year-olds perceived themselves as fat; and among the 18-year-olds, over 50 per cent reported that they were fat. In the USA in the late 1970s a study of 1000 teenagers attending high school showed that the girls were particularly preoccupied with their body shape and their weight. About half of them classified themselves as obese, although anthropometric measurements showed that only 25 per cent were obese by the criteria used by the authors, which were based on standard US weight, height, and age tables.

Fifteen years later, 2500 teenaged women aged 15 to 18 were surveyed. There had been little change in perceptions about body shape and weight and attitudes to being fat. Forty-three per cent of the girls perceived themselves as overweight and 31 per cent feared that they looked fat. Eighty-two per cent wanted to lose weight, 39 per cent worried about overeating and 18 per cent were fearful they would gain weight.

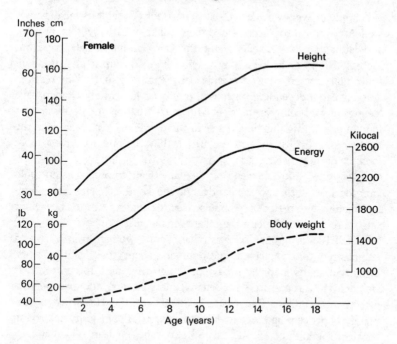

Fig. 3. Energy intake and growth of adolescents.

Faced with this preoccupation about their body shape and weight, it appears that between one-third and two-thirds of all teenaged women in the USA and similar developed countries, go on diets and one woman in six diets 'seriously'.

In Britain in 1976 an investigation of the eating habits of 16- to 17-year-old teenage girls showed that their eating behaviour could be described as disturbed. The amount of food eaten daily varied fourfold. The daily swings of food intake were super-imposed on a monthly pattern. Energy intake, mainly of carbohydrates, tended to increase in the week prior to menstruation and to decline following menstruation. At intervals after a period of strict dieting (usually by restricting carbohydrates) the girls would eat large quantities of food over a short period of time, choosing mainly carbohydrate-rich foods. In other words they were compulsive or binge-eaters. It is not possible to use these data to generalize about adolescent eating behaviour in other countries; this pattern of eating may have been peculiar to London teenagers at that time.

A study in Sydney made five years later showed that Australian female students aged 18 to 22 decreased their intake of carbohydrate, protein, and fat, and hence of energy, in the early premenstrual period but increased their intake in the day or two before and during menstruation. Individual women showed a wide daily variation in food intake, the amount eaten depending on how the women felt. Many women have feelings of well-being in the week after menstruation and decrease their food intake during this time. Later in the menstrual cycle, that is in the two weeks after ovulation has occurred, they feel hungry and eat more food, or even start binge-eating.

The Sydney study showed that the daily quantity of food eaten could vary fourfold. In the Swedish study, one-third of the teenage girls alternated dieting with periods of compulsive eating, and such eating behaviour was more common among the older teenage girls.

In 1981, four groups of Australian young women aged 15 to 25 volunteered to complete a questionnaire about their eating habits, menstrual status, and the behaviour which they used to control their weight. The groups were students, ballet dancers, anorexia nervosa patients, and bulimia (binge-eater) patients. Of the 106 students surveyed, 94 per cent had tried to diet at some time, the majority first trying between the ages of 13 and 18. Seventy-nine per cent said that they wanted to be a little or a lot lighter in weight and 31 per cent said that they had difficulty in controlling their weight.

Six years later another study of Australian women aged 19 to 29 showed that over 50 per cent had experienced difficulty in controlling their weight at some time. Four out of every ten teenagers considered that they had an on-going problem of weight control and one in three felt that the problem interfered with their daily lives. Like the Swedish and the American teenagers and young women, most of the Australian women wanted to lose weight from their thighs, bottom, hips, and abdomen (Table 1). Sixty-three per cent of the Australian young women said that they had episodes of overeating when they 'couldn't stop', in other words they had episodes of binge-eating. Eighteen per cent of the teenagers aged 15 to 18, and 23 per cent of the women aged 18 to 26 were habitual 'binge-eaters'. One woman in ten, aged 18 to 26 considered that binge-eating was a great problem for them. To control their weight most of the Australian young women avoided eating between meals, took energetic exercise, kept busy to avoid the temptation to eat, missed out one (or more) meals each day, chose low-calorie foods, or one of the other methods shown in Table 2.

Table 1. Areas of the body from which women want to lose weight

	1981 study	1987 study
	Per cent of women	
Thighs	64	75
Bottom	45	65
Hips	43	80
Waist/stomach	22	80
Legs	20	
Face	9	
All over	9	
Breasts	6	
Arms	6	

Table 2. Weight-losing behaviour used by 106 normal healthy women aged 15–25

	Per cent using
Avoiding eating between meals	78
Exercising alone	75
Dieting ('own' diet)	55
Avoiding eating breakfast	48
Keeping busy to avoid temptation to eat	46
Selecting low-calorie foods	41
Counting calories	34
Avoiding situations where food present	25
'Dieting with a friend'	22
Using illness as an excuse not to eat	21
Exercising with a friend	20
Drinking water before eating	18
'Natural' laxatives	16
Lying about amount of food eaten	16
Weighing self several times daily	15
Smoking cigarettes	14
Following a diet (from a magazine)	12
Keeping the larder empty	12
Avoiding eating with the family and 20 other methods	10

These weight-control strategies are similar to those used by women to resist binge-eating and are chosen by women diagnosed as having anorexia nervosa and bulimia nervosa.

Information obtained from several Western countries confirms that a preoccupation with body shape and size is common amongst young women, who try to change their body shape and size by using one or more of the methods shown in Table 2.

Teenage women first become aware of their body shape and weight, on average, at the age of 14.6 years. About a year later, many young women start trying simple and safe methods of weight control, such as not snacking between meals and exercising. By the age of 16.4 years young women may start on a diet which they believe will be successful in enabling them to lose weight.

Most women diet for shorter or longer periods, with about a quarter of those who diet doing so 'seriously'. Some women (14–30 per cent) fast for periods of time, usually a day or two, to try to reduce their weight quickly. Some women (25–65 per cent) exercise to lose weight and to change their body shape. About three women in every hundred self-induce vomiting, and between 1 and 5 per cent abuse laxatives.

By the age of 17 the minority of adolescent women who are having serious problems with eating, body shape, and body weight, recognize the fact. These women try the various methods of weight control just mentioned but the frequent use of dangerous methods of weight control, such as self-induced vomiting and laxative abuse, do not start until the young woman is aged 18.6 on average, and if chosen most young women will have used one or more of them by the age of 22.

As well as restricting food intake and exercising to lose weight, a number of women (variously reported as 14 to 46 per cent) go on eating binges, usually starting at about the age of 18.

Young women in Western societies are subjected to enormous pressures to be 'trim, taut, and tanned'. Television advertising and 'soap operas' portray the heroines as slim, young, and beautiful. The cinema, women's magazines, and popular newspapers further encourage the belief that to 'succeed' women should be slim. In these circumstances it is not surprising that a preoccupation with body shape and size is widespread amongst young women. The expanding 'weight-loss' industry is thriving. Each year considerable numbers of paperback books extol an 'exciting' new diet. Often these diets are nutritionally unsound. Some are dangerous to health. Women's magazines publish articles about diet in almost every issue. The efficacy of the diet books and articles in helping the reader achieve and maintain a reduced weight is questionable as new diets appear so frequently, and disappear as frequently, to be superseded by another 'fad' diet. It seems that the 20th century female desires a miracle diet which is effective, painless psychologically and physically, and can be adopted with no disturbance to her life-style. No such diet exists or can exist. Because of this, many women diet for a while then stop and, after an interval, start a new 'guaranteed' diet. This cycle of yo-yo dieting may continue over a number of years. Recent evidence from the United States suggests that the more diets a person tries the harder it becomes to lose weight. There is also a suggestion that these people are also at a greater risk of having a heart attack in middle age.

In spite of a constant barrage of propaganda extolling slim bodies among young people, and in spite of a constant stream of information about diets, the eating behaviour of many adolescent women is such that their weight fluctuates within the 'desirable' range for their height. However, the messages to be slim and successful induce many young women to diet. The dietary restriction often results in episodes of over-eating or binge-eating.

As we have mentioned, studies reported from Britain, the USA, and Australia show that up to one-third of adolescent women try periods of fasting to control their weight, and one-third of young women binge-eat from time to time. One woman in ten induces vomiting periodically as a means of controlling her weight.

A smaller proportion of young women choose a method or more than one method of weight control which may increase the health risks to the woman. These are some 'fad' diets, starvation, self-induced vomiting, laxative abuse, diuretic and slimming tablet abuse, and smoking.

The safety of 'fad' diets, meal substitutes, and commercial weight-loss programmes depends to a large extent on the person who chooses one or more of the methods. For example, a 'fad' diet which is nutritionally inadequate or dangerous, is harmless if the woman abandons it after a few days; and a commercial weight-loss regimen which is nutritionally sound becomes potentially dangerous if the user seeks to increase her weight loss by alternating the diet with periods of starvation.

Laxative abuse and self-induced vomiting are potentially dangerous methods of weight control. Laxative abuse, that is taking more than twice the recommended dose at least once a week for more than three months, may cause dehydration and in a few cases electrolyte disturbances. As more women have become aware that taking laxatives is an ineffective method of weight control, its use is declining. A recent survey showed that only 2 per cent of women aged 18 or less were using laxatives to control their weight compared with 5 per cent a decade ago.

In contrast, self-induced vomiting seems to be increasing and is being started at a younger age, as early as 13 years in some cases. Most teen-agers who use self-induced vomiting to control their weight do so infrequently, but one teenage woman in 20 induces vomiting more than once a week. Self-induced vomiting may cause dehydration or may damage the girl's teeth as the acid vomit eats into the tooth enamel. It occasionally leads to vomiting blood (haematemesis).

At a time when the health risks of smoking are becoming increasingly apparent, the use of cigarette smoking by young women as a method of weight control has emerged. Some young women start cigarette smoking and some older women continue smoking to control their body weight. Studies have shown that 14 per cent of young women who smoke, do so to control their body weight. In a study of pregnant women we conducted in 1989, we found that 4 per cent of the pregnant women continued to smoke during pregnancy in order to control their weight gain, in spite of having been advised not to smoke. Women with an eating disorder, particularly bulimia nervosa, may find it difficult to stop smoking as they fear that if they do their weight will increase.

They have reason to be worried as most women gain weight after ceasing to smoke. A study made in the USA of a large national sample compared the weight gain of continuing smokers with that of people who had quit smoking over a ten-year period. The Body Mass Index or BMI (see page 18) of women smokers increased from 25.5 to 26.5, whilst that of women who had quit smoking increased from 25.5 to 28.0. The average weight gain over the ten-year period among the women who had ceased to smoke was 3.8 kg and among the men 2.8 kg.

The study did not show when most of the weight gain occurred amongst the women who had quit smoking. If the weight gain occurs over a short period of time after giving up smoking, as many women believe it does, it may not be acceptable to them and may prevent them from quitting smoking.

Those people who were under the age of 55 and who smoked 15 or more cigarettes a day were more likely to gain weight. The authors of the study concluded: 'Weight gain is not likely to negate the health benefits of smoking cessation, but its cosmetic effects may interfere with attempts to quit'.

We believe that this is especially so among women who have an eating disorder.

Why tobacco smoking results in an artificially lowered weight is not known. It may be that smoking is a psychological substitute for eating. Other suggestions include: the possible effect of nicotine as an appetite suppressant; its possible action in preventing absorption or breakdown of certain nutrients from the gut; or its possible stimulatory effect on the nervous system.

The effects on health of the potentially dangerous methods used by people who have anorexia nervosa or bulimia nervosa are discussed in more detail in the appropriate chapters of the book.

A few young women follow a period of very restricted eating by an episode of gross overeating. This pattern may lead to a loss of control over their eating behaviour and may result in the development of compulsive binge-eating, or bulimia nervosa, which may disrupt the life of the woman considerably and, if dangerous methods of weight control—self-induced vomiting and laxative or diuretic abuse—are used, may lead to serious illness.

Other young women are so concerned about losing control of their eating behaviour that they starve themselves and start on a relentless pursuit of thinness. They eat minimal amounts of food, and many use the dangerous methods of weight control mentioned earlier. The result is that they become emaciated and their menstrual periods cease. They develop anorexia nervosa.

Although these two disorders predominantly affect young women in Western countries, recent information indicates that the same problems are beginning to be seen amongst young women in Japan and some other Asian countries.

Those teenagers who choose to ignore the social pressures to become and to remain thin, and continue eating more energy than they need for their bodily functions, gain weight progressively and become obese. In fact a person who is grossly obese (see Fig. 7 on p. 19) has at least 1260 MJ (300 000kcals) of energy stored in her body as fat.

The outcome of the young woman's concern about her body shape and her disordered eating behaviour is shown in Fig. 4. The onset of the eating behavior usually starts between the ages of 14 and 16.

It should be stressed that the eating disorders outlined—anorexia nervosa, bulimia nervosa, and obesity (especially morbid obesity)—are not *illnesses* in themselves. They become illnesses when they interfere with

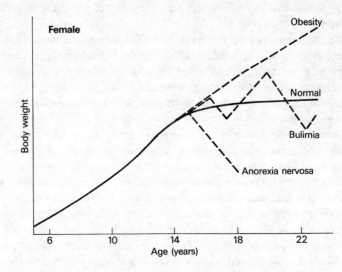

Fig. 4. The onset of eating disorders.

the person's physical or mental comfort; or if they are likely to produce severe medical complications; or disorganize the person's life to a marked degree; or so distort her or his life that those of close relatives are also disturbed and help is sought. Unfortunately, in severe cases, unless treatment is sought the eating disorder may lead to the premature death of the victim.

Pregnancy and eating behaviour

Although most eating disorder problems start in adolescence, a further challenge to some women's attitude to weight, body image, and eating behaviour may occur when they become pregnant.

We have studied the attitudes of 100 healthy pregnant women admitted consecutively to a teaching hospital to give birth to their first child. We questioned the women three to five days after the birth about their eating and weight control behaviours at any stage in their life before they became pregnant and during the pregnancy.

Before the pregnancy, the proportion of the women using methods of weight-losing behaviour, and the methods used, were similar to those used by the 106 normal, healthy non-pregnant women whose behaviours we have reported on page 7.

During the pregnancy, 71 of the women 'watched their weight', 52 reported that they were preoccupied with thoughts of food (eight reporting that this was a severe problem) and 41 women said that they had had problems controlling their weight gain. Forty-four of the women reported binge-eating (the same proportion as before pregnancy) and nine (three times as many as before pregnancy) said that they considered their binge-eating to be severe.

Because of their concern about weight gain, which may have been increased by the advice that they were receiving from their doctor, many of the women used one or more ways of controlling their weight gain. Most of the methods adopted were sensible. For example, nearly half of the pregnant women reduced their food intake modestly by choosing low energy foods, by avoiding eating between meals, by 'counting calories', or by exercising sensibly. Most of these women had used similar methods to control their weight before becoming pregnant. Eleven women adopted one or more methods of weight control which had the potential to harm their baby or themselves. Four of the 11 women took excessive exercise, four continued smoking cigarettes, three periodically starved themselves, two abused laxatives, and one woman self-induced vomiting throughout the pregnancy.

This study shows that many women who do not have an eating disorder are concerned about weight gain, body image, and eating behaviour in pregnancy.

Women with a history of an eating disorder respond to pregnancy in various ways. Some women who have anorexia nervosa may increase their weight in order to become pregnant. During pregnancy the woman may lose weight, try to gain weight, or gain weight in the expected range (10 to 13 kg) for a pregnancy. Women who have bulimia nervosa may cease binge-eating and self-induced vomiting or these behaviours may become worse. Obese women may gain a large amount of body weight, or may gain less weight than women whose pre-pregnancy weight was in the normal range or women whose pre-pregnancy weight was low (BMI less than 19).

2

Eating disorders

The human being is an open social system, each one, in its own way unique. My food problem is my somewhat unique reaction to a hoard of external and internal influences. Human beings prefer things in a state of organization, they dislike randomness and attempt to classify.

The various eating disorders are more easily discussed if the reader has a clear idea of how they are classified. In this, as in most other psychosomatic conditions, different authorities have slightly different classifications. However we can give a general definition for each disorder by putting together features most commonly described.

Anorexia nervosa

People may find it hard to believe or comprehend why a person, supposedly intelligent and quite attractive and with a good family upbringing would throw it all away for an obsessive need—no, desire!—to be slender and praised for the will power to diet so well and easily.

The term anorexia nervosa was first used by an English physician, Sir William Gull, in 1873. He described a young woman, 'Miss A', whom he had first seen seven years earlier:

Her emaciation was very great. It was stated that she had lost 33 lbs. in weight. She was then 5 st. 12 lbs. Height, 5 ft. 5 in. Amenorrhoea for nearly a year. No cough. Respirations throughout chest everywhere normal. Heart sounds normal. Resp. 12; pulse, 56. No vomiting nor diarrhoea. Slight constipation. Complete anorexia for animal food, and almost complete anorexia for everything else. Abdomen shrunk and flat, collapsed. No abnormal pulsations of aorta. Tongue clean. Urine normal. Slight deposit of phosphates on boiling. The condition was one of simple starvation. There was but slight variation in her condition, though observed at intervals of three or four months. . . . The case was regarded as one of simple anorexia.

Various remedies were prescribed—the preparations of cinchona, the bichloride of mercury, syrup of the iodide of orion, syrup of the phosphate of iron, citrate of quinine and iron, etc., but no perceptible effect followed their administration. The diet also was varied, but without any effect upon the appetite. Occasionally for a day or two the appetite was voracious, but this was very rare and exceptional. The patient complained of no pain, but was restless and active. This was in fact a striking expression of the nervous state, for it seemed hardly possible that a body so wasted could undergo the exercise which seemed agreeable. There was some peevishness of temper, and a feeling of jealousy. No account could be given of the exciting cause. Miss A remained under my observation from January 1866 to March 1868, when she had much improved, and gained weight from 82 to 128 lbs. The improvement from this time continued, and I saw no more of her medically. . . . The want of appetite is, I believe, due to a morbid mental state. I have not observed in these cases any gastric disorder to which the want of appetite could be referred. I believe, therefore, that its origin is central and not peripheral. That mental states may destroy appetite is notorious, and it will be admitted that young women at the ages named are specially abnoxious to mental perversity. We might call the state hysterical without committing ourselves to the etymological value of the word, or maintaining that the subjects of it have the common symptoms of hysteria. I prefer, however, the more general term 'nervosa', since the disease occurs in males as well as females, and is probably rather central than peripheral. The importance of discriminating such cases in practice is obvious; otherwise prognosis will be erroneous, and treatment misdirected.

Sir William was in error: anorexia nervosa patients do not have a lack of appetite. They are often hungry, but suppress their hunger and refuse to eat normally, because of their relentless desire to be thin, even to the point of becoming emaciated, and because of their fear that they will lose control of their eating behaviour.

The features of anorexia nervosa are as follows:

1. The woman is abnormally sensitive about being fat, or has a morbid fear of becoming fat, and of losing her control over the amount of food she eats. This fear induces her to adopt behaviour aimed at losing weight. Most anorexia nervosa victims drastically reduce the amount of food they eat, particularly reducing carbohydrate-containing foods (bread, cakes, sweets, sugar) and fatty foods. However, the diet which they choose usually reduces all food intake. Some anorexics use other methods of weight reduction, in addition to limiting the food they eat. The behaviours vary, but self-induced vomiting, the use of excessive amounts of laxatives or diuretics, and strenuous exercise are the most common.

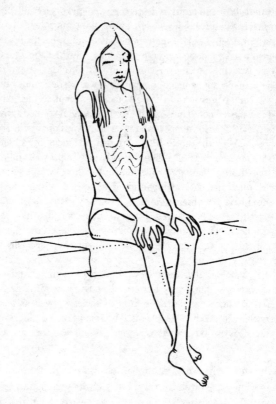

Fig. 5. A young woman suffering from anorexia nervosa.

2. A woman diagnosed as having anorexia nervosa has lost a considerable amount of weight, so that her weight is usually less than 45 kg (99 lbs, 7st 1lb). An obvious source of diagnostic error could creep in here. For example, women who have severe psychotic mental illness may believe that their food is poisoned, refuse to eat, and suffer considerable weight loss. Or the woman may be depressed and react by avoiding eating, because she cannot be bothered to eat. Marked physical diseases, such as terminal cancer and tuberculosis, may be associated with extreme emaciation. For these reasons, the woman must have no other physical or psychological illness, which might account for her loss in weight, before a diagnosis of anorexia nervosa is made. Once a physical or a mental illness has been excluded, a

woman whose weight is less than 45 kg (99 lbs, 7st 1lb) may have anorexia nervosa. However, merely to take a level of weight which makes no allowance for the person's height or age is simplistic, and doctors now tend to use a more sophisticated calculation. Three are used currently. In the first the woman is said to have lost at least 25 per cent of her 'ideal' or 'desirable' body weight, that is, the weight which falls into a range of weight-for-height calculated by insurance companies (Fig. 6). The second calculation takes into account the person's age, as well as her weight and height, and is called the Average Body Weight (ABW). It is obtained from a table prepared by the Society of Actuaries, which is printed in the Appendix (p. 192). If the woman's weight is less than 75 per cent of the ABW she may have anorexia nervosa.

The third calculation was devised in 1871 by a Belgian astronomer, Dr Quetelet, for diagnosing obesity. We believe it may be of value in reaching a diagnosis of anorexia nervosa. The *Quetelet Index*, which

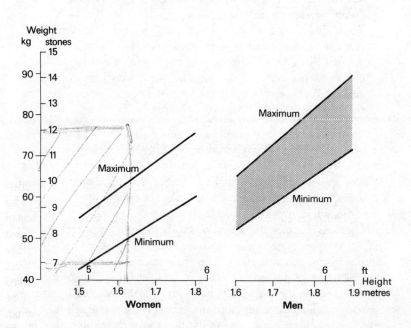

Fig. 6. Maximum and minimum ideal weights for men and women of different heights, wearing indoor clothing.

is now called the *Body Mass Index* (BMI), is calculated from the simple formula W/H^2, that is:

$$\frac{\text{weight in kilograms}}{\text{height in metres} \times \text{height in metres}}$$

The person is weighed in indoor clothing without shoes.

We have calculated the percentage of the ABW and the BMI for our anorexia nervosa patients and have found the latter to be a more precise measure of the degree of underweight or emaciation. If the person's BMI is between 19.9 and 15.1 she is underweight and, if the other criteria mentioned in this section are present, may have anorexia nervosa. If the index is 15 or below and she has no physical or mental illness she is emaciated and probably has anorexia nervosa (Fig. 7). A further advantage of the BMI over ABW tables is that the latter differ in different countries and change over periods of time. For example, the Metropolitan Life Assurance Company of New York has recently revised its tables upwards since the average weight of Americans has increased.

3. The third feature common to most descriptions of anorexia nervosa is that the woman ceases to menstruate—she becomes amenorrhoeic. Amenorrhoea may occur early in the illness before any great loss of weight has occurred, and menstruation invariably is absent in emaciated women. In fact most women cease to menstruate when their weight is in the BMI range of 17–19.

These features—a morbid fear of becoming fat; a marked loss of weight (which is not due to any physical or psychological disease), so that the woman has a BMI of 15 or less (or weighs less than 75 per cent of her ABW); and amenorrhoea—establish the diagnosis of anorexia nervosa. In addition, a woman suffering from anorexia nervosa may show other psychological or physical disturbances.

It has been claimed that a distorted body image—the woman perceiving her body as larger, wider, and fatter than it is in reality—is a specific feature of anorexia nervosa. This is inaccurate as many other women, such as pregnant women, who have recently changed their body shape, have the same distorted body-image. It is true that many severely emaciated women suffering from anorexia nervosa lose insight into how emaciated they are; in other words, they deny their thinness. These women have a grossly distorted perception of their body size. But it is also known that many women who have normal eating behaviour over-

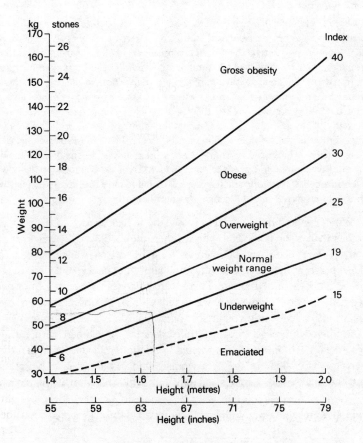

Fig. 7. Weight/height^2 index (Body Mass Index).

estimate their body size, and in some cases overestimate it considerably more than do women who have anorexia nervosa, especially when looking at their hip width and their body from the side. It is therefore unlikely that a distorted body image is a feature of anorexia nervosa, except perhaps among those who are severely ill.

It is also possible that some of the reports which say that a distorted body image is a specific feature of anorexia nervosa may be due to the patient deceiving the doctor, as in the following case history.

Case history: Clara

I've spoken to other anorexics and they realize just as I realize that at our lowest weights, we all knew we were damn thin. You'd have to be pretty stupid to think that you were not, but you have to hide it because if you let on to the doctors that you know you are thin, they will want to put weight on you. So you keep letting on you don't think you are thin but you think you are normal and they will think your way. I remember two anorexics who were so sincere to the Professor, telling him they were normal. I asked them if they felt like me, falsely sincere and secretive. They said they did. How could they think otherwise with their bones sticking out of their bottoms. The next day when I saw the Professor he said 'Clara, do you think you are thin?' My first reaction was 'see, he doesn't know, he must be dumb. Oh, I won't tell him though, because I want to stay like this: I feel safe, out of the world and men are too scared to touch me in case they break me.' So I answered him 'Of course I'm not thin.'

Women who have anorexia nervosa tend to look at parts of their body, rather than their body as a whole, when they look at themselves in a mirror. They see their abdomen as 'bulgy' and they want it to be flat. They perceive their thighs as ungainly, large, and heavy, and want them to be smooth and thinner. These perceptions also occur to normal women, as we found when we asked several groups of women the question: 'What would you prefer your weight to be?' The groups were of women who were students, ballet dancers, or women with eating disorders. Each of the groups wanted to be thinner (Table 3). When the perceptions of body image by a woman who has anorexia nervosa are further analysed, it becomes apparent that what the woman was saying

Table 3. What young women would like their weight to be

	Healthy women (106)	Ballet dancers (50)	Anorexia nervosa patients (22)	Bulimia nervosa patients (44)
	Per cent			
A lot heavier	0	1	9	0
A little heavier	1	1	50	0
Present weight	17	3	5	14
A little lighter	47	60	23	18
A lot lighter	32	30	14	64

was that when her weight was normal she saw parts of her body, for example her thighs, as too heavy, and, although she was now emaciated, she still saw her thighs as heavier and bigger than the rest of her body. In other words, although she knew that she was thin she *felt* that she was fat.

Anorexia nervosa patients have been divided into two groups. The first group, 'the dieters', lose weight by rigorously restricting their food intake (but may have episodes of abusing laxatives). The 'dieters' account for about 60 per cent of all patients. The second group, the 'vomiters and purgers', eat more food (some binge-eating) but try to prevent it being absorbed by self-induced vomiting and/or the excessive use of purgatives. In this behaviour they resemble many binge-eaters.

Bulimia nervosa

Looking back on the reason I started binge-eating, I think it was because of my obsession with dieting. And that stemmed from the fact that I thought I was overweight when in reality I was short and had inherited fatter arms and legs than the average person.

Binge-eaters are the second group of people who have eating disorders. A binge-eater can be described as a person who has a compulsion to eat large quantities of food over a short period of time, usually two hours or less. As in the case of anorexia nervosa, binge-eaters are usually female and the two illnesses have many features in common. However, although 40 per cent of anorexia nervosa patients binge-eat, many binge-eaters do not develop anorexia nervosa. In fact most binge-eaters are of normal weight or are overweight and at least 10 per cent of obese individuals go on eating binges. These facts have persuaded the American Psychiatric Association to differentiate the disorder of compulsive binge-eating from anorexia nervosa and to give the disorder the name of bulimia nervosa.

A problem in making the diagnosis of bulimia nervosa is that many people binge-eat from time to time. The difference between them and women who have bulimia nervosa is that the latter binge-eat frequently (more than twice a week) and feel that they have lost control over their eating. They have become 'foodaholics'. They divide their days into 'good' days when they have no desire to binge and 'bad' days when the compulsion to binge becomes irresistible. They are aware that anxiety, stress, or unhappiness may precipitate an episode of binge-eating.

To clarify the matter the American College of Psychiatrists has developed the criteria for the diagnosis of bulimia nervosa. The current criteria are as follows.

A person can be diagnosed as having bulimia nervosa if she or he indulges in:

(1) recurrent episodes of rapid consumption of a large amount of food over a discrete period of time (binge-eating);

(2) has had a minimum average of two binge-eating episodes a week for at least three months;

(3) has a feeling of lack of control over her or his eating behaviour during the binges;

(4) regularly engages in either strict dieting or fasting between binges, or takes vigorous exercise to prevent weight gain, and/or regularly practises self-induced vomiting, and/or uses laxatives or diuretics;

(5) has a persistent concern with body shape and weight.

Bulimia nervosa patients know that they have an eating disorder. They are fascinated by food and buy cook-books and read magazine articles about food and cooking. They enjoy discussing food and diets, and often use eating as a way of escaping from unpleasant stresses of life, to the extent that they have an all-consuming desire to eat. But they are aware that binge-eating is quite distinct from overeating. Between binges they may diet rigorously, and may try to resist the urge to binge-eat, rather as a dipsomaniac tries to resist the urge to drink. This analogy may be more exact than is obvious at first sight, as at least 20 per cent of bulimia patients abuse alcohol or drugs.

During an eating-binge (which usually lasts a few minutes or hours but may go on for days) the woman's resistance to eating fails, and she has an irresistible desire to eat. This leads her to ingest excessive amounts of food, far more than she needs to maintain good nutrition and far more than most other people in her culture normally eat. This causes her to be secretive about her binge-eating, at least in the early stages of the illness. She perceives binge-eating as a very private affair, and plans the binges secretively. It may sound bizarre, but in many cases the woman's husband, or partner, or her parents are unaware that she has been binge-eating three or more times a week for a number of years. Many of the women have a safe place where they can binge privately, and where, if they induce vomiting, they can vomit without discovery. When it becomes known by her parents, her partner, or close friends that she binge-eats, attempts to prevent her binge-eating may be met by hostility; or those close to her may condone her behaviour, in the hope that she will stop. As a woman who has bulimia is aware that binge-eating and overeating are distinct, and because she has a fear of putting on weight, she takes measures to make sure that the food she has eaten during an eating-binge will not lead to a weight increase. To achieve this she may adopt one or more of several methods. She may diet strictly or starve between eating-binges or she may exercise excessively, spending hours each day in the gymnasium, or jogging, playing squash, or swimming. If she finds that these measures do not control her weight, she may resort to a more dangerous method of weight reduction by making sure that the food she eats is not absorbed. She may achieve this by inducing herself to vomit or by taking large amounts of laxatives in the belief that the food she has eaten will not be absorbed.

More than half of bulimia patients induce vomiting during and at the end of each eating-binge, and all binge-eaters try to diet between binges, although many fail to keep to their chosen diet. A minority of binge-eaters do not induce vomiting and maintain a very strict diet between eating-binges, controlling their weight in this way. They find that eating 'anything' leads to binge-eating and they alternate starvation with binge-eating. Some bulimia nervosa patients also abuse laxatives or diuretics between binges in an attempt to keep their weight under control.

There are considerable variations in the weight-losing behaviour of binge-eaters, but, in general, 'vomiters' tend to have a longer history of binge-eating and to take more time in preparing food for the binge. They also seem to have a greater degree of 'feeling good' after a binge than non-vomiters, who are more likely to feel guilty or sad. In other words the feelings of unhappiness, anxiety, or stress which precipitated an eating-binge are relieved to a greater extent among those bulimia nervosa patients who induce vomiting than among those who use other behaviours to avoid weight gain. Some bulimic patients find that vomiting gives them so much 'relief' that they binge-eat in order to vomit.

Atypical eating disorders

Physicians who specialize in evaluating and treating patients with possible eating disorders have become aware that some of their patients have many, but not all, of the diagnostic criteria of bulimia nervosa or anorexia nervosa necessary to make a diagnosis of either. For example, some women binge-eat huge amounts of food, but only do so once a week. Other women have most of the features of anorexia nervosa, but their body weight is above the range necessary for diagnosis.

A further problem in diagnosis is that some women can be best described as 'chaotic eaters', with a seemingly unpredictable collection of eating and weight-losing behaviours. These women have no idea of 'normal' eating patterns or of the appropriate amount of food necessary for health and to maintain a steady weight.

These groups of women have been classified by the American Psychiatric Association as having an 'eating disorder not otherwise specified' but a better diagnostic term is that they have an 'atypical eating disorder'.

Women with an atypical eating disorder recognize that they have disordered patterns of eating, that they are preoccupied with thoughts of food and body weight and they are aware that their eating disorder affects and interferes with their daily life.

Some of the young women falling into this category of eating disorder may be in the process of developing all the features needed for a diagnosis of bulimia nervosa or anorexia nervosa, or may be in the process of recovering from one or other of these disorders when first seen. Other women may have avoided developing all the diagnostic criteria for anorexia nervosa or bulimia nervosa but have become obsessed with exercise. They exercise excessively and are developing an 'exercise disorder'.

Several studies have shown that 30 per cent of healthy young women in the community, when questioned, said that they had had an episode of disordered eating, and more than half of them said that they had had recurring episodes over a period of 12 months. Half of these women, when questioned, said that their disordered eating had caused them problems and 23 per cent of those aged 18 or more considered their preoccupation with body shape to be a problem. These women are more likely than the others to adopt dangerous methods of weight control.

Women with atypical eating disorders need help from health professionals and community services. Such help may prevent the development of bulimia nervosa or anorexia nervosa in the future. Their concerns should be taken seriously.

Obesity

There is considerable controversy among nutritionists as to whether obesity can be classified as an eating disorder. The problem is that people whose weight is 'normal' often eat erratically, sometimes putting on weight, sometimes losing weight. Recently a study was made of over 5000 food choices at various restaurants, snack bars, and cafés. The conclusion of the study was that the major influence on how much people ate was *where* they ate, and that obese people had as wide a range of eating behaviour as 'normal' people. On the other hand many researchers have shown that obese people choose to eat more food and eat it more quickly than non-obese people. Other researchers have argued that obesity, and particularly severe (or morbid) obesity, occurs in people with a psychiatric problem. However, a study of severely obese people in the United States showed that anxiety, depression, low self-esteem, and poor body image reported by severely obese people were a result, rather than a cause, of their obesity. The study added support to the theory that severe obesity is a habitual disturbance of eating. The experience of nutritionists who try to induce severely obese people to lose weight also suggests that obesity is an eating disorder.

The first decision a severely obese person has to make is that she wants to lose weight, either because she finds her body unattractive, or because others remark about her obesity, or because she learns that morbid obesity is dangerous to her health, or that it is aggravating an existing disease such as osteoarthritis or hypertension. The decision to lose weight induces her to consult a doctor, who offers advice and suggests a stringent diet. In most cases of obesity it is difficult for an obese person to adhere to a stringent diet, which contains less than 5040 kJ (1200 kcals) per day, because previously she has eaten at least twice and often four-times this amount of energy each day. In this she resembles a 'binge-eater'. She wants to keep to the diet but she is tempted to eat. The decision to keep to a diet becomes even harder when a severely obese person has already lost substantial weight. Every day, in every social situation, she has to make a decision, and keep to it, that she will not eat food which other people are eating freely. She knows that she should keep her weight down, for whatever reason she first chose to reduce her weight, but she finds it frustrating to do so. She begins to think about food and to plan a diet. The more she plans, the more she becomes preoccupied with food and the harder it is for her to keep to her diet. She may decide to abandon all attempts to diet, or may start binge-eating. Another choice is to seek to have some form of operation which will protect her at least partially from eating readily available food.

The main key to weight loss is the motivation to keep permanently to a strict diet. It is also evident that most obese people must have eaten more food over the years than non-obese people or they would not be so fat.

In these two respects, obesity is an eating disorder, and its correction must involve methods by which the obese person finds it 'better', psychologically and physically, to reduce weight than to remain obese. The treatment of obesity therefore involves the person in changing her eating habits.

Further evidence that obesity is an eating disorder are the comments made by severely obese patients when placed on low-energy diets. Most have adverse emotional reactions. The main problems are a preoccupation with food (65–75 per cent), irritability (60–70 per cent), nervousness (40–50 per cent), and depression (35–45 per cent). These symptoms are similar to those voiced by bulimic patients and women who have anorexia nervosa.

Obesity can be defined in several ways, some of which require complex investigations and are only practical in research. Other definitions are less complicated, and enable a person to determine if she is obese. A simple and effective method is to use the Body Mass Index (W/H^2) (see p. 18). Using the index, four groups (or grades) can be identified:

Grade 0 : W/H^2 = 19–24.9   : Normal range of weight
Grade I : W/H^2 = 25–29.9   : Overweight
Grade II : W/H^2 = 30–39.9   : Obesity
Grade III : W/H^2 = 40 or more : Severe or morbid obesity.

Generally overweight and obesity are defined as an excess of body fat, but a few very muscular men may be classified as overweight (on the W/H^2 formula) although they have no excess of body fat. However, the W/H^2 ratio of these men does not exceed 29, so they are not obese, by definition, although they may appear overweight. They can be differentiated from other overweight people relatively easily.

The grades are to some extent arbitrary, but help to emphasize that, with increasing weight, distortions of the person's life-style may occur and help may be sought. When the person's weight places her in the classification of morbid obesity, medical conditions which are potentially life-threatening become more common and help is more urgently required.

As mentioned on page 18, the formula W/H^2 can also be used to define underweight and emaciation. If this is accepted, the various ranges of BMI for late adolescent and adult women are as follows:

	BMI range
Emaciated	less than 15
Severely underweight	15.0-16.9
Underweight	17.0-18.9
Normal weight range	19.0-24.9
Overweight	25.0-29.9
Obese	30.0-39.9
Severely (morbidly) obese	40.0 or more

The prevalence of eating disorders in the community

The exact prevalence of eating disorders in the community is difficult to determine accurately. Most surveys are made of groups selected for the ease of surveying, such as women attending school, or are obtained by advertising in women's magazines. Women who have an eating disorder, particularly if it is severe, may be unrepresented in these surveys either because they do not want to disclose their problem or because they were absent from their place of study or work, or were being treated in hospital when the survey was made.

It is increasingly clear from a review of published studies, that women of all social classes and of many racial groups may have an eating disorder, and the older belief that bulimia nervosa and anorexia nervosa were almost exclusively found in middle-class women is incorrect. The prevalence of obesity is more difficult to estimate, as obesity increases with age and reaches its peak prevalence in both women and men between the ages of 50 and 70.

Current information suggests that the following figures give a reasonable estimate of the prevalence of the eating disorders in women aged 15 to 30.

Anorexia nervosa:	less than 1 per cent
Bulimia nervosa:	2 per cent (range 1–4 per cent)
Atypical eating disorder:	15 per cent (range 10–34 per cent)
Obesity:	5 per cent.

3

Why do eating disorders occur?

What made me anorexic in the first instance seems to be unimportant to what keeps me as thin as I am. I've come to the right conclusion that my anorexia is just a bad habit and a crutch for any failings I may wish to excuse myself from making.

In spite of a considerable amount of research in the past three decades no consensus has been obtained to answer the question: Why do some adolescents have an eating disorder? Four explanations have been advanced, but none of them has been proved conclusively. They are (1) the developmental and learning theory explanation; (2) the social explanation; (3) the psychological explanation; and (4) the physiological explanation. These theories are not mutually exclusive and referring to more than one may give a closer explanation.

The developmental and learning theory explanation

From the earliest days of its life the quality of care a mother gives to her baby, and the love she lavishes on the baby, are related at least indirectly to the amount of fat covering its body. A chubby baby is seen by the mother and her neighbours as a well-cared-for baby. In childhood, too, the provision of substantial amounts of food, often rich in refined carbohydrates and fat, is seen as a way of showing love for children, as well as ensuring that they are adequately nourished. In our culture, which has an abundance of food, children learn to increase progressively the amount of food they eat, and often increase the quantity of energy they ingest beyond that needed for growth, body functions, and the demands of exercise. In the three years before puberty, a biological spurt of growth occurs, and the food intake is increased still further.

Studies have shown that in boys the energy requirements for growth, and the spurt in growth, occur at about the age of 15; and because boys increase their muscle mass after this age, additional energy continues to be needed. The growth spurt in girls occurs between the ages of 12 and

14, earlier than that of boys, and the girl's energy requirements peak over the same period. By the age of 16, the girl's energy requirements have fallen considerably, as girls do not increase their muscle mass like boys. If the girl continues to eat the quantity of food she ate in early adolescence obesity is inevitable. As she becomes increasingly aware of her body weight, she learns that she can control weight gain either by dieting or by using other measures which will help her to stop her absorbing the food she eats. On the other hand, some adolescents may reject the need to control their weight and may enjoy eating, while limiting the amount of energy expended in exercise. Inevitably this will lead to obesity. Some of the adolescents who diet and control their weight successfully may become so concerned about food and about weight control that their eating behaviour escapes from what is considered 'normal', and they decide to pursue thinness—becoming anorexia nervosa victims. Some of those who diet unsuccessfully either develop bulimia nervosa or become obese.

Case history: Vera

Vera first became concerned about her weight when she was aged 14 and started dieting. However her preoccupation with food caused her to gain weight in spite of the diet she had chosen. She was teased about her body by her friends and in an attempt to lose weight effectively began taking large quantities of laxatives when she was 16. Soon after she began to abuse laxatives, her menstrual periods ceased. The next year, a series of family problems and her continued concern about her body image induced her to adhere to a weight-reducing diet (5040 kJ (1200 kcal) a day) with resultant weight loss. By the age of 18 her weight had stabilized at the level she desired and has been maintained, with fluctuations of 1–3 kg (2.2–6.6 lbs), for the past five years.

Case history: Kate

Kate began to 'watch her weight' when she was at boarding school, as did many of her contemporaries. However, the nature of the food and the discipline imposed on the students limited her ability to control her weight. She left school at 18, having graduated from high school, and became increasingly conscious of her weight. She decided that she wanted to lose weight by 'avoiding eating rubbish'. She was now at university, and began binge-eating, interspersing the bulimia with stringent dieting, which resulted in wide swings of weight. In an attempt to control her weight gain, at the age of 19 she began to self-induce vomiting and abused both laxatives and diuretics. This behaviour coincided with a decision to leave university and to move to another city to take up fashion modelling. To some extent her behaviour controlled the swings in her weight, but she continued to have episodes of binge-eating, although these became less frequent, but it was not until she was aged 24 that she achieved a body weight in the low range of 'normal'. She has since stabilized at this weight by dieting, and no longer uses potentially dangerous methods of losing weight.

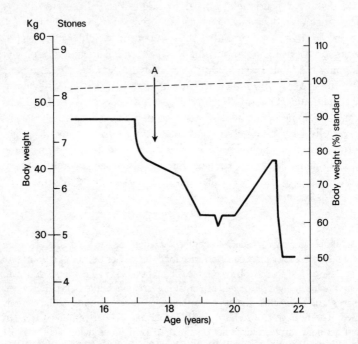

Fig. 8. Robin started dieting at the age of 14. By the age of 17 she had developed anorexia nervosa (A) and this has persisted in spite of treatment since that date.

Onset of severe weight loss can also follow a period of sensible dieting with realistic weight loss or, in some of the younger patients, it appears to occur immediately, with no prior unsuccessful or realistic attempts. On the other hand, the young women may reject the need to be or to become thin and may continue eating the quantity of food she has learned to eat and enjoys eating. If she was fat during early adolescence, the degree of obesity will increase. Obesity occurs in some families, and may be due to the family having a continuing fantasy that 'our family have always had healthy appetites and have been large people'. A child brought up in such a family is comfortable over-eating and becoming obese because she can share an identity with the other members of her family. She has no need to limit her food intake in adolescence to conform with prevailing fashions because the strong influence of her family outweighs those of prevailing fashion.

The social explanation

In Western culture two contrasting messages about food and eating are offered by society, and particularly by the media. The first message is that a slim woman is successful, attractive, healthy, happy, fit, and popular. Canadian teenagers, for example, believe that being slim will help them to be chosen for a good job, find a boy-friend, be popular with their peers, be and look fit and healthy, and get on well with their family (provided that most of the family is overweight or obese). To become slim, with all that this implies, is deemed to be a major pursuit of many women. The second message is that eating is a pleasurable activity which meets many needs, in addition to relieving hunger, and women have a right to have these needs met. In women's magazines these two contrasting messages tend to appear inextricably mixed. In nearly every issue the magazines publish 'exciting' new diets which 'guarantee weight loss with minimum discomfort or motivation', and these diets are often followed by recipes for, and superb photographs of, luscious cakes and foods with rich sauces. It is difficult to watch television without being confronted by an advertisement for a substitute diet-food alternating with a fast-food advertisement, or its equivalent. The social (and usually family) pressures are also contradictory: you must eat everything other people give you but you must not get fat.

The provision of food is seen in our culture as a major sign of caring; and sharing food at a meal is seen as one of the prime social contacts. These cultural imperatives place a burden on a mother to provide abundant quantities of food, and on her loving daughter or son to eat that food. It is not surprising that in the face of the psychological bombardment of two contradictory messages, most young women diet. Some become 'foodaholics' and develop bulimia nervosa. Others become preoccupied with food and the avoidance of weight gain, developing bulimia or anorexia nervosa. Some decide that dieting is too disturbing to their way of life and return to eating more food than they require, becoming obese. These women may also find obesity protective against acceding to current social attitudes to sexuality, which they fear. Hidden in a fat body, they give the message that they are not attractive and do not want to form a sexual relationship.

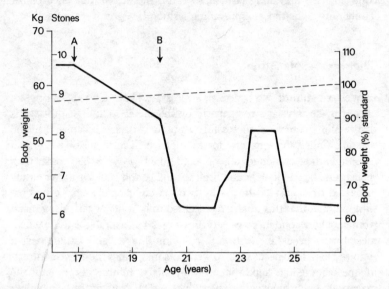

Fig. 9. Cheryl felt herself to be overweight when she was aged 17 and started dieting. At that time her weight was 110 per cent of the standard weight (A). The dieting resulted in a slow weight loss until the age of 20, when she broke up with her boy friend and had a sudden weight loss, leading to a diagnosis of anorexia nervosa (B).

The psychological explanation

Because eating is such a basic instinct it has been postulated that those people who suffer from an eating disorder have an identifiable personality, being more obsessional or neurotic than normal eaters. The *Oxford textbook of psychiatry* defines personality as 'enduring qualities of an individual shown in his or her ways of behaving in a wide variety of circumstances'. Some studies, using personality questionnaires, suggest that some women suffering from anorexia nervosa are indeed more 'neurotic' or 'obsessional' than women whose weight is in the 'desirable range'. The studies also suggest that those women who have lost weight by dieting and excessive exercise are more introverted, more anxious, and more dependent than women whose weight is normal or women with anorexia nervosa who use self-induced vomiting and purgation as methods of losing weight. No distinctive personality profiles are available for women who have bulimia nervosa or obese women.

The *Oxford textbook of psychiatry* defines an abnormal personality as occurring 'when the individual suffers from his own personality or when other people suffer from it'. The American Psychiatric Association defines a 'personality disorder' as being present when 'the constellation of behaviours or traits causes either significant impairment in social or occupational functioning or subjective distress'. Could it be that patients with eating disorders have an abnormal personality or a personality disorder?

The American Psychiatric Association has suggested a further subgroup of personality disorder which they term a 'borderline personality disorder'. For this diagnosis to be made, the person must have at least five of the following eight features: unstable relationships; impulsive behaviour that is harmful to the person (including spending, sex, substance use, shop-lifting, reckless driving, and binge-eating); variable moods; undue anger or lack of control of anger; recurrent suicidal threats or behaviour; uncertainty about personal identity; persistent feelings of boredom; and frantic efforts to avoid real or imagined abandonment. This definition may cause diagnostic problems. For example, does a young male, living in a slum neighbourhood, who shop-lifts, steals cars for joy-riding, has undue anger and is often in fights, has an unstable relationship and persistent feelings of boredom, have a personality disorder when, in his culture, these behaviours are so common that they are considered normal? This suggests that a major problem in accepting the concept of a borderline personality disorder is that it is imprecise and can depend on environmental and socio-cultural influences.

Women who are in the usual age-group for diagnosis of an eating disorder may have several of the features required for the diagnosis of a borderline personality disorder. However, in women with an eating disorder, some of the features are due to the biochemical and psychological changes (discussed later in this chapter) resulting from the eating disorder—for example, variable moods and feelings of chronic boredom. If they are added to other of the features needed to make a diagnosis of a borderline personality disorder, the total may appear to clinch the diagnosis, whilst in reality, the woman does not have a personality disorder. She may have a temporary change in her personality soon after the onset of the eating disorder, or episodically during the disorder. Such a change has been reported frequently by the family or by people with whom the woman lives.

Until a more precise definition of personality disorder has been made, all that can be said is that a woman may have both an eating disorder and a personality disorder, but not that most people who have an eating disorder have a personality disorder. Further problems about accepting a psychological explanation for the eating disorder are, first, that many women who have anorexia nervosa or bulimia nervosa have been found, after careful testing, to have a 'normal' personality and second, the personality scores of normal people and those who suffer from eating disorders overlap considerably. This may mean that the tests are too crude to identify a personality problem, or that the psychological explanation has no foundation.

Other psychological explanations have been suggested, one of which is the concept that some obese women use eating as a substitute for love. A person who feels lonely, empty, and unloved unless she has constant company may eat to compensate. The emptiness of her life is soothed if she takes food to fill her empty stomach. The more she eats the more complete and full (or fulfilled) she feels. Food, and particularly beverages such as milk or beer, become mainstays of her life, suppressing lack of self-esteem and providing satisfaction. As she becomes increasingly obese she develops a need to remain obese and so avoid the resurgence of her feeling of inadequacy.

Furthermore, according to the personality defect theory, some women suffering from anorexia nervosa have a fear of 'growing up' and of becoming physically and sexually mature. By avoiding eating, the woman's body contours become those of a prepubertal child, her menstrual periods either do not start or cease, she is able to withdraw from the social occasions which make her ill at ease and anxious, and is able to deny her sexuality. This explanation may apply to a few anorexia nervosa patients, but in most cases of eating disorders the concept does not apply.

From this it follows that although psychological factors may be involved in explaining why individual patients who have an eating disorder persist with their eating behaviour, no single psychological explanation is available.

The physiological explanation

Recent research has shown that many people who embark on a strict diet feel 'flat and down in mood'. These people have been found to have low levels of tryptophan in their blood. After eating food, particularly foods with a high carbohydrate content, the level of tryptophan in the blood is raised. The increase is due to a release of insulin following the absorption of the food, which increases the ratio of tryptophan to other amino acids.

The raised circulating level of tryptophan permits it to cross from the blood into the brain where it stimulates the production of serotonin (5-hydroxytryptamine or 5HT). The raised brain level of serotonin decreases the person's appetite and improves the person's mood.

Recently, in a double-blind, placebo-controlled study we gave tryptophan in a high dose of 3 g a day and vitamin B_6 in a dose of 50 mg a day (which is said to improve the uptake of tryptophan into the brain) to 11 women being treated for bulimia nervosa. The drug and the placebo were in identical capsules and neither we nor the patients knew which was being taken. Each woman filled in a Mood and Behaviour Questionnaire each night just before going to bed.

When the results were analysed we found that during the time that the women were taking the tryptophan, they reported an improvement in mood, less binge-eating, less overeating, and less 'picking behaviour'. In addition, when they did binge-eat the amount of food eaten was reduced. However the changes in binge-eating were small which suggests that the tryptophan theory does not in itself fully explain why people binge-eat (Table 4).

It has also been found that the changed blood tryptophan levels following a carbohydrate 'load' are of the same magnitude in women who have

Table 4. Tryptophan and pyridoxine in the treatment of bulimia nervosa (11 women studied in a randomized, crossover, double-blind trial)

	Average daily scores *	
	Women taking tryptophan	Women taking placebo
Total mood score	43.3	47.3
Binge-eating	0.32	0.52
Overeating	0.59	0.85
'Picking'	0.30	0.52
Eating out of control	0.55	0.73
Amount eaten in binge	0.41	0.78

* The lower the average daily score the more improvement shown

bulimia nervosa and women who have no eating disorder. This suggests that factors other than tryptophan/serotonin are involved in explaining why some women develop bulimia nervosa and some do not. One explanation is that some women who have bulimia nervosa overeat or binge-eat because this makes them feel relaxed or less depressed.

The tryptophan/serotonin theory may also be involved in the development and persistence of some cases of obesity. It has been suggested that some obese people are 'carbohydrate cravers' and are more likely than other people to snack on foods rich in carbohydrate in the afternoon and the evening. This would increase the levels of serotonin in the brain and they would feel 'better' after the snack. The more often they snacked, the better they would feel and the more obese they would become.

As we will discuss in Chapter 9, about obesity, a new drug, dexfenfluramine, which increases the level of serotonin in the brain, has been shown to reduce the food intake and to decrease selectively the carbohydrate content of snacks by about 40 per cent in obese 'carbohydrate cravers'.

Anorexia nervosa is more difficult to fit into the tryptophan/serotonin theory. Anorexia nervosa patients initially deny themselves eating an adequate amount of food and do not respond to the 'messages' to eat more food and feel better. If they continue to eat inadequate amounts of food for their bodily functions over a period of time, one hypothesis suggests that an increase in opioid activity occurs in their brains. This leads to an elevation of the person's mood and causes the person to continue restricting food because it makes her feel 'good'. As time passes, the elevation of mood can only be maintained by reducing the food intake further, and 'addiction' to increased brain opioids may be inevitable if withdrawal symptoms are to be avoided.

Anorexia nervosa patients who have episodes of breaking their strict diet and who have small eating binges do not reach such low weights and find it easier to gain weight than women whose eating behaviour is restrictive. The theory could explain this finding by suggesting that these women do not become so 'addicted' to high brain opioid levels and can respond, at least episodically, to the need to eat.

Exercise is also thought to cause the release of opioids into the brain and the more strenuous the exercise the greater the opioid release. The need for some people to increase the amount of exercise that they undertake can be explained by their need to maintain the release of brain opioids.

Many women who have anorexia nervosa exercise excessively when at low body-weight and during weight loss, or during and after refeeding. This behaviour may be explained by a brain opioid 'addiction'.

These theories await further clarification. If they are correct, anorexia nervosa patients may be trying to stimulate their mood and they equate euphoria with a decreased food intake. Bulimia nervosa patients and some obese patients eat because the food induces the release of brain serotonin which may improve their mood to help them relax, which they equate with increased food intake.

The combined explanation

All the explanations given in this chapter may be relevant but no single one is sufficient by itself. The developmental and learning theory explanation and the social explanation may answer the question of why eating disorders are more likely to occur in women and the onset is more likely to occur in the late teens or in the early 20s; but not why only some women develop an eating disorder, or why the eating disorder persists for many years in only a few women. Perhaps the psychological or physiological explanations may help to explain this.

What is an eating disorder? A sufferers view

One of our patients wrote this letter to her parents.

Dear Mum and Dad,

I thought that I would write this letter in an attempt to try and explain what an eating disorder actually is. From talking to you about it on various occasions I have come to realize that both of you still view an eating disorder as a diet. The truth of the matter is that we focus on food and weight so that we don't have to feel any emotions or feelings that may be uncomfortable, such as anger, sadness, anxiety, or guilt. We have been conditioned from childhood to suppress these feelings for various reasons, such as that it is not 'ladylike' to express them and that no one wants to be around someone who is upset. We may have seen people become out of control with their anger and this could have scared us into believing that's what would happen to us if we became angry. The longer we suppress these feelings the more painful it becomes and thus the more we focus on our food in a desperate attempt to block them. It soon reaches a stage when all the emotions that we feel are indeed connected to our food, weight, and shape. We grow to believe that we are void of all feelings. Inside us a big hole develops and in attempt to get out of it we either try to fill it with food by bingeing or we try to starve it away. However this hole is bottomless and will not disappear.

It is only when we come to a place like this clinic that we slowly begin to realize that our problem is not anything to do with the food we eat or avoid and that this is just a symptom of our underlying problems. It is only when these issues are discussed and help is given that the food and weight issues can become less of a problem.

One thing that I feel you do not really understand is that when we leave this clinic we are not 'better' completely. We will still have to fight hard against falling into all the old habits. Depending on how long the eating disorder has been around and on how severe it was, the time that we will take to recover will vary.

A person does not 'recover' from anorexia nervosa just because they have reached a normal, healthy weight. Unless they have managed to work on a few of the problems that led to their eating disorder they will continue to focus on the food and they may well lose all the weight they have gained.

I think that in order to get better you have to really want to—one hundred per cent! You have to get to the stage when you are so sick of all the behaviours involved with the eating disorder and want to get rid of them, that you are willing to go through whatever pain is necessary to get over—and there is pain!

A stay in a clinic is not relaxing and fun at all, like you seem to think. Because we have all blocked our emotions for so long, once we begin to eat 'regularly' and shift the focus from food, sometimes the pain that we have to feel is too much for us. It is only when you are ready, that you can work through all the emotions that have been building up inside of you over the years that the eating disorder has been around. Obviously the more years that the eating disorder has been there, the more feelings there are to get through.

I know that all of this must sound pretty confusing to you. I feel that the most important thing for you to remember is that *food* is not the problem. Most anorexics do not set out with the aim of losing weight to any extent. However once it has begun it is extremely difficult to control. Then you need help in order to stop the destructive pattern and to regain some normality in your life. So just being taught to eat properly does not mean that you can simply eat normally when you leave here.

I hope that this has helped a bit to explain what an eating disorder is. It is a bit confusing to us, so I can imagine that to non-sufferers a lot of the behaviours would be incomprehensible. Why would someone starve themselves to a near death? Why can't they start to eat when they look like a skeleton? Why don't they get to see how thin they are? I think most anorexics do realize that they are thin when they are badly underweight, but they still feel fat and big. That never changes.

Anyway that is about all I can say about what I see an eating disorder as being about. It is caused for a variety of reasons. Often it is not just one event but a chain of events that builds up the stress that has been suppressed.

The writer then goes on to explain about her personal problems, which, to preserve her anonymity, we will omit.

4

Eating disorders and sexuality

Often I used to go out and eat for my sensual sexual experience of the day. I actually would be turned on by it.

Coming to terms with one's sexuality is a major challenge facing adolescents. It appears that many women who have an eating disorder perceive an association between eating and sexuality. The sexual knowledge, attitudes, and behaviour of women with eating disorders covers a broad spectrum. This is not surprising as many are over-concerned about their body image and their relationships with others. We have found that there is an association between eating behaviour and sexual behaviour of the women we have studied. We have identified four categories: sexuality denied; unsure of sexuality; sexually passive; and sexually active.

Sexuality denied

The woman avoids challenge to her sexuality and suppresses her sexual feelings. She has negative attitudes to puberty, menstruation, masturbation, and sexual intercourse. These attitudes may be aggravated by her lack of knowledge of her genital anatomy, of menstruation, of contraception, and of sexual behaviour. She avoids reading about sexuality and is rigid and obsessional in her attitudes to life. She avoids looking at her body in a mirror, and does not touch her genitals. She uses external sanitary pads for menstrual protection and has never attempted to use tampons. Most of the women in this group have no sexual experience, and neither masturbate nor date. They become embarrassed if a discussion relates to sex, but often wish that they had a close companion. These women lose weight exclusively by strict dieting and exercise, and often are emaciated.

Case history: Clarissa

Clarissa is aged 28, is an only child, and is a highly intelligent, personable, neatly dressed woman, but rather obsessional and anxious. She finds it difficult to relate socially. She learned about menstruation when she was 13 from her mother, who was embarrassed and not very informative. Six months later she had her first menstrual period. She was ashamed and embarrassed about menstruating, and described her periods as 'messy', 'dirty', 'disgusting', and 'inconvenient'. She was unable to touch herself 'down there', and used sanitary pads, which she continues to use. She feels unable to use tampons. She received no information about sexuality or sexual intercourse from her mother, and felt unable to ask anyone else because of her shyness. She has avoided reading any books about sexuality, and says that 'there is no point because I wouldn't remember any of the information'.

At the age of 20 she had her first relationship, but it broke up after two years of courting because she believed that the man was 'making demands on her', and because she couldn't cope with his desire for heavy petting. She has since avoided any physical contact with a man. She finds it difficult to say words describing sexual functions, and found kissing 'disgusting' although she permitted her boyfriend to kiss her occasionally. The idea of sexual intercourse revolts her, particularly as she would be forced to look at and touch the man's genitals. She has a dread of exposing her body and of looking at her breasts, abdomen, or thighs in a mirror.

She began dieting soon after her relationship ended. Her object in dieting was to reduce the size of her breasts (which she saw as large and ugly although her boyfriend had complimented her on their shape) and to take weight off her abdomen. By the age of 23 she was considerably underweight and her menstrual periods had ceased. She says that she is pleased about this as she hated menstruating and she uses her thinness to avoid social situations and sexual challenges. She is 'up-tight' and fastidious in her appearance and, at work, her employer refers to her as 'a most excellent secretary'.

In the past five years she has had episodes of dramatic weight loss, due to stringent dieting alone, which have required admission to hospital for refeeding. She has never induced vomiting, having a fear of its effects, nor does she abuse laxatives or diuretics. Her rigid dieting and her sexual attitudes appear to be part of a constant preoccupation with 'self control' and a desire for perfection. She is not sure what masturbation is and would never attempt it. She denies any sexual feelings and says she has never accepted that she 'could have a libido'. However, the thought that she might be a lesbian causes her to avoid female company. She is 'disgusted' by homosexuality. She is often lonely and wishes for a male or female companion, but avoids making friends, believing herself unable to cope with an intimacy that could lead to a sexual challenge. Amenorrhoea has been 'a relief' which she hopes will continue.

Unsure of sexuality

These women appear to use their eating behaviour to delay sexual encounters until they feel that they are ready for them. The woman tends to find it difficult to form a warm, mature relationship, although she may marry, when she tends to be dependent on her husband. She is anxious to conform and has conflicts about her sexual feelings and her sexual behaviour, always trying to be what she believes is 'normal'. She is shy. She may masturbate occasionally but worries because it may not be 'right' to masturbate. If she is given reassurance that her sexual behaviour is 'normal' she begins to enjoy it. She is shy, and, although she may look at her naked body in a mirror, does not feel comfortable when doing it. She is also shy about menstrual protection and prefers sanitary pads to tampons, as she finds the latter 'difficult' to insert. Her anxiety about vaginal insertion extends to sexual intercourse, which usually first takes place at an older age than average. She believes that she is not easily aroused, but sometimes reaches orgasm either by clitoral stimulation or during sexual intercourse. She would like to learn about sexuality but is too shy to initiate a discussion.

Women in this group lose weight predominantly by dieting and exercising. If they decide to use laxatives or diuretics, they only take small quantities for short periods of time. Usually they have anorexia nervosa but may be obese.

Case history: Samantha

Samantha is aged 26 and is an attractive 'elfin' woman who is dependent on others and needs continual reassurance and approval about her relationship with both sexes. She learnt about menstruation and sexuality from a book (given to her by her mother) when she was 12 years old. She went to a boarding school run by nuns, and was worried when her menstrual periods failed to start, as all the other girls in her class were menstruating. She became increasingly anxious and apprehensive about starting to menstruate, and was embarrassed when, at the age of 15, her first menstrual period began during a dancing class. Sex education was not provided at school, but she was told that it was wrong and unhealthy to masturbate. When she tried masturbation she felt guilty and ashamed and did not repeat the experience. During her last two years at school, she dieted, unsuccessfully, with school friends, and her weight increased slightly, although it stayed within the 'desirable' range. She was self-conscious about the small size of her breasts, and the fact that whilst her school friends *needed* bras she just *wore* one.

She left school and entered university, where she began dieting. This resulted in weight loss and her menstrual periods ceased, which pleased her, saying she 'felt lucky they had stopped because she hated them'. Towards the end of the first year in university, she formed a relationship with another student. She knew herself to be sexually ignorant and although her ignorance worried her she did not seek any sexual information. She permitted nothing more than kissing in the relationship. The relationship lasted two months, and after it ended she continued to diet strictly and lose weight. When she was 20 she met her future husband. By this time she was very thin. During their four year courtship she limited sexual contact to kissing, and occasional breast fondling, although she did not enjoy this because of the small size of her breasts and her guilt. Before the marriage at the age of 24, she visited her family doctor who induced 'menstru-ation' for two cycles using hormones. She tried to use a tampon during the first episode of bleeding but reverted to pads as 'it was difficult and uncomfortable to put the thing in'. At marriage she was emaciated and fulfilled the criteria for anorexia nervosa. She had a romantic opinion about marriage and believed that once married she would 'blossom'. The first attempt at sexual intercourse was a 'dismal failure', which disillusioned her. Subsequent intercourse has often been painful and the couple tend to avoid sex. She alternates between blaming herself and her husband who she says is 'undersexed'. She has never discussed sex with him because of embarrassment and the belief that she is 'frigid'. When they have sexual intercourse, she tells him she enjoys it, and has fantasies of responding more if they could vary positions during sexual intercourse, but feels too inhibited to suggest the idea. She has never had an orgasm during sexual inter-course, but says she can sometimes reach orgasm if her husband stimulates her clitoris, although she believes it is 'not right to do it'. Her husband enjoys swimming but she refuses to go with him as she thinks she is too thin and is embarrassed about her small breasts. At times she wishes she was 'soft and cuddly' like most women.

Sexually passive

Women in this group (which includes those who have anorexia nervosa, bulimia, or who are obese) also appear to use their eating disorder to avoid having to make a sexual commitment until they want to. The woman's eating behaviour offers her a chance to place an 'intermittent moratorium' on her sexual activity. She experiences wide swings in weight, binge-eating alternating with periods of fasting or strict dieting. If she is bulimic, she rarely reaches a low weight and if she does she maintains the low weight only for a short period of time, before binge-eating and gaining weight. Between underweight and overweight episodes, women in this group become involved in sexual relationships, but are unresponsive, denying that they enjoy their experiences. Because they do not wish for a commitment they tend to choose partners who are married, and with whom a long-term relationship is not possible. In the relationship they prefer to cuddle and be held, and accept sexual intercourse to achieve this rather than because they enjoy the experience. They are able to touch their genitals and use tampons for menstrual protection, but their ability to look at their body depends on their weight at the time.

Case history: Harriet

Harriet, who is aged 25, is an attractive obese young woman who desperately wanted to lose weight in order to attract a boyfriend and to 'live a normal life'. Before she had menstruated (when she was 13 years old) her mother had told her to expect 'a brown spot on her pants' and had taken her to a 'mother and daughter night'. For two years she suffered from pain and vomiting with her menstrual periods and wished to be rid of them. She used external pads until changing to tampons when she was 18. At the age of 14 she had a brief lesbian relationship at school but felt it 'did nothing' for her. When she was 16, she decided to 'stop eating rubbish' and reduced her weight by dieting. At the age of 17 she applied for and was accepted for a teachers training course and began alternating between binge-eating and stringent dieting. In addition she abused laxatives. During the course and subsequently when teaching in primary school the eating behaviour caused at least five rapid swings in weight. She wanted to lose weight from her 'bottom, stomach, and thighs' and would look at her body in a mirror when her weight was low, but avoided looking when she was 'fat'. She dressed to camouflage her body when she was obese but not when she was thin. Over a three-month period her weight could vary from 44 kg (97 lbs, 6 st 13 lbs) to 57 kg (126 lbs, 9 st).

Throughout the six years her menstrual pattern was quite irregular and she did not bother to record when she menstruated. She considered premarital sex 'normal' and wished to lose her virginity 'as quickly as possible', in order to 'satisfy curiosity', 'to rebel against' her parents, and to achieve 'maturity'. She believed sexual intercourse was necessary to attract and keep a boyfriend. At the age of 19 she had intercourse six weeks after meeting her first boyfriend. She described her first experience of penetration as 'fantastic because of the pain'. Later experiences were not painful but 'never satisfying'. During the 12 months of her first sexual relationship her weight fluctuated within the normal range. She used the contraceptive pill throughout the relationship. She ended the relationship because of recurrence of bulimia and consequent weight increase. Renewed dieting lowered her weight but when she began binge-eating her weight continued to rise. Her second sexual contact was during a five-month stabilization of weight. She had hoped to gain a friend by agreeing to have sexual intercourse but felt obliged to terminate the relationship after renewed binge-eating. Desperation with weight gain culminated in a suicide attempt by an overdose of sleeping tablets. She has 'never really enjoyed' orogenital sex and prefers to be the recipient. She will only use a passive, supine position for sexual intercourse.

She feels guilty about masturbating and states that she has turned to binge-eating as a 'substitute'. After the commencement of treatment and an initial weight reduction she maintained her weight within the normal range for 10 months during which time she resumed sexual activity with two older, married men which she enjoyed but found sexually unrewarding. She ceased to abuse laxatives and the frequency of the eating binges was reduced from weekly to monthly episodes. The relationships were terminated during a brief episode of bulimic behaviour with a resultant rise in weight of 4 kg (9 lbs). Her weight has subsequently been stable within the normal range for six months and sexual activity has resumed.

Sexually assertive

Women in this group mirror their eating behaviour, which consists of binge-eating followed by episodes of self-induced vomiting and laxative abuse, with their sexual behaviour. They are unable to form a long-term relationship and have frequent casual sexual encounters. They usually have had their first sexual experience at an early age; they masturbate and have oral sex, but are rather negative about both of these. They talk about sex freely and have no anxiety about being naked, either when alone or with others. They tend to be histrionic, and socially active, but underlying this is a feeling of loneliness.

Case history: Brenda

Brenda is an attractive well-groomed blonde of 24 who has a rather histrionic manner. She is preoccupied with sex and likes talking and reading about it. However, she is preoccupied by doubts about her sexuality. She says she only feels feminine when her stomach is completely empty. Her mother discussed sex and masturbation with her before she went to boarding school at 12 years of age. She and a girlfriend would often explore and embrace each other in bed. She started menstruating when she was aged 14, which she described as 'unpleasant and a nuisance'; and it was associated with cramps requiring bed rest. She has continued to feel that her menstrual periods are 'hateful' and wishes she could 'do away with them'. For the first two menstrual cycles she used external pads and has since used tampons exclusively. She felt 'pressurized' into first intercourse at age 15 and found penetration painful and unpleasant. Subsequently she has enjoyed intercourse at times, including 'rough' intercourse. She sometimes reaches orgasm. She regrets having had sex outside marriage and wishes she could have been a 'virgin bride'. She has had many casual sexual partners since the age of 15. Following a 'pregnancy scare' at age 17, she developed an increased fear of pregnancy, dreading changes in body shape and the pain of childbirth, but did not use contraceptives. At age 18 she became more conscious of her weight, and dieted by avoiding 'rubbish foods'. She became engaged when she was 19, but decided she didn't really like her fiancé, and broke off the relationship. When the man married her closest girlfriend she was deeply upset and decided to move to another city where she could 'start again'. Her progress there was a disaster at first. She began binge-eating and because her weight increased she began to self-induce vomiting, and abused laxatives. She found it impossible to keep to a diet and began to drink alcohol to excess. She was very social, hated being alone and said that on her 'good days she was the life of the party'. Increased vomiting and purging led to a steady decrease in her weight. At the lower weight she became intensely preoccupied, almost narcissistic, about her appearance and the size of her abdomen, her hips, and her thighs. Because of her appearance she obtained a job as a cosmetic representative which she enjoyed. She had multiple sexual relationships and began taking the pill. When taking oral contraceptives her menstrual periods became scanty, which pleased her. By the age of 24 her preoccupation with her body and her weight increased and she started dieting strictly, induced vomiting, and abused laxatives with the result that her body weight fell and she became emaciated. Her menstrual periods ceased when her weight was low, but she continued with multiple sexual relationships, which often involved oral and anal sex, although the latter revolted her. She says that she 'craves orgasm' and tries to get it any way she can, masturbating in the absence of other outlets. She has now been binge-eating and vomiting for five years. She has frequent invitations to parties and frequents bars and restaurants. She avoids eating before going out and prefers to wear loose fitting clothes. After returning home she induces vomiting. She feels she is most likely to vomit in a situation where she fears both sexual challenge and a temptation to 'overeat'.

5

Investigation of eating disorders

I don't want to be like this, but what I eat still rules my life so that at times every working minute seems occupied with thoughts of food and the day passes in the measured times between when I last ate and when I'll eat again. I'm still plagued with guilt about everything I consume unless I nearly fast. I dream of the perfect day when I have no appetite, no thought, desire, or temptation for food or to eat. I often despair of ever finding a solution.

Weight loss and excessive weight gain may be caused by several physical and psychiatric conditions. For example, starvation causes emaciation, as does advanced terminal cancer and tuberculosis; gross obesity may be due to a brain tumour or to an endocrine disorder. Among psychiatric disorders, depression poses a diagnostic problem. Many women who have an eating disorder, particularly bulimia, show clinical signs of depression. However, it is unclear if the depression led to the eating disorder or if the eating disorder led to the depression.

It is important to exclude medical and psychiatric disorders when making a diagnosis of an eating disorder. This can be done by obtaining a good history and after an appropriate physical examination by a doctor. This examination includes careful measurements of the person's weight and height, so that the Body Mass Index can be calculated. Alternatively, measurement of the height and weight for the person's age enables the doctor to determine how much the person's weight deviates from the Average Body Weight (this information is obtained from a table; see Appendix, p. 192).

Most people with eating disorders either have a fear of becoming fat, or are obese and perceive themselves as ugly, massive, undesirable, or flabby. Both groups have poor self-esteem and a poor body image. For this reason it is important for the health professional (who may be a doctor or a psychologist) to make a psychological evaluation of the woman before starting any treatment. There are several psychological tests, and the information obtained from these can be converted into mathematical scales to help in this evaluation, each test having its adherents. Many of the tests are complex and the findings contradictory. Before deciding if any psychological tests are to be made, it may help to ask a few simple questions. But before they are asked, the appearance of the woman seeking help may determine which questions should be asked. As well as estimating her body size, other observations may be made. Is she wearing clothes which reveal her body shape or has she chosen loose-fitting garments to try to hide her body shape and weight? Does she have calluses on the back of her fingers? These may be associated with self-induced vomiting. Are her fingers and feet puffy? These signs may occur following the consumption of large amounts of food over a short period of time. Are her teeth discoloured or damaged? These conditions may follow frequent episodes of self-induced vomiting.

The purpose of the questions is to try to establish whether the patient is prepared to alter her eating behaviour, to lose or gain weight, and if she has sufficiently high motivation and fortitude to make the changes. If her motivation is low, a great deal of time will be expended, both by the health professional and the patient, with little benefit.

The following questions have been tested and found to be helpful in establishing a patient's motivation to change her disordered eating behaviour.

1. Do you really want to change your eating behaviour?

If the patient is unwilling to change her eating behaviour there is no point in starting treatment. In mild cases her enjoyment of her present behaviour may outweigh the long-term consequences of emaciation or obesity. This implies that in some cases the person has to get worse, becoming even more emaciated, or more obese, or more disordered in her eating, before she is sufficiently motivated to accept treatment. In extreme cases when the illness may threaten her life, pressure must be placed on her to accept treatment.

Some women deny that their problem is one of disordered eating behaviour. These women insist that they can gain or lose weight easily if they want to, and after admitting that they binge-eat or induce vomiting, say that they could easily stop the behaviour if they wanted to. In other words they, too, are ambivalent about starting treatment. One strategy to suggest to these women is that if they wish they can try to change their eating behaviour on their own, but to recommend that they should return after about four weeks for a further evaluation. During this period nearly all the women will have failed to change their disordered eating and may be more ready to accept treatment.

2. What is your occupation?

Certain jobs which involve business entertaining, catering, extensive travelling, shift work, or long periods of relative inactivity and boredom make dieting difficult and may frustrate the woman's attempts to change her eating behaviour. Knowledge of the patient's occupation helps the health professional to suggest strategies for resisting the compulsion to eat. Occupations which require the patient to be thin, such as fashion modelling or ballet dancing, have to be accepted, and treatment may have to be modified so that the desired weight fits in with the occupation. Another example is the woman whose occupation is involved with food preparation or who is a waitress, because her occupation may reinforce her preoccupation with food.

3. What is your weight now?

Assessment of the patient's current weight and her 'desirable weight range' enables the health professional to estimate how long it will take for the woman to achieve her desirable weight if her motivation is high and if she adheres to the recommended diet, whether this is to achieve refeeding or weight reduction. Knowledge of the woman's present weight may also give some indication about further medical investigations which should be made to avoid aggravating a possible vitamin deficiency or a metabolic disturbance, such as low blood potassium, which could cause cardiac arrest.

4. What weight would you like to achieve?

It is important for this to be discussed as the patient may have unrealistic expectations, which may frustrate her attempts to change her eating behaviour and may require modification. It is also helpful to explore the reason a particular weight was selected as the 'desirable' personal weight, if she is to recover from her eating disorder.

5. What is the heaviest you have ever been?

This question establishes whether the person has previously attempted to reduce, or to increase, her weight; whether she failed or achieved partial success; and how she coped.

6. What is the lowest weight you reached?

The question has greater applicability to people who have anorexia nervosa and gives an indication of weight changes, at least those reported by the patient.

7. *Have you maintained your weight over a period of at least six months without much effort?*
This question gives a reasonable indication of a weight range which the patient could aim for, and it may help her recognize that she can maintain a body weight without being preoccupied with food.

As many women believe that their weight should be the 'ideal weight' proclaimed in many articles in women's magazines, it may be helpful to her to introduce the concept of a desirable weight-range as defined by the BMI, and dissuade her from seeking an ideal weight.

8. *How do you think changing your weight will change your life-style?*
Many patients try to generalize in answer to this question saying that 'I'll probably feel better' or 'I read that I should lose weight'. The question requires to be answered more specifically, and the patient should try to state clearly what things she hopes to do after weight change which cannot be done while she is emaciated or obese. It may help the patient if she makes a list of the reasons why she wants to gain or to lose weight. She may find difficulty in answering this question at the beginning of treatment, but later, with more insight into her eating disorder, this may help her to understand her eating problem. As an example, a patient who has anorexia nervosa who changes her weight may feel that she will lose control, not only of her eating behaviour but of her life-style, and may also lose the feeling of 'safety' she had when her body weight was low.

9. *Are you on a diet at present?*
If the answer is yes, it is important to establish exactly what the diet contains, and how rigorous the patient has been in keeping to it. For example, many obese people try new fashionable 'fad' diets, but the diet is not really effective and the dieter has insufficient motivation to keep to it. Information about the patient's chosen diet is even more valuable when she has anorexia nervosa or bulimia. Starvation diets are more likely to end in an episode of binge-eating than 'sensible' diets, rather in the way a person who misses breakfast and lunch because of work or other circumstances feels hungry when dinner-time approaches and is likely to eat more at dinner than normal. It is also useful to find what the diet contains, as some 'health' foods contain considerable amounts of sugar, and many obese people do not consider beverages as food, although they contain sugar. Even 'low-calorie' foods and drinks provide

a considerable amount of energy if the person eats or drinks quantities of them, believing that they will not put on weight.

Many women with eating disorders lose their perception of how much they need to eat, or not to eat, if they wish to maintain a constant weight. Obese people tend to over-estimate their food needs, while patients with anorexia nervosa tend to underestimate how much they should eat to maintain a constant weight. Bulimia nervosa patients usually under-estimate their requirements because they do not include the food eaten during a binge as normal eating.

10. *Have you previously tried dieting to lose or to gain weight?*
If the person has dieted previously and has failed to gain or to lose weight while dieting or has kept to the diet for only a short time, it is important to establish this fact, as well as finding out why previous attempts at dieting were abandoned.

11. *Have you used any other ways apart from dieting to lose weight?*
People who have failed to lose weight because they have not kept to their diet often try other methods such as self-induced vomiting, or laxative or diuretic abuse, or excessive exercise in an attempt to lose weight. This applies to bulimia patients, anorexia nervosa patients, and obese patients. In fact over 40 weight-losing behaviours were reported in a recent study made in Sydney (Table 2, p. 7). Some of the methods are potentially dangerous, but most patients only resort to them when simpler methods have apparently failed. It may help the patient understand her eating disorder if the reason why the methods failed to work is talked about or thought about. As some of the methods are socially unacceptable it may be difficult for some patients to admit that they have used them. But the patient and her therapist should try to explore them, since much of the management of eating disorders is directed to changing eating and weight-losing behaviours. The question also enables the physician to decide if further medical and laboratory investigations are needed.

12. *If you keep strictly to your 'meal plan', how quickly do you think that you will gain weight if you have a weight-losing eating disorder or will lose weight if you are obese?*
A woman who is trying to gain weight will find it relatively easy to increase her body weight by eating a little more food in the first two weeks of her new 'meal plan', but it is unrealistic for her to expect that

her weight gain will continue unless she progressively increases her food intake.

Similarly in the case of an obese woman, unrealistic expectations about losing weight (usually obtained from reading about 'fad' or crash diets) can be clarified by asking the question. For example, many people know that on a strict diet it is relatively easy to lose 3 kg (7lbs) in the first week, but expect to be able to continue losing weight at this rate which is unrealistic (this is discussed further on p. 158). They find that they do not lose weight rapidly after the first week and may give up the diet assuming that it is 'no good'. It also helps the patient to know that the weekly weight loss or weight gain may fluctuate even though she has adhered to the diet. A person who says 'I have only to look at food to put on weight' is playing games with herself, and is either eating snacks or practising 'picking behaviour'; so is a person who says to herself that 'a piece of cake, or a chocolate, won't do any harm'—and goes on eating pieces of cake and chocolates.

13. *An obese woman may be asked: 'Do you expect to lose weight without dieting?'*
The question may seem stupid at first. Of course, the person will answer that she does not: but when the subject is explored further it will be found that most people seek magic cures for obesity or for losing weight while continuing to binge-eat. Many of these women spend considerable quantities of money following 'fad' diets or attending various courses guaranteeing painless weight reduction.

14. *Are you taking any medication at present?*
This question is designed to determine what medication the patient has been given, why the medications were prescribed or bought, and whether they are really needed. It explores the matters raised in question 11.

15. *Tell me about your family?*
The question is deliberately vague. It seeks to determine if the parents of the patient were fat; whether siblings or children are fat; what sort of life the family leads; what pressures are put on the person by the other family members; who does the cooking and who the shopping; if other family members are dieting. Family dynamics may have a considerable influence on the patient's opinion of herself and disclosure may help in changing eating behaviour.

This question may help to clarify if the person has inherited 'fat genes' (see page 145), since if she has, it may be necessary to modify treatment goals.

16. *Tell me about your life-style*
The information obtained from this question enables the therapist to decide on the strategy which is most likely to succeed in inducing the person to change her eating behaviour and to persist with the new eating habit.

17. *Have you had problems becoming pregnant?*
Some married women may be asked this question, as infertility is not uncommon amongst women with an eating disorder, and women being investigated for infertility are not usually asked about their eating behaviour. A woman who has an eating disorder or is recovering from an eating disorder and who becomes pregnant requires increased care in pregnancy and after childbirth. This is discussed on pages 83 and 132.

6

Management of eating disorders

When this all started, I used to always use a knife to eat an apple, and a teaspoon to eat cereal or desert—I suppose it took longer, and therefore felt as if I was eating more. I always left a bit of potato/rice/noodles on my plate, no matter how much was served to me—as a test of willpower. The whole exercise of putting on weight, to me, is a breakdown of my iron willpower, because I know only too well that I enjoy eating. That is what still revolts me—the amount of food actually to be consumed in order to put on one stone. I've always maintained that I would so much prefer to have one stone in weight 'sewn' on instead of having to 'eat' it on.

Eating disorders occur because a person loves food and either seeks to control this love rigorously (anorexia nervosa) or intermittently (bulimia nervosa and atypical eating disorders) or has a lack of control over the amount of food eaten (obesity—although many other factors are involved in obesity, as we discuss on pages 144-9). It follows from this observation that the reversion of an eating disorder to 'normal' eating depends on several decisions. The first is that the person perceives that she has an eating disorder. The second is that the person believes that if the disordered eating continues it may cause a serious problem to her life-style or to her health, or both. In other words, she has to decide that the benefit, or reward, of changing the disordered eating behaviour exceeds that of the cost of continuing with it, at a physical, psychological, and social level. Having made these decisions, she has to experience or show a readiness to change her present eating habits. This implies that she will accept the help given, but understands that the change will only occur if she is prepared to achieve the change herself. It is relatively easy to lose (or to gain) weight so that it lies within the desirable range: it is much harder to *maintain* the weight within the desirable range.

   To achieve weight alteration and to stabilize it within the desirable range, the person has to change her life-style and eating behaviour and habits. It is important to be aware that eating disorders do not exist in isolation; they are a result of altered eating behaviour, which in turn may be a reaction to events in a person's life. Because of this, treatment must take care of the other problems and needs of the individual, and help the person to learn to cope with the problems in ways other than resorting to eating or avoiding eating. She will also need to obtain insight into her eating behaviour and why she is behaving in this way.

The aim of treatment is to help the woman learn normal eating behaviour which allows her to maintain her body weight in the normal range (BMI 19–24.9), without having to resort to dangerous methods of weight control. Different strategies have to be adopted for women who have a weight-losing eating disorder and those who are obese. For example, women who have anorexia nervosa need to lose their fear of becoming fat, and learn to eat more, to achieve weight gain; obese patients may need to learn how to avoid episodes of overeating, whilst on a weight-reducing programme, so that a slow but steady decrease in body weight occurs.

If the individual is to achieve the needed change she requires motivation, fortitude, persistence, and a continuing stimulus to change. This will only be achieved when she becomes aware of the factors—physiological, psychological, social, and familial—which induce her to continue her disordered eating. She also needs to become aware that what triggered the disordered eating habit is not necessarily the reason why it is continuing. For example, if a disturbed family relationship was one of the factors which led to the onset of anorexia nervosa, it may be necessary not only to explore this relationship but also to use other treatments. She may have to learn that although she has a morbid fear of becoming fat, it is safe for her to try to increase her weight, and that she will not lose control of her eating and other behaviour. On the other hand, unless a grossly obese individual can be induced to lose her urge to eat, starting a strict diet may lead her to take one of two actions. First, she may pander to her urge to eat and so break her diet. At first the food gives her pleasure, but then guilt may follow and lead to depression. Alternatively, she may keep to her diet and suffer 'stress' because she does not accede to her urge to eat. This can lead to anger, frustration, or depression. If an obese person continues eating because of loneliness, boredom, or stress at work this must be examined.

As far as is possible the patient and her therapist have to agree to try and be honest with each other. The problem is that patients with eating disorders tend to 'play games' and to manipulate the therapist. In spite of this the patient should try to answer honestly that she is complying with the menu plan they have jointly chosen and should try to discuss how her altered eating behaviour is affecting other behaviour. As it is important to 'track' changes in behaviour as well as of weight during treatment the patient must be able to have confidence in and trust the therapist.

If the patient is obese, changes in weight can be tracked by regular weighing at weekly or two-weekly intervals, or by tracking weight changes by measuring skin fold thickness changes. Another method is to track progress by using a Weight Reduction Index * which is as follows:

$$\frac{\text{Weight loss (in kg)}}{\text{Weight in excess of normal weight range}} \times 100$$

Eating behaviour and mood diary

It often helps the woman to keep a daily diary of her moods and eating behaviour. She fills in the diary every night before going to bed. A diary which we use for patients who have bulimia nervosa is shown in Table 5 (page 58). At the end of each month, the daily points of each component of the diary are joined up and the sheet is rotated so that the woman can see a graph of her changes in mood and eating behaviour over the past month. The diary also permits the woman to see the associations between her feelings, moods, and eating behaviour, to observe changes in her eating behaviour, and to note changes in her menstrual cycle.

Often when a patient feels that she is not improving in spite of treatment, checking back on the diary and talking about it with her therapist shows that her feeling is false and that she is improving.

During the recovery period, some women who have bulimia nervosa may observe by referring to the diary that they move from recording binge-eating to recording overeating (with no gain in body weight). In other words, the nature of the binge has changed and the decision to eat or not to eat has been recognized. For some women, knowing that they have to record their bingeing or vomiting may be sufficient for them to change their behaviour.

The diary was designed to minimize the woman's preoccupation with body weight, body shape, and eating behaviour.

Food diaries, that is, a diary in which the woman is asked to record everything that is eaten and drunk for long periods of time, may be

---

* The weight reduction quotient is more accurate:

$$\text{Weight reduction quotient} = \frac{\text{Kg lost}}{\text{Kg overweight}} \times \frac{\text{Initial weight (kg)}}{\text{Desired weight}} \times 100$$

helpful if the patient is obese, but if the patient has anorexia nervosa, a food diary appears to have the potential to increase the patient's pre-occupation with food and to hinder recovery. However, a food diary kept for a few days may be necessary from time to time to help the dietician devise a menu plan suitable for and accepted by the patient.

Changes in life-style

It is important for the patient continually to be aware that changes in life-style are as important as changes in weight and that the two are inter-linked. During treatment the woman needs to become aware that the decision to change her eating behaviour to achieve and to maintain her weight in the normal weight range may have to be reinforced for many years, and that she may need support and help at intervals to maintain her resolve and her weight. With this support she will gain insight into her behaviour and learn to cope without relapsing into a disordered eating behaviour.

If she has a weight-losing eating disorder, she needs to be aware of the dangers of abusing laxatives and diuretics, and the problems which arise from self-induced vomiting.

If the problem is obesity, she needs to be provided with a comprehensive 'weight-reducing programme' which is easy to understand and to follow and which does not distort her eating pattern too greatly. She must be very aware why she has to take in less energy than she expends each day. This implies that she learns to *choose* appropriate foods rather than being taught to *avoid* inappropriate foods. She needs to know the importance of regular exercise as a complementary way of losing weight.

Self-help groups

Many women who experience an episode of disordered eating can receive help in the community. The self-help groups which help women achieve a loss of weight (such as Weight Watchers International, TOPS—taking off pounds sensibly, Overeaters Anonymous) are firmly established. Self-help groups for women with anorexia nervosa and bulimia nervosa are increasing in number in many countries. Providing that these groups are properly organized and run by responsible people they provide great help to many women.

Table 5. Eating Behaviour and Mood Diary

MONTH _____   ID _____

Date	Mood					Binge-eating			Overeating			Preoccupation†			Vomiting			Laxatives			Other/exercise			Menses		
	0	1	2	3	4	0	1	2	0	1	2	0	1	2	0	1	2	0	1	2	0	1	2	0	1	2
1	o	o	o	o	o	o	o	o	o	o	o	o	o	o	o	o	o	o	o	o	o	o	o	o	o	o
2	o	o	o	o	o	o	o	o	o	o	o	o	o	o	o	o	o	o	o	o	o	o	o	o	o	o
3	o	o	o	o	o	o	o	o	o	o	o	o	o	o	o	o	o	o	o	o	o	o	o	o	o	o
4	o	o	o	o	o	o	o	o	o	o	o	o	o	o	o	o	o	o	o	o	o	o	o	o	o	o
5	o	o	o	o	o	o	o	o	o	o	o	o	o	o	o	o	o	o	o	o	o	o	o	o	o	o
6	o	o	o	o	o	o	o	o	o	o	o	o	o	o	o	o	o	o	o	o	o	o	o	o	o	o
7	o	o	o	o	o	o	o	o	o	o	o	o	o	o	o	o	o	o	o	o	o	o	o	o	o	o
8	o	o	o	o	o	o	o	o	o	o	o	o	o	o	o	o	o	o	o	o	o	o	o	o	o	o
9	o	o	o	o	o	o	o	o	o	o	o	o	o	o	o	o	o	o	o	o	o	o	o	o	o	o
10	o	o	o	o	o	o	o	o	o	o	o	o	o	o	o	o	o	o	o	o	o	o	o	o	o	o
11	o	o	o	o	o	o	o	o	o	o	o	o	o	o	o	o	o	o	o	o	o	o	o	o	o	o
12	o	o	o	o	o	o	o	o	o	o	o	o	o	o	o	o	o	o	o	o	o	o	o	o	o	o
13	o	o	o	o	o	o	o	o	o	o	o	o	o	o	o	o	o	o	o	o	o	o	o	o	o	o
14	o	o	o	o	o	o	o	o	o	o	o	o	o	o	o	o	o	o	o	o	o	o	o	o	o	o
15	o	o	o	o	o	o	o	o	o	o	o	o	o	o	o	o	o	o	o	o	o	o	o	o	o	o

16	o	o	o	o	o	o	o	o	o	o	o	o	o	o	o	o	o	o	o
17	o	o	o	o	o	o	o	o	o	o	o	o	o	o	o	o	o	o	o
18	o	o	o	o	o	o	o	o	o	o	o	o	o	o	o	o	o	o	o
19	o	o	o	o	o	o	o	o	o	o	o	o	o	o	o	o	o	o	o
20	o	o	o	o	o	o	o	o	o	o	o	o	o	o	o	o	o	o	o
21	o	o	o	o	o	o	o	o	o	o	o	o	o	o	o	o	o	o	o
22	o	o	o	o	o	o	o	o	o	o	o	o	o	o	o	o	o	o	o
23	o	o	o	o	o	o	o	o	o	o	o	o	o	o	o	o	o	o	o
24	o	o	o	o	o	o	o	o	o	o	o	o	o	o	o	o	o	o	o
25	o	o	o	o	o	o	o	o	o	o	o	o	o	o	o	o	o	o	o
26	o	o	o	o	o	o	o	o	o	o	o	o	o	o	o	o	o	o	o
27	o	o	o	o	o	o	o	o	o	o	o	o	o	o	o	o	o	o	o
28	o	o	o	o	o	o	o	o	o	o	o	o	o	o	o	o	o	o	o
29	o	o	o	o	o	o	o	o	o	o	o	o	o	o	o	o	o	o	o
30	o	o	o	o	o	o	o	o	o	o	o	o	o	o	o	o	o	o	o
31	o	o	o	o	o	o	o	o	o	o	o	o	o	o	o	o	o	o	o

Mood 0—very good/happy/bright/confident
2—average
4—very bad/unhappy/dissatisfied/inadequate

† with body weight and eating

Other 0—absent
1—present
2—severe

Professor S. Abraham
University of Sydney
1988

Self-help groups have many advantages: (1) the leaders of the group have been able to alter their own eating habits and have achieved and maintained their weight goal: they are therefore able to serve as a model for the other members of the group; (2) the person finds it easy to join and to leave the group (this may be more difficult in treatment by a therapist, as she may feel an obligation to the therapist); (3) the group exerts a 'dynamic effect' which may help the person counter the psychological and social pressures which encourage relapse; (4) the method helps the person feel that she has achieved the changes of eating behaviour by her own efforts without a 'professional' taking over her treatment, although this negative effect is reduced if the professional is well-trained, skilled, and empathetic; (5) the person is not converted into a 'patient' with a 'disease'; (6) usually the courses provided by self-help groups are cheaper than those provided by health professionals, a factor which may be of some importance for compliance; and (7) some groups, notably those which help women with anorexia nervosa and bulimia, have people who are accessible at all times to help a woman who perceives herself to be in 'crisis'.

Recently people involved in self-help groups have obtained better training and it may be expected that the groups will be increasingly effective in helping women with disordered eating. Self-help groups may not be appropriate to help women who have a severe eating disorder, or a complicating medical or psychiatric problem. However, most responsible self-help groups 'screen' women with an eating disorder and recommend that women whose eating disorder is severe or who have a psychological or a medical problem receive additional help from a medical specialist.

Self-help groups have some dangers. The members of the group may teach each other bad habits, such as self-induced vomiting, or to compete to be the worst or best in the group. They may reinforce the woman's preoccupation with weight and food. They may have no routine assessment procedures to determine if the person needs to seek the help of a specialist. They may indirectly persuade the woman to keep her eating disorder so that she can continue to obtain the support of the group for other problems which she may have.

Disordered eating and compulsive exercising

Regular enjoyable exercise is beneficial to the health of all people and is particularly useful in helping obese people, who embark on a weight reduction programme to continue to lose weight (see page 157). A number of women who have one of the other eating disorders use exercise, not as a way of keeping fit but as a way of losing weight. They become compulsive exercisers. They may exercise compulsively during the time that they have anorexia nervosa or bulimia nervosa, and on recovering from these disorders may continue to exercise compulsively. In other words they replace their eating disorder with an 'exercise disorder'.

One such woman is Belinda. Belinda had bulimia nervosa. As she became free from her preoccupation with food and weight control, her eating habits returned to normal. For the past three years she has maintained a BMI of 22, and is happy with her appearance. But she is a compulsive exerciser.

Belinda wrote:

Each day of my life I try and fit my day around at least one session of quite strenuous, routine exercising—usually either 20 laps of a 50 metre pool or a 45 minute strenuous aerobic workout. If I cannot fit in my usual daily piece of exercise I feel guilty, worried, and up to a point anxious. Exercise has become an important part of my life. I should say that the main reason I exercise is for the actual feeling of being fit and feeling relaxed, not because I want to lose weight or look thin. I like me as I am now.

I do have the willpower to reduce exercising to only one session a day but I itch to keep pushing myself to it, even if my body just wants to flop. So I drive myself to do it and afterwards I feel really happy that I had pushed myself to do it, even though I didn't enjoy doing it at the time. I feel so sick of it all but would feel so unhappy and insecure if I stopped altogether. When I am emotionally upset over something important to me, I punish my body even more severely and increase the exercise. I feel weakness and no strength during an exercise session but I cannot stop doing it. I feel that I couldn't cut out my exercising completely but I am a strong-willed person and I feel positive about being able to live with myself if I reduce the intensity gradually. My aim is to keep doing three or four classes of aerobic exercise each week and have the occasional swim. Exercise used to be a really enjoyable feeling for me—now it is an addiction.

A woman who has Belinda's problem needs continued support and the chance to talk to her therapist whenever she feels that she needs to, so that she can express her feelings about the amount of exercise she does and can be helped to reduce it to a level which she can control.

The advantages of having an eating disorder

Women who have eating disorders may see advantages in continuing with 'abnormal' eating behaviour. The advantages may be perceived by the woman as being greater than the disadvantages of the disorder, so that she is more comfortable persisting with the behaviour than changing it. The advantages vary and depend on whether the person has anorexia nervosa, has bulimia, or is severely obese.

An eating disorder may become an all-absorbing hobby and lead to the exclusion of most other age-related activities. In this way the sufferer is able to avoid making decisions and can reduce the challenges made on her. If the challenges are sexual, the woman may use her emaciation, or her obesity, to avoid them, claiming that her distorted body shape would repel rather than attract men. One of our patients said 'when my body weight is normal I am scared of people's expectations of me, and have to resist men who make advances. But when I am fat, I am able to avoid these problems'.

Other patients find that their emaciation, or obesity, makes other members of the family concerned. The woman becomes the centre of concern and induces the family to make expressions of love and to go to great lengths to 'look after her'. In this way she may be able to manipulate the family and obtains satisfaction from her behaviour. Other women manipulate close relatives by adopting 'illness behaviour'. Because the woman is perceived by her relatives as being 'ill' she is looked after. She is able to feel dependent, without feeling guilty, and may use this 'illness' to avoid a social or a family situation. For example, one of our patients lost weight each year in November and December so that she could be admitted to hospital for Christmas rather than having to spend it with her family. Another patient used her illness to justify her behaviour towards her husband, saying that 'my husband knew that he was marrying a sick person. If I get better he may not like me and we may separate'. By being ill she forced her husband to concentrate on her needs to the exclusion of his needs.

In other cases the person uses her eating disorder to avoid discussion of other problems in her relationship with her husband or family, or to avoid going out to social functions, at which she is uncomfortable. The person's emaciation or obesity may be used as an excuse to avoid competition. One of our patients ceased competitive swimming at the age of 12 and began putting on weight. By the time she was 19 her weight had risen to 108 kg (238 lbs, 17 st). She wrote:

All the girls were too competitive. I'm out of that now, and can get on with everyone. When I was swimming people picked on me if I didn't do as well as they expected me to have done. Now I can do what I like, and do the things I like well. Now I'm fat, I find that people come and talk to me. They can see I have a problem. They can see I have a weakness of character, or I wouldn't eat so much. They have problems too. Other people can't see their problems, but as my problem is obvious they feel comfortable with me.

Another of our patients wrote about her eating disorder:

I feel I have always needed the food to give me 'the rush' to make me high and happy. I know I use it as a protection barrier against experiencing and expressing emotional feeling with others and against physical and mental intimacy with a man. I have the need to break down this barrier and take charge of my life. You asked me what did I think would change if I lost the weight. I don't think the actual weight loss (or gain) would change anything, but if I could cease to look upon myself as a compulsive eater and feel relaxed about my food intake, then I feel I could tap the vitality and creativity that has eluded me all my life—I would feel I was functioning as a whole and not the several personalities I feel I am.

Obesity may also be a camouflage in families who are overweight. Being fat enables the person to fit in with the family and to behave as they do.

Some women feel a sense of achievement in being able to reduce their weight so that they become emaciated. One of our patients, aged 20, who had anorexia nervosa and who had, in her words, 'done nothing with my life' wrote to us saying 'At least I've done one thing well. I enjoy being my Doctor's worst patient.'

Most people have an idealized view of how they should appear: they want to be socially attractive, happy and outgoing, and popular. When the person realizes that she cannot achieve her ideal, she may adopt disordered eating behaviour, either losing weight and becoming thin or gaining weight and becoming obese. In this way she has an excuse which explains why she can't achieve her ideal. But at these extremes of weight she looks in a mirror and doesn't like her body image. She then tries to return to the normal weight range, by dieting and other methods.

7
Anorexia nervosa

I just wish that anorexia would get the blazes out of my life! From 1982 to now, everything I do, have done or didn't do centres around my fear of food. For those of you not familiar with the demonic workings of anorexia—fear of food and getting fat are its basic elements.

Anorexia nervosa affects females fifteen-times more commonly than males and usually begins during adolescence or in early adulthood. It is rare for the illness to occur for the first time to a woman who is over the age of 25, and, if it does, the eating disorder is usually associated with severe mental or physical problems. Anorexia nervosa seems to be occurring more frequently among young women in the developed countries. The illness affects at least one woman aged 13 to 25 in every thousand, reaching a peak incidence of one in 200 amongst adolescent girls aged 15 to 18. It cannot be called an epidemic.

Fig. 10. Anorexia nervosa.

Case history: Alison

Alison was a tall, slim girl, who at the age of 15 had begun dieting with the other members of her class at school. She did this to feel part of the group rather than because she needed to lose weight. She managed to stick to the diet better than most of her peers, her weight falling from 52 kg (115 lbs, 8 st 3lb; BMI 20.4; 90 per cent of Average Body Weight) to 47 kg (104 lbs, 7 st 6 lbs; BMI 16.9; 80 per cent of ABW). 'I was able to keep to the diet because my family are health freaks, and I began to feel guilty if I ate "bad fattening" foods.' About this time she began to be teased by the other girls about her small breasts and became self-conscious about them and her bottom, which she said 'stuck out too much'.

Alison was ambitious and wanted to do well at school. In her last two years she seldom went out to social events, because she felt she had to study, which she did conscientiously. 'Perhaps I was rather obsessional about study', she said, 'but I wanted to do well'. As well as studying hard, she cooked for the family, making cakes and biscuits (which she avoided eating) in addition to cooking the main meals. She perceived her household duties as helping her mother, who had a full time job, but her sister perceived them as trying to be a 'goody goody'.

She passed her school examinations and enrolled in a catering course because she enjoyed the practical aspects of cooking and preparing food. About this time she began to weigh herself each day, and continued to diet so that she became thinner. Her sister left home, and told Alison that in her opinion she had only 'lost weight to get all the attention of the family and put her sister's nose out of joint.' The sibling rivalry was marked.

Over the next two years, Alison continued with her course and proved an outstanding student. During this period her father's weight increased by about 14 kg (31 lbs, 2 st 3 lbs) whilst his daughter's weight continued to decline, so that at graduation Alison weighed 32 kg (70 lbs, 5 st; BMI 12). Her father was diagnosed as having a high blood pressure and instructed to lose weight which he found difficult to do. Alison tried to help, informing him what to eat, and worked out diets for him, 'counting the calories' of the food in the diets she devised.

She recognized that she was very thin and that she no longer menstruated, but she felt she was eating as much as other people, and if she ate more she would 'put on weight rapidly and become fat'. She felt safe as long as her weight did not increase. She also felt it was wrong to eat more than others when 'there were so many starving people in the world'.

When she was 19 she visited a doctor about constipation which worried her and which she did not connect with her small intake of food. She was diagnosed as having anorexia nervosa and admitted to hospital for refeeding which was not successful. She responded to out-patient treatment and over seven months her weight increased to 44 kg (97 lbs, 6 st 13 lbs). She wanted to put on more weight but was worried that if she did she 'would lose control and become fat'. With persuasion and persistence she was induced to gain weight and by the age of 20 had stabilized at 49 kg (108 lbs, 7 st 10 lbs). She now believed that if her weight increased to 50 kg (110 lbs, 7st 12 lbs) she would 'lose control', but was happy to keep it at about 49 kg (108 lbs, 7 st 10 lbs).

At this time she moved to a city 125 miles away to run a restaurant, and began to write letters. Two months after her move she wrote:

> Well, I weighed myself recently and I'm just 47 kg (104 lbs, 7 st 6 lbs). I'm not consciously trying to lose weight, but its obvious I'm not eating enough. I'm not missing out on any meals and eat a varied diet—including supposedly fattening foods. But my brain still ticks in the same way as before —that I'm not allowed to get fat. What's wrong with me? I can't go through life needing someone to reinforce the fact that I have to be at a higher weight before my hormones will start functioning. I still feel the need to be reassured that it's OK to be 52 or 54 kg (115 lbs or 119 lbs, 8-8½ st)—whatever I'm supposed to be. Now it's only me, telling me I'm not allowed to get fat. I can't believe I'm so thick headed!

Two months later

> One positive fact is that I haven't lost any weight. But how true that at a low weight, your moods are more erratic and depressed and mental functioning is impaired. I can't believe it—people keep telling me I don't eat enough but the whole day is 'a meal'. I can't stuff anymore into me. If my bowels would function normally maybe I would have more appetite. I've been more tense in the last 3 or 4 weeks, it upsets me terribly. The more depressed I become the less I want to be with people. I could quite happily exist alone— I'm constantly accusing myself of things and apologizing to other people. I talk to other people but do not listen to what they say. I know I must be a pain but I can't seem to do anything about it. I don't want to come back because I know I would run home to the family for protection—they'd assure me that everything was OK when I know damn well it isn't. I'm wasting my life—it is a chore just to get through the day. I want to come back and talk to you when I get my holidays later this year.

Three months after her last letter, Alison returned to the Clinic. She was neatly, even elegantly, dressed but looked thin. She weighed 46 kg (101 lbs, 7 st 3 lbs). Over the next few months she increased her weight at the rate of 1 kg (2.2 lbs) a month and has now maintained a body weight of 50 kg (110 lbs, 7 st 12 lbs) for the past two years. She has formed relationships and has a steady boyfriend. She continues to excel in her work as manager of a restaurant.

Most anorexia nervosa patients have a preoccupation with food and control of their weight. Food and its avoidance becomes an all-absorbing hobby to the exclusion of most of the other activities they would normally indulge in at their particular age, especially social occasions when food is usually present and eating expected. The preoccupation with weight is such that most patients can give a detailed history of their weight changes, including changes as small as 0.5 kg (1 lb) over periods as short as a week. The preoccupation about food and weight control and the overwhelming urge to become thin leads anorexia nervosa patients to use a range of eating behaviour to achieve their desire.

Young women whose weight has usually been in the normal range before their eating disorder began generally lose weight by the simple method of eating less and by avoiding situations in which they have to eat. In order to avoid eating they make excuses such as 'I don't feel hungry at the moment so I'll eat some later' when told by parents that a meal is ready. Other excuses offered are 'I have eaten already'; 'I've decided to become vegetarian'; 'I have an allergy to . . . (certain foods)'; 'I feel sick'. The young women tend to avoid social occasions, and may lock themselves in their room and ask not to be disturbed. They may be competitive and are often obsessive about their work, which enables them to avoid social occasions where food is eaten. In addition to strict dieting, they may use exercise as a method of losing weight. This may involve jogging, playing squash, attending 'health farms', or 'working out' at a gymnasium for long hours.

Case history: Jennifer

Jenny was 15 when she went on holiday on her own. At the sea-side resort she entered a beauty contest and came second. That night she got drunk for the first time and had her first experience of sexual intercourse. She felt guilty about being drunk and about having sex. At school she was a good student, worked hard, and excelled in sports, being in the school swimming, hockey, and basket-ball teams. On her return from holiday she believed that she would have won the beauty contest if she had been slimmer and if her thighs and bottom had been smaller. She decided to go on a diet to lose weight, and this resulted in arguments with her mother, who thought that Jennifer was already too thin.

Jenny compromised by offering to do the cooking (in reality it was to help her have control over the calorie content). During meals she moved the food about the plate so that she appeared to be eating. She avoided cream and fatty foods, telling her family that they made her feel sick. She spent long hours alone in her room studying and in the evenings attended dancing classes. In her room she exercised strenuously, for 15 to 20 minutes every two hours, and played music to hide the noise of her exercises from her parents. She told them that the music helped her concentrate upon her studies. She became obsessional about her weight, weighing herself before and after meals, before and after bouts of exercise, and before and after going to the toilet.

At about this time she was chosen to represent her state in a folk-dancing championship and increased her daily exercise, telling her parents that she had to be 'super fit to help my team win'. With increasing exercise and a limited food intake, Jennifer's weight dropped from 53 kg (117 lbs, 8 st 5 lbs) to 45 kg (99 lbs, 7 st 1 lb). She wore loose clothes to disguise her low weight from her family. However, one morning her mother saw her naked and was horrified. Jenny promised to eat more, but again managed to disguise the amount she ate and whenever possible slipped food from her plate to the family dog.

As the time of the folk-dancing championships approached Jenny increased the amount of exercise she did daily, and, because she still felt she was too fat, restricted her food intake still further. Two weeks before the championships she collapsed and was admitted to hospital. Her weight was now 30 kg (66 lbs, 4 st 10 lbs). In hospital she was given sedatives. She felt that she was no longer in control of her weight, she became agitated, and was given additional medication. With refeeding she gained 8 kg (17 lbs) and with her parents' agreement discharged herself from hospital.

At home she continued to exercise excessively and again collapsed. She was readmitted to hospital and remained in hospital until her weight had increased to 51 kg (112 lbs, 8 st; BMI 19.3; 90 per cent of ABW). During this hospital admission she agreed to and worked out a diet with the dietitian. Since discharge she has maintained her weight at around 46 kg (108 lbs, 7 st 10 lbs; BMI 18.7; 85 per cent of ABW). At first she was terrified that she would gain weight and began exercising again. This has become an obsession, so much so that she jogs in the streets if her doctor is running late with his appointments. However, in spite of a strenuous exercise programme, she eats sufficient food to maintain her body weight.

The second group of anorexia nervosa patients, who have more often been overweight before the start of the illness, and whose weight tends to fluctuate during the illness, use potentially dangerous methods to lose weight. In this behaviour they resemble binge-eaters. They usually deny that they have any concern about their weight. In public, or among the family, they may appear to eat normal amounts of food. However, having eaten, they make excuses to leave the group and induce vomiting, and may combine this with the excessive use of laxatives. Because of their eating habits, phases of severe weight reduction, causing emaciation, are interspaced with periods of weight gain. They tend to be fairly social, and are less obsessional than the 'dieters'. In some cases, the woman has been a binge-eater for several months, or even years, before a decision to lose weight relentlessly precipitates her into anorexia nervosa.

Case history: Barbara

Barbara thinks that she began binge-eating when she was ten. The binge usually consisted of eating a packet or two of biscuits, several ice creams, and whatever she could find in the house when she came home from school. By the age of 13, Barbara weighed 70 kg (154 lbs, 11 st; BMI 28.4, 143 per cent of ABW) and began to menstruate. A year later she became interested in boys, became aware that she was fat, and stopped eating sweets and cakes. She knew she was overweight but was popular and had an active social life. As she was intelligent she achieved high grades at school. Over the next five years her weight decreased slowly so that by the age of 18 she weighed 63 kg (139 lbs, 9 st 13 lbs). At this time problems in her parents' marriage were becoming apparent. She obtained entry to university and enjoyed the experience, but at the end of the second year she decided that she must lose weight for the coming summer and began dieting. She also avoided eating whilst studying. As a result her weight fell to 57 kg (126 lbs, 9st) over a period of four months. She restricted her diet further, began counting calories, and started jogging. In addition she started taking laxatives daily because of constipation. Her parents had now separated and after trying to live with her father she moved into her mother's house. By winter her weight had dropped to 32 kg (70 lbs, 5st) and her periods had ceased. She abused laxatives and on days of overeating took emetics so that she would vomit afterwards. She was also able to obtain diuretics from the family doctor for her 'fluid retention'. With these medications, the dieting, and the vomiting she became sufficiently ill to be admitted to hospital for refeeding. In hospital she lost control of her eating and ate everything she could obtain, with the result that her weight increased rapidly and she was praised by the staff. Her weight was now 43 kg (95 lbs, 6 st 11 lbs; BMI 18; 88 per cent of ABW) and she was discharged 'cured of anorexia nervosa'.

Her preoccupation with being extremely thin had ceased, but she still had an eating disorder. This became apparent later that year when she went to India with a group of students to visit Kashmir. She wrote to the clinic from there:

I spent the first 3 weeks of the holiday trekking in Kashmir which is astonishingly beautiful. I was enjoying the fantastic scenery, the fresh air, and the exercise and seemed to escape my problems up here high in the mountains. But on the last days of the trek, I got extremely sick with acute dysentery, fever—the works—and reached Srinagar in great distress doubled up by unbelievable cramps. I had to stay in bed for several weeks feeling pretty rotten. Four of my friends got hepatitis and the hospital was appalling. So what did I do? I ate, believe it or not! Few but ex(?) anorexics could eat with such gusto, in spite of abdominal pains, but somehow I managed and I have continued to eat since I came home. I am now even fatter than before—I'm 66 kg (145 lbs, 10 st 5 lbs) and still have diarrhoea and cramps at times. But these will go; the stool tests are negative. What I'm rather distressed about is my weight (what else!) as I feel it is slowly destroying my ability to cope with everyday life. Just as my eating behaviour is out of control, my life seems to be getting the same way. My social life is eventful and fun, on the whole, and I'm not withdrawn, but I have that frantic sense of imminent doom and I'm incredibly fearful of putting on more weight. I've tried many ways to overcome whatever it is that makes me eat but I can't break the pattern for more than 2 or 3 days. I've thought of the alternatives—getting fatter, vomiting, starving—even suicide . . . but actually I'd give my right arm to have the whole lot sorted out. I'm enjoying Uni, and the course which is full of interest (when I'm not occupying my mind with stagnant thoughts of weight and food). I'd rather anything than spending half my time (and all my money) on food. And it was this feeling that made me diet, and become anorexic, two years ago.

I am lying down listening to Mozart. I should be writing an essay but I ate so much yesterday that I have bad cramps plus an upper abdominal pain from eating too much today. Musing over how long it will take to lose 19 kg (42 lbs, 3st) in the shortest quickest way—etcetera, etcetera—and it sure is a BLOODY WASTE of TIME. I've got a lovely family, some good friends, a fantastic boyfriend, lots of material assets—and instead I retreat into this *awful* life I've created for myself. Is it going to be like this forever? I couldn't stand it for much longer. I feel like it is moving in upon me and asphyxiating me. I can't get much done at all as I'm so caught up in this 'vicious circle'—I'm just as obsessed with food as I was 2 years ago and I want to escape or it will be 3 years, 4 years—ad infinitum. An unbearable thought.

Anorexia nervosa in males

Anorexia nervosa occurs in males fifteen-times less frequently than in females. It begins in the same way and its course is similar. Most males with anorexia nervosa are compulsive exercisers, spending long hours each day jogging, doing press-ups, and other exercises. They are as obsessed about food as women but are less likely to show the same interest in cooking and cook-books. Why males should pursue thinness so relentlessly is obscure, as adolescent men seek to be muscular rather than thin. Men who develop anorexia nervosa may also binge-eat; an example is John who explained why he binge-ate in a letter.

Whenever I get worried about the fact that I have anorexia nervosa and that I binge-eat as well (and I have to admit vomit after the binge) my thoughts turn to Uncle Harry and his character, personality, and his periods of depression. I don't know him too well so the following is only a theory but it seems to fit to our—his and my—personality traits and our mental histories. The theory came into my mind when I was talking to Bill about my eating problems; I don't talk to many people about them but I did to Bill. Bill said 'You set your standards pretty high'. He's right, of course, I do and it may explain my recent overconscientiousness and overconsciousness—an overconsciousness of myself which has trapped me in a small world of self so that I have found it hard to work, to study, to relax, to sleep, to concentrate or even to communicate with others. I have become overconscious of everything I say and do. So when Bill said 'you set your standards pretty high', at first I thought it sounded like flattery. But when I thought about it more I realized that it may have some truth in it.

I have to admit that prior to moving here I had a method of relaxing and releasing this tension. I'd binge. Certainly I felt guilty as I was a strain and burden on Mum and Dad. Since moving I have tried to have as few binges as possible. In all fairness, I have cut down on binges. (I try not to keep count, but I must maintain this positive attitude.) However, regardless of any physical success I *may* have had, the mental impact of telling myself 'I can't' and 'I must not' or 'I intend to go the next three weeks without a single binge', creates much tension and depression. Remember, I no longer have 'bingeing' as an outlet for any 'natural' everyday type tensions. As a matter of fact, the desire to *stop* bingeing has become a tension-maker within itself.

The result is that my tension and depression builds to the point of desperation when I feel I am near insanity and even contemplate suicide. It never gets any further than this as (and I am sad to admit this, but it seems true) I end up having a binge. Somehow, I end up feeling more relaxed.

However, I then promise myself to make a more determined effort to beat the bingeing and the cycle starts again. This tension 'build-up' cycle not only applies to my bingeing. It also applies to other projects, plans, and aspects of my life. I seem to set a goal that *may* be just that little bit too high for me. I don't accept myself and my own limitations. I seem to set myself up for failure.

Everyone suffers tensions. Those who handle them best seem to have some way of relaxing. I *used* to have by bingeing. Although I still have binges *physically*, I now seem to have placed a *mental* prohibition on binges. The *mental* prohibition itself creates tension which sometimes causes a *physical* binge and thus not only becomes ineffective, but also becomes a causal factor itself.

In other words, I either have to find another method of relaxation or, at least for the time being, accept my human weaknesses and, by this, I mean accept an at least limited amount of bingeing. Two important points: first, another form of relaxation will probably have to come about naturally. I don't think I will be able to consciously search for one. If I try to search for one the mere fact that I am conscious of it can prevent relaxation. Second, I find it hard to mentally accept a limited amount of bingeing in the future. Both because I have become determined to defeat it (once again setting my goal too high??) and because of my insecurity, especially financially, as I no longer live with Mum and Dad. Although Mum and Dad have assured me that they would always help me (and I believe trust and love them) there is a large physical distance between us. I also fear that if I let up my 'guard' against bingeing to allow 'limited' bingeing (by limited I mean once, maybe twice, a week), I may end up slipping back and bingeing more. Would Mum and Dad help me then?? . . .

Anyway, I digress. Uncle Harry is a person who sets high standards for himself. I don't feel I'm guessing. He's achieved a hell of a lot in his life; but instead of being proud of it, he is only ashamed/guilty (for the want of better words) for what he hasn't achieved. Look!! He played first class cricket, he's been a successful headmaster. He's had a successful family life (many don't these days) and he's raised three healthy, intelligent and successful children. He's been superannuated and is just as well off as he was when he worked. (This might not be a fantastic achievement, but how many people can retire at 50 yrs. with the prospect of leading a secure, fulfilling and useful life). Me? I haven't achieved any of these things (and actually don't seem to have achieved much), except being thin.

Anyway, the key to Uncle Harry's and my problems is *tension!!* This tension isn't caused by external factors (such as family, work or social problems) but internal standards we set ourselves. I seem to continually set myself up to fail by setting goals that are not within my reach (at least in the time span I allow and expect). It is probably about time we accept our own weaknesses (food may be mind but I'll never admit or accept it??), our inevitable failing, our limitations, and the limits of the human body and mind. We can only do our best and unfortunately our best may sometimes be less than what we, ourselves, expect. Don't worry about whether other people accept us—if they can't accept us as we are with our limitations, that's *their* problem, *not* ours. . . .

Uncle Harry's and my basic problem is the self-inflicted tensions we impose on ourselves. In the past, I have used bingeing to relieve my tensions. I sometimes fear I may suffer nervous breakdowns if I can't find a way to relax. Just lately, especially with my at least attempted mental (if not physical) non-acceptance of bingeing, my fears of having some sort of breakdown have been far from a fantasy. Anyway, the answer for Uncle Harry and me may be this: *accept* ourselves for what we are; *accept* our limitations. For Uncle Harry this may be accepting that he was not meant to be some of the things he feels he should have been or had a duty to be or do. For me, this may mean accepting (and I still don't want to admit it) bingeing to a small extent while I allow some other element to replace it naturally (but by God, I'll still search hard and experiment until I find this other element).

I also have a great need for affiliation, friendship, love and a need to feel needed. But as I said, if others can't accept us as we are, that's *their* problem. There will always be someone to accept us as we are (these people are friends worthy of having).

If we accept ourselves, we can relax. Tension and our inner self-competitiveness will float away. We can then concentrate on giving to others and the world, those good points we have *AND EVERYBODY* (no matter who they are) has good points!! *EVERYBODY!!!*

The onset of anorexia nervosa

Anyway, when I first started to diet I set myself a specific amount that I was allowed to eat each day—usually birdlike portions. I would suffer endlessly if my plan was disrupted by an invitation to lunch. To eat a large meal in the middle of the day was a source of a most guilty conscience for days after, that was the extent of my paranoia! I stuck to my diet religiously. But my reward was always a Coconut Honey Log on Friday afternoons, and, I allowed myself to eat bread during the weekend.

The decision to diet in order to become thin is triggered in a variety of ways, depending on the woman's personality and the particular circumstances in which she finds herself. Often the onset of anorexia nervosa in a young girl follows an awareness that she does not like the shape or size of her body. As has been mentioned, concern about body shape and size is common among adolescent girls; but, in the case of those who have anorexia nervosa, it becomes an obsession. The young woman's preoccupation with her body and her weight often follows a challenge; for example, her family or her friends may tease her about her shape and her weight, or it may follow a competition with a friend to lose weight. Family stress may be a factor of considerable importance in triggering the onset of anorexia. The most common factor is an independence/dependence struggle between the young woman and one or both parents, who give mixed messages, for example, 'you must be independent but we need you at home'. In other cases the young woman is confused: wanting to be independent yet dependent. For example, she may say 'I want to do things my way but I want the security of home'. In other instances the onset of anorexia is associated with a series of events which are stressful in themselves, such as a break-up with a boyfriend, the first experience of sexual intercourse, an unwanted pregnancy, marriage, a major examination, or with a period of further deterioration in already stressful circumstances such as parents separating; or increasing pressure on the girl to 'achieve' at school in extra-curricular activities such as sport or dancing.

The physical features of anorexia nervosa

Before I started to lose weight I weighed about 52 kg (115 lbs, 8st 3 lbs) and had reached my present height. Common sense tells me that my weight was not heavy for that height. But common sense had left me and I wanted to weigh about 43 kg (95 lbs, 6st 11 lbs). And I achieved it! The strange this is that whenever I went to buy new clothes I always saw how revoltingly thin my image in the mirror actually was. But I still felt fat.

The physical symptoms of the illness may result from the behaviour which the girl has used to achieve a loss in weight or from her low body weight itself. When a woman becomes emaciated, her insulating layer of fat is largely lost and in consequence she becomes sensitive to hot and cold temperatures; her hands and feet feel cold and often look blue; her skin may become dry; her hair brittle, and a soft downy hair, called lanugo, may appear on her face, back, or arms. Her heart rate slows down, and her blood pressure falls, probably because her body tries to adjust to the low energy intake by using less energy. In spite of this, the response of patients suffering from anorexia nervosa to exercise is normal and their heart rate increases to the same extent as that of 'normal' women. The bowel motility of many anorexia nervosa patients diminishes because there is less food in the intestines to stimulate peristaltic activity, and constipation is usual. If the women has been on a starvation diet she may develop a vitamin deficiency which can be quite severe.

Oedema may occur in some women, particularly following attempts to gain weight by eating more food. If the woman notices the swelling it may discourage her from attempting to increase her weight further or may induce her to use diuretics. Oedema may also occur when the woman ceases to take diuretics or purgatives because of 'rebound' fluid retention in her body. The oedema may alarm her so much that she starts dangerous methods of weight control again.

Case history: Sandra

Sandra was a tall, quiet girl who was considerate, competent, and well-liked at school. In consequence she was given responsibility both at school and at home.

When she was 14 years old, her weight was 67 kg (148 lbs, 10 st 8 lbs; BMI 23.7; 107 per cent of ABW). She felt that she was too fat and decided to lose weight. Her elder sister had been told by a modelling school that one way was to induce vomiting by putting a finger down her throat. Sandra decided to do this but was disappointed that little weight loss occurred, so she accepted her existing weight as normal and ceased to worry about it. She began swimming competitively and by the age of 17 felt fit, competent, confident, and had lost 6 kg (13 lbs).

Her eighteenth year was one of tragedy. Her mother was killed in a car accident, leaving two younger children. Her older sister became a drug addict and Sandra injured herself so that she had to give up swimming. She felt she could no longer cope and deferred taking her higher school certificate for a year. Sandra took over the responsibilities of housekeeper and looked after her younger sisters. During this period her feeling of confidence and competency disappeared. She wrote in her diary:

I know what I should be doing. I should be going out. But meeting people is a major effort and hassle for me as I feel so uncomfortable and inept in company, especially in arranging to go to new places and meeting new people, that I end up settling for my own company. Food and eating has become such an integral part of everything. I don't want to be like this but what I eat rules my life so that every waking minute seems occupied with thoughts of food and the day passes in the measured times between when I last ate and when I'll eat again. I dream of the perfect day when I have no appetite and no thought, desire or temptation for food or to eat.

When she was 19 she returned to complete her higher school certificate at the local technical college, where comments about her 'emaciation' induced her to eat more. Increasing her food intake was associated with episodes of binge-eating which alarmed her. She began to induce vomiting (remembering her sister's advice) by putting her fingers down her throat. Soon she was inducing vomiting up to ten-times a day. It became increasingly difficult to dispose of the vomit. She resorted to vomiting into plastic bags and disposing of these in the garbage bin. Her father found out what she was doing and insisted that she visit a doctor, who made a diagnosis of anorexia nervosa as her weight was 39 kg (86 lbs, 6 st 2 lbs). He arranged for her to be admitted to hospital to help her gain weight and to stop her vomiting. In hospital she was co-operative and liked by the staff. A psychiatric consultation showed no major psychiatric illness. She was able to continue studying while in hospital and after discharge sat for and passed the examination. Her weight was now 46 kg (102 lbs, 7st 4lbs). She persisted in dieting and in self-induced vomiting and became weak. This induced her to seek re-admission to hospital. The vomiting led to a low level of potassium in her blood and tissues. She was treated with potassium supplement and an intravenous infusion.

Over the next three years during a university course she had six re-admissions to hospital for the effects of self-induced vomiting which led to a low body potassium and dehydration. These in turn caused heart-beat problems (cardiac arrhythmias) and a degree of renal failure. The admissions followed periods of increased binge-eating and vomiting which Sandra related to stress from family problems. She battled against treatment saying that her illness was 'all my fault because I will go on vomiting' and resolved each day to stop. But each day she broke her resolution when she panicked about becoming fat and when she ate food. Although she was watched by her family she managed to dispose of her vomit by hiding it in the garden or in plastic bags which she took to the university where she disposed of it. Sandra's illness became the scape-goat for the family's problems which were considerable.

Her father remarried during this time and on obtaining her degree Sandra left home. Over the next three years her weight increased slowly and is now 53.9 kg (119 lbs, 8 st 7 lbs). She no longer induces vomiting. When last contacted she said 'I look back in horror and wonder if it was some terrible nightmare.'

Behaviour aimed at achieving weight loss, such as starvation, self-induced vomiting, the abuse of laxatives or diuretics, and excessive exercise may cause psychological, physiological, and biochemical disturbances. The psychological disturbances include lassitude and emotional lability (violent swings in mood). The physical disturbances include dilatation of the intestines which gives the woman a feeling of extreme bloating and may aggravate existing constipation. As well, some women bruise easily.

The biochemical disturbances have more serious implications (Fig. 11). The main disturbances are dehydration and changes in the levels of some electrolytes in the blood. The levels of potassium and chloride fall, and the blood becomes alkaline to some degree, producing a metabolic

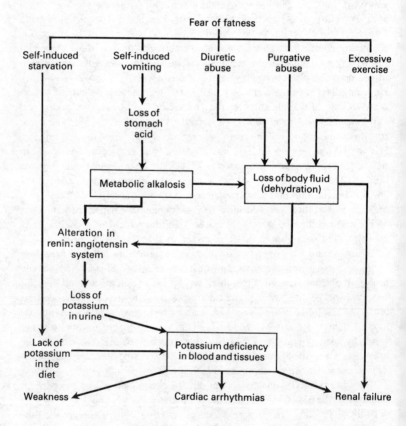

Fig. 11. Electrolyte problems in anorexia nervosa.

alkalosis. Dehydration and low body potassium levels may cause weakness and fatigue. The metabolic alkalosis may impair neuromuscular function, the woman developing tingling in her hands and feet and involuntary hand clenching similar to that found in tetany. The low body potassium and the alkalosis may cause heart-beat irregularities and alterations in the electro-cardiogram.

In spite of the severity of the weight loss and the potentially dangerous nature of the methods used to achieve it, it is surprising how few patients with anorexia nervosa develop severe potassium deficiency. This probably reflects the physiological compensatory mechanisms which occur and the fact that the diet is relatively nutritious, apart from being very deficient in energy. Many women who have anorexia nervosa are aware that their weight losing behaviours may cause potassium depletion and choose foods which are low in energy but rich in potassium (such as tomatoes, orange juice, and capsicum).

Many patients suffering from anorexia are hyperactive, always doing things, and unable to relax. The hyperactivity may be the cause of insomnia, especially early morning walking, which is a feature in some patients with anorexia nervosa.

People with anorexia nervosa (and bulimia nervosa) are more likely to shop-lift than 'normal' eaters. In one study reported from the USA, one anorexic patient in three either shop-lifted or stole, and many tended to hoard.

Case history: Debbie

Debbie was caught shop-lifting two children's pillow-cases and a box of chocolates. Ten days later she wrote:

> For the life of me I cannot believe why I did such a stupid and criminal act. Do I put it down to another destructive coping mechanism like that of anorexia and bulimia which has been so familiar to me for the past ten years? That is what I have to believe in order to come to terms with it and at the same time learn that I need to find other methods of coping with whatever pressures I may be under. The humiliation of that day and the repercussions are just not worth it. How could I explain to the lady who caught me what I was going through and that she should know that normally I just wouldn't do something like this? I actually tried but she told me that I was just the same as all the others and that it's a shame people like me don't go to jail. The silly thing is that I had more than enough money in my purse to pay for the things I'd taken and I think that only made things worse.
>
> From here on, I think my body and mind relented to whatever was to happen and so as I was escorted from the shopping centre by two police

officers, pushing my 21-month-old baby in her stroller, I convinced myself
that people weren't staring at me and anyway this wasn't happening. Even at
the police station, being questioned, finger-printed, formally charged, and a
Court date given, I was oblivious to the reality of all that had happened and
left the police station in a very dejected state, knowing that I had to explain all
of this to my husband.

Dental problems also occur among anorexia nervosa patients, particularly those who induce vomiting. The main problem is a loss of dental
enamel, due to the effects of acid vomit on the teeth. In addition,
dehydration, by altering the quantity and composition of the saliva,
increases the likelihood of dental decay.

Menstrual disturbances in anorexia nervosa

*I haven't had my periods for the last 10 years. I have forgotten that it is
normal to have periods—and not normal to be without them. Even
though it seems a lot easier and convenient for them to be non-existent,
I'm also aware that I'm not experiencing the emotional state of a fully
developed woman because of the shut-down of my hormonal system.
I find that I am feeling deprived of this privilege but the only way to
regain my periods, is to do the positive thing that will remedy this
situation—eat!*

A major physical problem among females who have anorexia nervosa is
that they fail to reach menarche, or their menstrual periods cease, often
before much weight has been lost. Indeed, the absence of menstruation
(amenorrhoea) is one of the features essential for a diagnosis to be made.

The explanation of the menstrual disturbances is rather complex, as it
involves the interplay of a number of hormones (Fig. 12, p. 80). The
control of these hormonal relationships is situated in the area of the brain
called the hypothalamus, which in turn is influenced by messages from
other parts of the brain, and from outside, such as an emotional shock.

In childhood, before puberty, throughout the reproductive years, and
into old age the hypothalamus secretes and releases several hormones
into small blood-vessels which carry them to the pituitary gland where
they induce the synthesis and release of pituitary hormones, which have
profound effects on the body. Because they cause the pituitary gland to
release hormones, the hormones made in the hypothalamus are called
releasing hormones.

The releasing hormone concerned with ovulation and menstruation is called the gonadotrophic releasing hormone or GnRH. In childhood, a small but constant amount of GnRH is released, but in the years just prior to the onset of menstruation a change occurs and GnRH begins to be released in pulsatile surges throughout the day. These pulsatile surges begin when the girl begins to grow rather rapidly in the three or four years before menarche. When her body reaches a 'critical' weight, or more accurately when the proportion of fat in her body exceeds a critical level, she menstruates for the first time, reaching menarche. Once menarche has been reached, GnRH continues to be released in a pulsatile manner throughout the reproductive years, the quantity varying from day to day. For example, during menstruation a large surge of GnRH occurs and this stimulates specialized cells in the pituitary gland to synthesize and to release follicle-stimulating hormone (or FSH). As its name implies, FSH stimulates the growth of a number of egg-containing structures (follicles) in the ovary. At puberty each ovary contains over 200 000 follicles. Each month between puberty and menopause, 10 to 20 follicles are stimulated to grow, one of them out-stripping all the others. As they develop, they synthesize the female sex hormone, oestrogen, and release it into the circulating blood. Oestrogen is taken up preferentially by the tissues of the genital organs and the breasts, particularly by the glandular lining, or endometrium, of the uterus and that of the breasts which are induced to develop, increasing in thickness. At the same time the rising amounts of oestrogen in the blood 'feedback negatively' to the hypothalamus and to the pituitary gland, leading to a slow fall in the amount of GnRH released and consequently a fall in FSH. At mid-cycle, that is about 16 days before the next menstrual period, a surge of oestrogen secretion occurs, causing a 'positive feedback' to the hypothalamus and to the pituitary. In response the pituitary releases both a surge of FSH and a surge of a second hormone, the luteinizing hormone or LH. LH, in turn, acts on the largest of the growing follicles, which is three-times as large as all the others, measuring about 23 mm in diameter. The follicle, by this time, has stretched the surface of the ovary. The follicle 'bursts' and releases its ovum (or egg). Ovulation has occurred. LH also causes changes in the character of the collapsed follicle, now called a 'corpus luteum'. It becomes yellow and begins to synthesize and release a second female sex hormone, progesterone. Progesterone develops the endometrium further, so that it is ready should the ovum be fertilized. If fertilization fails to occur, the corpus

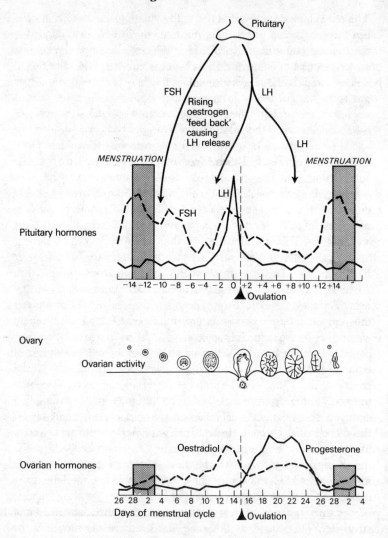

Fig. 12. The control of menstruation.

luteum dies, and ceases to produce hormones. This leads to menstruation and a repetition of the hormonal cycle.

It has been observed that the close interrelationships of the hormones can be interrupted by a number of factors. If the body weight falls below a critical level, the hypothalamus fails to release GnRH in pulsatile surges. In consequence, the pituitary fails to release sufficient FSH to stimulate the ovaries, and menstruation ceases. Once the body weight increases above the critical level, the menses resume, often after a delay. It is also known that excessive exercise inhibits pulsatile GnRH release with consequent amenorrhoea. A woman whose weight is below normal, but above the critical level, and who exercises excessively, for example a ballet dancer, also fails to menstruate, becoming amenorrhoeic.

The hormonal changes discussed provide an explanation for the menstrual disturbances. When a woman's BMI (see p. 18) falls to 15 or below, or her body weight falls below the critical level of approximately 80 per cent of Average Body Weight, GnRH ceases to be released in a pulsatile manner, and the surges of GnRH are replaced by a steady low secretion, similar to that which occurred before puberty. Because GnRH is no longer released in surges, the pituitary fails to release FSH and LH at levels sufficient to stimulate the ovaries to secrete sufficient amounts of the female sex hormones and amenorrhoea results.

If the period of amenorrhoea lasts for longer than six months, the woman should consider taking an oral contraceptive pill or, if she prefers, the regimen of hormone replacement recommended for menopausal women. The reason for this advice is that oestrogen deprivation over a period of months leads to a loss of bone density, in other words, the bones become less strong. In healthy women who eat a good diet containing at least 1 g of calcium a day, the quantity and the strength of their bones increases until the age of 40. After the age of 40, the bone density decreases, and the decrease is more marked in the ten years after the menopause. The less dense bones of the spine (the vertebrae) are likely to collapse in late middle age causing back pain and a decrease in the woman's height, while the less dense bones of the forearm and the hip may fracture after a minor fall. The less dense bones are said to be osteoporotic and the woman has osteoporosis.

Women who have anorexia nervosa will not increase the quantity and strength of their bone during the time they have amenorrhoea, because their ovaries do not secrete oestrogen, and consequently it would be wise of them to take oestrogen supplements to reduce the risk of osteoporosis in later years.

It is interesting that between 10 and 20 per cent of anorexia nervosa patients develop amenorrhoea before any weight loss has occurred (in fact their weight may even be increasing). Menstruation usually starts again when the woman's body weight increases to reach a BMI of 19 or more, but some women recommence menstruating at a lower body weight.

Because of the uncertainty about when ovulation and menstruation will recommence, sexually active women who do not intend to become pregnant (and babies born to women of low body weight have an increased chance of being underweight for age at birth) should not rely on lack of menstruation as protection. The woman or her male partner should use a contraceptive method even when her body weight is low.

On the other hand, some women do not start menstruating again for some months, or even years, after returning to a normal body weight range. If a detailed history is taken from these women it is usually found that they have been using weight-losing methods such as excessive exercise, self-induced vomiting, and laxative abuse before weight loss or during and after weight gain. In these cases the menstrual disturbance is almost certainly associated with the weight-losing behaviour.

However, not all patients who continue to have amenorrhoea before they have lost much weight, or after refeeding, use such methods, so that some other explanation is possible. At present we do not know what it is.

Case history: Maria

Maria is the attractive youngest daughter of a family who emigrated to Australia before she was born. At the age of 14, a year after her menstrual periods started, she became aware that her family were fat, and she did not want to become fat like them. Her weight was within the desirable range at 47.5 kg (105 lbs, 7 st 7 lbs, BMI 20.6; 100 per cent of ABW) and she was teased at school as being a 'sexy Italian'. She bought some slimming tablets from the chemist, but after taking them for 5 days stopped because they 'did no good'. As her friends at school were dieting, she decided to do so too. Her plan was to eat normally for one day and starve the next day. She tended to overeat when not starving so that after two months she had gained, not lost, 4 kg (9 lbs). She heard that if she took laxatives she would lose weight, and as her mother had put out laxatives for the family when they had not opened their bowels each day, felt she had 'permission' to use laxatives to lose weight. She also started exercising, spending 1 or 2 hours a day in exercise, telling the family she was preparing for the school sports.

Within a month of starting the exercise programme, her menstrual periods ceased, although she had only lost 2 kg (4 lbs). Maria was secretly pleased that she had no periods but was worried that people might know and wonder if she was normal. For the next five months, in spite of exercise and laxatives, her weight remained the same. In desperation to lose weight Maria refused to eat with the family as the food was 'all pasta and unhealthy'. By the age of 16, she was dieting rigidly and was abusing laxatives. Her weight began to decrease and on her 18th birthday she weighed 31 kg (68 lbs, 4 st 12 lbs; BMI 12; 65 per cent of ABW). Her parents now intervened. She was admitted to hospital with a diagnosis of anorexia nervosa and started on a refeeding programme.

After three months when she was discharged from hospital her weight had increased to 49 kg (108 lbs, 7 st 10 lbs; BMI 18.5; 90 per cent of ABW) and she had a menstrual period. At home, she continued to be afraid of becoming fat and returned to using excessive laxatives and dieted carefully to maintain her weight at about 44 kg (98 lbs, 7 st). She had no further menstrual periods until a year later when she found a job and a boyfriend of whom her parents approved. She started menstruating in spite of the fact that her weight had fallen to 42 kg (93 lbs, 6 st 9 lbs).

Infertility and anorexia nervosa

Although we have discussed the possibility of an unexpected pregnancy occurring during or after treatment of anorexia nervosa, studies made in Canada and our own studies, suggest that many women who have anorexia nervosa or bulimia nervosa are likely to be infertile.

One of our Canadian colleagues examined 66 women attending an infertility clinic for the presence of an eating disorder, using a reliable psychometric test and an interview. She found that 1.5 per cent of the women had anorexia nervosa, 6 per cent had bulimia nervosa and 9 per cent had an atypical eating disorder. This is a higher proportion than would be expected in the community. In each case the cause of the infertility was a lack of ovulation.

In our study of 14 women in whom the only reason for infertility was anovulation and who were to be treated with gonadotrophic releasing hormone (a fertility injection), we found that ten of the 14 women had a prior history of anorexia nervosa, one had had bulimia nervosa, one had an atypical eating disorder, and one woman was a compulsive exerciser. At the time we conducted the study, six of the 14 women still had an eating disorder and the compulsive exerciser was still compulsively exercising.

Pregnancy and anorexia nervosa

Pregnancy, particularly if unexpected, may pose several challenges to women who are recovering or who have recently recovered from anorexia nervosa. The women respond in several ways. Some women look forward to the pregnancy, feeling that during pregnancy and when caring for a child they would be less preoccupied with body weight and eating and that 'pregnant women are supposed to be fat'. These women often find that pregnancy provides a relief from their eating and weight-losing behaviours. Some women's desire to become pregnant can be sufficiently strong to induce the woman to increase her weight and to try to recover from anorexia nervosa.

Other women become distressed, feeling that they cannot cope with 'putting on weight'. These women and others may continue their eating disorder behaviours during pregnancy. If these behaviours include the dangerous methods of self-induced vomiting, diuretic, or laxative abuse, the woman is more likely to have complications during pregnancy and to give birth to a low-birth-weight baby compared with women who have normal eating behaviour. If the woman fails to gain weight between antenatal visits during the pregnancy, admission to hospital may be required. She is less likely to breast-feed as she believes that lactating women lose the weight gained during pregnancy less quickly and to a lesser degree than women who choose not to breast-feed.

The woman's concern about her previous eating behaviours and attitudes may interfere with her care of the child. She may be over-concerned about her child's shape and weight and this may transfer and affect the child's behaviour. From time to time the woman may relapse and limit the food available in the house. This may help her, but may be detrimental to her family.

One of our patients wrote:

It is all coming together, gradually. I just hope that I am not going to do too much damage to my kids whilst I 'grow up' and that I have enough time left to enjoy being me and that the fears and depression and isolation never overwhelm my mind again. On the basis of past experience I suppose that's a lot to ask—but who would have believed that I would have two kids of my own either!

I hope that everyone who is trapped in anorexia nervosa or any other 'lonely obsessive trap', and who realizes their misery and wants to escape, finds someone to trust and help them, as I did.

The possible problems which may occur during pregnancy and child-rearing, particularly if a low-birth-weight baby is born, suggest that women who have had an eating disorder should recover completely before becoming pregnant, or if they have not should have someone they can trust to help them during the pregnancy and after the birth.

Pregnancy may act as a challenge to a woman who has apparently recovered from anorexia nervosa, even if she has maintained her body weight in the normal range for some time. Normally, a woman may be expected to gain about 11 kg during a pregnancy. Of this weight gain, half is contributed by the baby's weight, the weight of the placenta, and the growth of the uterus and breasts. One-tenth is from the increase in the volume of blood. This leaves just over 5 kg, half being due to increased fluid in the body and half due to increased fat deposited.

Many women who have apparently recovered from an eating disorder tend to gain less weight during the pregnancy. Most of the reduction in weight gain is due to a lack of fat deposited, because the woman eats less food.

Case history: Anthea

Anthea had gained very little weight during her first pregnancy. In her second pregnancy she was repeating this pattern and sought help. After discharge from the Eating Disorders Unit, she wrote:

> What a battle it's been trying to gain weight so that I can have a healthy baby and at the same time still have the desire to keep my weight down. As you know, I tried hard on my own but didn't have much success. After ten years of having an eating disorder, the fact that I was carrying a child was not strong enough for me to stop my behaviour. I kept thinking back to my first pregnancy—no morning sickness, healthy and fit the whole way through, and I have birth to a perfectly healthy and beautiful baby girl—knowing that my weight gain and eating habits throughout that pregnancy were far from normal. But I was anxious the whole time that my lack of weight gain would harm the baby.
>
> I knew that I couldn't take the same risks again and so spent eight weeks at the Unit. The time I spent there was more than helpful, although the separation from my baby and husband was more difficult than I had ever imagined.
>
> My weight gain in hospital was quite considerable initially and quite difficult to come to terms with, so I had to keep remembering exactly why I was there. The sooner I came to terms with that, the sooner I'd be back at home with my family.
>
> My first week home was quite difficult, the hardest thing being the rejection given me by my daughter. Daddy was her hero and I'd taken the back seat. Feeling very sorry for myself, I found myself quite depressed and very tempted to return to former eating habits. I must admit that I had some difficult moments but managed to fight these bad times.
>
> After being home now for six weeks and with about ten weeks to go I feel so proud to be pregnant! I know that my weight gain has slowed down, but my eating habits are a lot more normal than in my first pregnancy which makes me very content and very ready for the birth of another baby.

The thing for me to remember is that after I've had this baby, my body isn't going to return to normal straight away. At this stage I don't know how I will react, but will face it when the time comes.

The diet of anorexia nervosa patients

As has been mentioned earlier, anorexia nervosa patients are preoccupied with food. They collect and read books and magazine articles relating to food, dieting, and body weight. Often they take over cooking for the family. They have a better knowledge of nutrition than the general public. Several investigators have shown that many women who have anorexia nervosa avoid carbohydrates in their diet, and that a low carbohydrate intake is the distinctive feature of the diet chosen so that they will lose weight. However a recent study in Sydney places some doubt on whether 'carbohydrate starvation' is the distinctive feature of anorexia nervosa. Seventeen patients who had been ill with anorexia nervosa for less than 15 months volunteered to be interviewed by a dietitian on two occasions: from these interviews typical daily food intakes were reconstructed, and the diet eaten by the women at the peak of their illness was compared with that of 'normal' women of similar age. The diet of a patient with anorexia nervosa contained one-sixth the energy, one-sixth the carbohydrate, one-third the protein, and one-ninth the fat of a normal woman's diet. When the proportion of energy obtained from carbohydrate, protein, and fat was calculated, the amount obtained from carbohydrate was similar in both groups. This indicates that the anorexia nervosa patients reduced all items of their weight-losing diet and did not preferentially starve themselves of carbohydrate. These findings suggest that they have a better than average knowledge of nutrition, but these women, although scoring higher in a test of nutritional knowledge as a group, showed wide individual variations.

The treatment of anorexia nervosa[*]

It's about time I got over my anorexia, and I agree that I've wasted enough time on it. But at times I think that I hang on to my old patterns of eating behaviour, or really non-eating behaviour, as the only secure thing I can fashion from such a changing and, as I feel sometimes, topsy

[*] See p. 101 for a summary

turvy life. I often feel that is the only part of my life over which I can exercise any sort of control, though it ends up in the absurdity of feeling that every bit is an act of losing control.

Before any treatment is offered, the therapist must have taken a careful history to confirm that the woman has anorexia nervosa and not that her body weight is low as a consequence of experimenting with dieting, her choice of a career, or her life-style.

An example of the importance of making this distinction is that of Zoe.

Zoe had always wanted to be a ballet dancer, and at the age of 15 was selected by her ballet teacher to compete for a place in a prestigious full-time ballet school. Her teacher had impressed on her the need to be thin and had weighed her once a week from the age of 12, praising her for keeping thin. Zoe said she had never had to control her weight consciously as she went to ballet classes three evenings each week, and didn't eat between school and the class. When she was weighed six months before the selection process her ballet teacher told her that she would have to lose some weight or she would not be selected. At that time her BMI was 17.5 and her weight was 85 per cent of the Average Body Weight.

She started dieting and soon her weight loss was noticed by the headmistress of her school who contacted Zoe's mother fearing that Zoe was another girl who had anorexia nervosa. Her mother at once took Zoe to a doctor who arranged for her to be admitted to hospital for refeeding. Her BMI was now 16 (78 per cent of Average Body Weight). In hospital she refused to eat, or gave her food to other patients. She adopted this strategy because she believed that if she gained weight her chance of selection to the ballet school would be jeopardized. Her resistance to refeeding confirmed to the health professionals that Zoe had anorexia nervosa. She was also considered by them to be uncooperative, untruthful, and difficult.

After three weeks in hospital she had failed to gain any weight, and after discussion was taken home by her parents. She was then referred to one of us. When we talked to Zoe, her fear of not being selected for the ballet school became clear. We reassured her that in Australia, ballet dancers needed to have a BMI of at least 18 (80 to 90 per cent of Average Body Weight), or they would 'not look good on stage'. Zoe accepted the reassurance and gained 2.5 kg (5½ lbs) in the next five weeks, which brought her weight into the desired range.

She was selected to train at the ballet school and has maintained her weight within the range acceptable for a dancer since that time. She does not appear to be more preoccupied about food, dieting, or her weight than the other students, and is enjoying the training at which she has been very successful.

The reverse situation of that of Zoe can also occur, when the diagnosis of anorexia nervosa may be difficult as many young women who have the disorder initially deny that they have it.

Anorexia is a psychosomatic disorder, during which physical symptoms may develop because of the self-induced starvation and other methods of inducing weight loss. The main treatment is psychological, involving cognitive behaviour therapy, supportive psychotherapy, counselling about eating and potentially dangerous methods of losing weight, and, when appropriate, other psychological supports, such as relaxation, family therapy, and marital therapy.

In the past many treatments for anorexia nervosa have been suggested and used, such as insulin shock therapy, force-feeding, tube-feeding, 'sleep therapy', and using medications to stimulate appetite. These treatments are still being used and the results are presented at various conferences. It is true that they may work and the patient may put on weight while she is in hospital, but in no case has a follow-up period of over 12 months been reported. These treatments should not be used as they do not allow patients to learn or relearn normal eating behaviour and they often cause feelings of loss of control, and panic. Drugs are seldom necessary but they may be needed in certain cases; for example, if a patient is clinically depressed she may need anti-depressants or if she has an infection she may need antibiotics.

Anorexia nervosa patients are individuals. They have different problems, different needs, and are at different stages of their illness when they come for treatment—they need treatment by a person who can offer sympathetic understanding and individual treatment. This can be done by a multidisciplinary team as long as there is one consistent person in the team to whom the patient can relate and who can co-ordinate treatment.

The varied needs of the anorexic frequently call for a multidisciplinary approach, including help from a dietitian or a social worker. The time being spent with an individual health professional depends on the patient's current needs and the relationships formed—for example, the dietitian may be the main therapist in certain cases.

The principal problem in treatment is that the patient wants to eat but is terrified that if she does so she will lose control of her eating and be unable to limit her weight gain. For this reason the hope expressed by parents, partner, or friends of an anorexia nervosa victim that 'All she has to do to get better is to eat' is unrealistic and counter-productive. The fear of losing control often extends to other aspects of the patient's life, but is particularly relevant to body weight and to food intake. For example, the fear of losing control over body weight prevents the patient from eating more than the amount she has set herself as she believes that if she eats what 'other people eat' she will put on weight rapidly. Because of this fear, patients weigh themselves daily or more often, and if they find that they have gained 1 kg (2.2 lb) for no apparent reason, immediately restrict the amount of food they eat or use some other method of losing weight. Even when they are emaciated they often find it safer to underestimate the amount of food they eat, rather than risk losing control over eating. As anorexia nervosa patients love food, this need to control their food intake may cause psychological turbulence. They are fearful that if they permit themselves to eat, they may be unable to stop, and that they will go on an eating binge. As many have experienced binge-eating before and after developing anorexia nervosa, the fear is real to them and it requires considerable patience by the therapist to dispel it. The therapist must be aware, constantly, that treatment has three objectives.

The first objective is to help the patient increase her weight so that it is within the normal range. The choice of where her weight should lie, within the normal BMI range, is a balance between the weight a woman is likely to accept (usually it is the range of a BMI of 19 to 20) and the weight which is likely to be associated with a successful outcome (that is a BMI of 21 to 23). Although it is a bit on the thin side of the normal range, the reason for choosing a BMI of 19 to 20 (which is about 90 per cent of Average Body Weight) is that in this weight range most physiological functions, such as temperature control and menstruation, will have returned or will soon return to normal at this weight. The weight level is also realistic as it helps the patient avoid feeling anxious about becoming fat.

The second objective is to help the patient learn to re-establish normal eating behaviour and to avoid other methods such as excessive exercise, self-induced vomiting, or laxative abuse. The third objective is to explain the physical symptoms in a way which is understood by the patient.

Increasing body weight

Although anorexia nervosa is a psychosomatic problem, the first priority in treatment must be to achieve weight gain, as most patients do not respond to psychological treatment at low body weight or when failing to gain weight. It is important for the patient to realize that the long-term aim is for her to learn to increase her weight and to maintain it within the normal desirable range for her age and height. This does not mean that she has to control her weight to within 0.5 kg (1.1 lbs) on a day-to-day basis. In fact, weighing more than once a week is meaningless (unless the woman is in hospital receiving treatment) as it is normal for the weight to vary by more than 1 kg (2.2 lbs) over a period of days. Although a weight corresponding to a BMI of 19 is set as a target weight, this is the minimum weight for normal physiological function such as the return of menstruation. At this weight, the patient is still on the thin side of normal and as many women look better at a higher weight she may be encouraged to attempt this. There are certain exceptions; for example, if the woman is a fashion model or a ballet dancer she may not accept a weight corresponding to a BMI over 19 as desirable, and she and her therapist have to agree that a lower weight is appropriate in her case. They may also have to agree that she is likely to remain preoccupied with her weight and to limit her food intake, so that she may retain the body shape expected of her profession.

Weight gain is achieved by 'refeeding'. During refeeding the patient learns that as she gains weight she will feel physically better and this will help her to cope with her everyday problems, particularly if she has had anorexia nervosa for many years. Weight gain may be undertaken with the woman as an out-patient, or admission to hospital may be necessary, or preferred, by the woman.

In either case, she should be alerted to the possibility of a rapid weight gain when refeeding treatment begins. This results through the expansion of the extracellular compartment of the body (the tissues between the cells), and an increase in the body's glycogen-water pool (p. 141).

Because of this, which is to her a disturbing change, she should be reassured that the weight gain, which is due to rehydration, will resolve spontaneously if she continues to eat the prescribed food menu.

In hospital the woman is first given the opportunity to be responsible for her own weight gain, with the support of the dietitian and the nursing team. During this time she is ambulant, doing mild exercise, talking with trained nursing staff, and attending discussion and educational groups with other women, to help her gain insight into her problems. She is encouraged to pursue interests such as relaxation craft, painting, and typing. Most women respond to this lenient approach.

If the woman does not respond, a more structured programme should be implemented. In extreme cases the woman may have to be observed continually or kept in somewhat extreme isolation in a single-bedded room and have to stay in bed until the 'target weight' is reached by refeeding. This strategy is necessary because many patients try to find methods to avoid eating (by disposing of food in the WC, or wash basin, or elsewhere) or to get rid of food by inducing vomiting or abusing laxatives (see Table 6).

Table 6. Cheating with food intake as told by patients

1. Hide food in table napkin
2. Leave the crust of toast or bread on the plate, discarding the rest
3. Dispose of food into vases, stuffed toys, cupboards, or out of the window
4. Keep food in the mouth and discard it when cleaning the teeth
5. Surreptitiously feed the family dog under the table

If she eats the amount of food expected and conforms to treatment by avoiding weight-losing strategies, and starts gaining weight, she is offered a 'reward' or a 'privilege'. For example, she may be allowed to get up and have a shower, or to watch television. On the other hand, if she fails to put on weight she knows that privileges may be taken away and she may be ordered to go back to bed and stay there. Most authorities insist that the patient is weighed each day at the same time of day on the same scales, but some believe that, because minor daily changes in weight occur, it is preferable to weigh the patient twice a week, not daily. Weighing has to be done to a ritual and the nurse has to make sure that the patient doesn't cheat, for example, by putting weights in her pockets or by drinking a large amount of water just before being weighed (Table 7).

During refeeding in hospital the patient is expected to eat a varied diet providing between 9200 kJ and 10 400 kJ (2200 to 2500 kcals) each day. The aim is for a weight increase of 1–1.5 kg (2.2–3.3 lbs) per week. In the early stages of refeeding this increase can be achieved with a smaller amount of food eaten providing about 8400 kJ (2000 kcals). In the later part of the programme an increased amount of food is usually necessary. The diet is devised to contain an adequate amount of complex carbohydrate so that the metabolic problem of ketosis is avoided.

Table 7. Cheating to apparently increase weight as told by patients

---

1. Drinking large amounts of water the night before being weighed
2. Avoid emptying bladder before being weighed
3. Drinking bath or shower water
4. Binge-eating the night before
5. Wear heavy jewellery or heavy clothing (such as ski braces)
6. Sew weights into night-clothes or insert the weight into her bra early in the morning when about to be weighed

---

Out-patient treatment is appropriate for some patients. The advantages are that as an out-patient the patient can increase her weight at her own speed, so that she feels safe and in control; she has to take responsibility for her eating and, with support and guidance from the therapist, can relearn eating patterns which are appropriate to her life-style. Some women may be helped if the woman and her therapist agree that she may remain at the same weight for some weeks before a further increase in weight is attempted.

This strategy helps the patient to gain confidence that she is in control. With her therapist's support and encouragement she learns how much she needs to eat to control her weight at an appropriate level. She has to be made aware that she will not be rewarded for gaining weight rapidly, as this may merely indicate that she is binge-eating.

The therapist also has the responsibility of helping the patient to adjust to the other problems (such as relationship problems) which may have arisen because of the patient's fear of losing control.

The therapist's function is to explore these problems with the patient, and to encourage her motivation to return to 'normal' eating. She must also give the patient the confidence to continue with treatment and must teach her to maintain her body weight within the normal range.

As the therapist becomes aware of the patient's fear of losing control and her resistance to changing her eating behaviour, it may become apparent that treatment will have to be delayed until the patient is 'ready to get better', even though this means that a few patients will become severely ill and have to be rescued from impending death by urgent admission to hospital. Other patients who require admission include those who are severely ill when first seen, those who fail to make progress as an out-patient, those who persist in continuing with their weight-losing behaviour, and those who are incapable of responding to treatment as a result of the physical and mental consequences of the very low body weight. In other cases the patient's doctor may feel she should be admitted to hospital, or she herself may prefer to be treated in hospital.

During the time that she gains weight, the patient often feels 'full' and her stomach may bulge. She needs to be told that this will happen, and needs to be reassured that the abdominal swelling will not remain. Unless this is done, she may feel that she is losing control. These are temporary symptoms which the patient has to suffer to achieve her goal. The abdominal swelling is due to distension of the intestines, and, once intestinal function becomes normal, the abdomen becomes flat, whilst fat is deposited on her limbs and body. During refeeding the patient should avoid buying tight-fitting clothes, such as jeans, because within two or three weeks after her desirable weight has been achieved and the distension has subsided they will be too big. The appearance of a 'bulging stomach' is usually more marked among patients who are refed in hospital and who are not permitted to exercise, than among patients who are allowed to undertake supervised exercise.

When a reasonable amount of weight gain each week has been obtained, it will be found that the amount tapers off as the 'target' body weight range is approached. At this stage women who are patients in hospital should remain in hospital for two or three weeks after their weight is in the desirable weight range to make sure that the weight is maintained, and that they gain confidence that they can maintain their weight in the desired weight range, and can learn how much to eat.

After reaching a body weight in the middle of her target weight range, the patient must continue with her refeeding diet, that is, a diet containing more energy than would normally be expected to be necessary to maintain a weight in the normal weight range, for about a month. This strategy prevents a sudden drop in body weight to below the desired weight range when refeeding stops.

Some women require higher than expected energy intakes for some weeks, or even months, if they are to maintain their desired body weight. The reason for this is not known.

Establishing normal eating behaviour

As most anorexia nervosa patients restrict the number of different foods they eat, the second aim of treatment is for the patient to learn to choose from a wide range of foods. This wide choice provides her body with the many nutrients it needs. She is helped to stop seeing foods as 'good' (that is, with a low energy content) or 'bad' (high energy content), and learns to eat a wide variety of foods in sensible amounts. Eating sensibly includes learning to eat in front of people, at different venues and in social situations, and to be comfortable about this. For example, if someone who has had anorexia nervosa goes to a social function, such as a wedding or a Chinese banquet, she may eat far more than her body requires that day and has to learn to accept that this is normal. She also has to conquer her preoccupation with food and her urge to weigh every item of food she eats and to calculate its calorie content. Many patients have no idea of how much they can eat without weight gain and have trouble recognizing cues for hunger and satiation. During treatment they learn to recognize these cues and are taught the elements of dietetics. Many patients who have an eating disorder do not know what 'normal' eating is. To help them be aware of normal eating, we have listed some of the criteria in Table 11 on page 127.

A major concern is to change the potentially dangerous weight-losing behaviours resorted to by many women who have anorexia nervosa. Many patients respond to information about the short- and long-term effects of vomiting and abuse of purgatives, diuretics, and slimming tablets, and are willing, at least initially, to reduce the frequency of these behaviours. They find reassurance on learning what effects to expect when they stop vomiting and using laxatives, for example, that they may undergo a temporary weight gain as they become rehydrated, and that constipation may persist for some time, as well as abdominal fullness and cramps. As the patients are preoccupied with body weight and abdominal fullness, these are the very symptoms which make them anxious and may make them return to vomiting and laxatives unless they know that these symptoms are to be expected.

Women who have anorexia nervosa may be manipulative and un-truthful when they are questioned about their food intake and their methods of losing weight. The therapist may have to confront the patient before treatment is started, to establish, as far as possible, whether she is prepared to agree to try and eat more food. Truthful common-sense con-frontation is also required during treatment if the patient is discovered cheating. For example, she may appear to take all the food offered and then dispose of most of it surreptitiously down the sink, or place weights in the pockets of her dressing gown when she knows that she is to be weighed. She may also secretly resort to self-induced vomiting or abuse laxatives when she decides that she has reached a certain weight and does not want to gain more, as she is fearful that she is losing control of her eating.

Explaining the physical symptoms

Some patients are content that they no longer menstruate, but if they are in their late-teens or twenties they may need reassurance that menstruation will return if they maintain their higher weight, stop extreme methods of weight control, exercising excessively, and abusing laxatives and diuretics, although the return of menstruation may be delayed for several months. As the patient gains weight she may want her menstrual periods to start again as she sees this as a demonstration that she is getting better. Other women require discussion and reassurance that their dry skin, broken hair, and lanugo hair will disappear as their nutrition improves.

The place of exercise during treatment

Studies have shown that women who have anorexia nervosa gain body weight faster if their activity is limited during treatment. For this reason, it would appear sensible to limit a woman's activity when she is admitted to hospital, both to reduce her time in hospital and the cost of treatment.

There are other factors, however, to be considered. These include the quality of the patient's life, how she feels and looks, and the need for her to learn or relearn what is 'normal activity' and what is 'sensible activity'. Treatment is also directed to encourage the weight gain to be partly lean (muscle) body weight as well as the increased deposition of body fat.

In the general community, exercise is encouraged so that conditions such as obesity are avoided, the chance of having a heart attack is reduced, and the mobility of joints is maintained. Most people say that they feel better about themselves and their body if they exercise regularly. Also, women who are trying to gain weight find that regular exercise reduces the size of the abdomen by redistributing fat and increasing intestinal tone.

Graduated, controlled exercise during the refeeding period of an anorexia nervosa sufferer increases the recovery of lean body mass by increasing the muscle mass. As some women who have anorexia nervosa immediately reduce their food intake once they have reached their target weight range and in consequence lose some of the fat they had deposited during refeeding, the greater the proportion of weight gained as lean body mass, the better the long-term outcome may be. This avoids a woman being discouraged by observing her temporary loss of body weight.

As we noted earlier in this chapter, many anorexia nervosa patients exercise excessively and many others appear to be continually active or hyperactive. If these women are denied the opportunity to exercise whilst in hospital, the result may be agitation and the woman may continue exercising in secret. In most cases the woman does not know how much exercise she is doing and cannot equate her secret exercise with what is appropriate for her after refeeding.

It seems sensible for an anorexia nervosa patient, if she so wishes, to embark on a graduated exercise programme whilst under treatment so that she may learn and accept a sensible exercise programme which is appropriate for her and which aims to achieve the levels of exercise she is likely to do after leaving hospital. This allows the woman to learn what exercise is safe and 'normal'. However, if the woman is not gaining weight whilst being refed, the amount of exercise she does must be reduced or may have to stop.

There is further benefit. An exercise programme which the woman does during refeeding and during the maintenance of her body weight in the target weight range may prevent her from replacing the eating disorder with an exercise disorder. In this, the pursuit of thinness and a preoccupation with body weight, shape, and food intake is replaced by a preoccupation with exercise and body shape, which can be just as disabling as the previous eating disorder.

These comments apply also to some women who have bulimia nervosa, as we described in Belinda's story on page 61.

Dealing with associated problems

Some patients say that when they are in control of their food intake and their body weight, they feel in control of their lives. For example, when preparing for an examination the patient may feel it would be 'good' to put on weight but resists this because if she starts to lose control of her eating behaviour she fears she will lose control of her self-discipline, will not study, and will fail the examination. Her control of her eating behaviour may continue for other reasons. It may become part of a reward–punishment system. She may argue: 'If I eat one extra thing, something dreadful will happen to me'. It may be used to manipulate parents or her husband, to gain attention, or as an excuse if she does not perform as well as they expect: 'If I am thin, people know there is something wrong and do not expect as much.'

On the other hand, some anorexia nervosa sufferers have problems which upset them and which affect their behaviour. For example, the preoccupation with weight control and with food may be used to prevent the patient thinking about her other problems. The eating disorder may also permit the woman to escape from having to make decisions and from participating in events which she fears.

Patients of ours have told us that 'people do not expect as much of you when you look sick'; and 'people treat you more gently if you have an eating disorder'; or 'it keeps my parents talking to each other'; or 'my husband will leave me if I get better'. These last two comments show that the family may be involved in producing or maintaining the eating disorder.

Although most anorexia nervosa patients, particularly if the woman is young and lives at home, have a supportive, sharing, communicating family, some form a part of a 'dysfunctional' family. These families tend to have rigid, unbending attitudes and values, or are over-protective of their children, the parents being unable to allow their children to be independent, or the family is chaotic and disorganized. These families seem to be unable to resolve problems which arise within the family, and may need a 'sick' member to enable the other family members to communicate with each other, or to take sides in parental quarrels.

Some older anorexic nervosa patients may feel that they cannot recover from their eating disorder whilst in their current relationship. The situation is more likely to arise if the woman married after the onset of anorexia nervosa. At that time, her husband had been attracted by a thin, fragile, dependent woman who had a problem. He may have sought a woman whom he could care for and derived much satisfaction from looking after her. If she now recovers and becomes less dependent, he may feel uncomfortable and may feel that his enjoyable role has diminished. This can lead to family problems which may need professional help to be resolved, or the couple may separate or divorce.

If family problems are revealed during talks with the sufferer, she may be helped if she talks with a therapist who has expertise in relationship and marital problems, or in family therapy. Indeed in some cases this help is essential if the eating disorder is to be resolved.

Some women who have anorexia nervosa are helped considerably after they have been refed and helped to overcome their immediate problems, by joining a *self-help group* composed of anorexia nervosa sufferers and those who have almost or completely recovered from the disorder. An alternative is to join in *small-group therapy*, in which a health professional acts as a facilitator for a group of sufferers, who discuss their problems and the ways they are being helped to overcome them. Both groups are often successful if the group is made up of people of similar ages, those who are employed, those who are undertaking tertiary education, those who are married, those who are single, those who have children, and those who do not have children.

In addition, parents of young women who have anorexia nervosa may need support. Support groups for parents can provide information and reassurance, and also enable the parents to gain insight into the eating disorder. Similarly if the problem is one of adjustment to adolescence, a problem of sexuality, or is a gynaecological problem, the woman may welcome the opportunity to talk to an appropriate expert who is empathetic and able to communicate well.

The problems, and strategies for their relief, discussed in this section apply equally if the woman has bulimia nervosa or an atypical eating disorder.

The outcome of anorexia nervosa

The aims of treatment are: first, to help the woman achieve a weight within the normal body weight range, that is, a BMI of 19 or more (between 90 and 110 of the 'Average Body Weight'); second, to help her to eat normally for her age and life-style; third, to enable her to avoid extreme methods of weight control; and fourth, to enable her to gain insight so that she no longer needs her eating disorder to help her cope with problems of her daily life.

About 70 per cent of anorexic patients achieve these aims after therapy lasting from six months to six years, but many need continuing counselling, particularly when they encounter stressful situations. The support from a therapist over a period of years may be necessary.

Kylie's story typifies the problem. In the previous three years she had had four admissions to hospital for refeeding. Each admission had lasted for at least two months. After being discharged from hospital for the fourth time she wrote to her doctor:

I know that I still look too thin, but I just don't seem able to regain the weight I lost in the last four months. It may be because I left home then. I was very worried about how I'd cope when I started living away from home again, and tried to be strict with myself about 'cutting back' on food. I don't think I did 'cut back', but suppose I'm a lot more active now at work than I was when I was at home leading a life of (enforced) leisure. However, I find it almost impossible to let myself eat more. As you may remember, my problem has always been an 'eating-food' one, rather than a concern with weight. Basically I still think the same way as I have for a long time, and I don't suppose this will ever change now.

Anorexia now seems to be becoming increasingly common, and receiving a lot of publicity. I don't know whether the publicity is all for the good—I have the feeling it may be becoming almost 'fashionable' among young girls, without their realising its long-term consequences. If I could but turn the clock back about twelve years; wishful thinking!

A year later, Kylie wrote again:

Considering everything, I've been keeping quite well. I've maintained my weight since I left the Clinic (over a year ago now!) though I haven't put any more on. I'm still not over-confident about how I would cope on my own, i.e. if I was preparing and responsible for all my own food. So many of the old attitudes are still lying dormant and I have to be ever vigilant that they don't exert too much influence. All in all it's still not terribly easy, though I must admit that I do think less and less about being an 'anorexic'.

Between 15 and 25 per cent of anorexia nervosa patients continue to have an eating disorder. These women may continue to have anorexia nervosa or may develop bulimia nervosa, but most have an atypical eating disorder (page 23).

The remaining 10 to 20 per cent of anorexia nervosa patients continue to suffer from anorexia nervosa, requiring intermittent therapy over many years. The last two groups of patients require the support of, and to be counselled by, a therapist at intervals for several years after refeeding, because life and developmental stresses may precipiate a recurrence. Refeeding, re-education of eating habits, and explanation of physical symptoms are only initial goals in the treatment of anorexia nervosa.

Helping the woman to understanding what is happening and to give her reassurance about these matters and her beliefs about eating is equally important. Although this information is given during the refeeding period, most patients have more insight and understanding about their feelings and behaviours as their weight approaches or is within the normal weight range. In these sessions the aim is to help the woman continue to escape from the preoccupation with weight gain and food that she had when she was ill, and help her cope with life stress and other problems which may arise, without resorting to her previous disordered eating behaviour.

Continuing therapy may have to be available for many years. This means that the woman may need to know that she can contact her therapist and make an appointment or a series of appointments even if she has not had treatment for months or years.

Death due to anorexia nervosa gets newspaper headlines, particularly if a celebrity such as Karen Carpenter is the victim. However, fewer than 3 per cent of patients die from the effects of the eating disorder (half of whom die following a drug overdose). In short-term studies, predominantly of adolescent women, the death rate is about 2 per cent. Long-term studies, which include the 20 per cent of chronic anorexia nervosa sufferers, suggest that 6 per cent of these patients will die over a period of years. However, with a greater community awareness about anorexia nervosa so that victims seek help earlier in the illness, and more physicians trained to manage the illness, the death rate is likely to be lower in the next decade.

Summary of treatment of anorexia nervosa

---

* Age: 18 or more
* Clinically not seriously ill
* Failure of hospital treatment previously

* Age: less than 18
* Severely ill on clinical examination
* Failure of out-patient treatment
* The woman expresses a preference

———————— Evaluate biochemical status ————————

Usually treat as out-patient

Offer suggestions and support to help patient:

* increase weight slowly
* stop using weight-losing behaviour
* learn sensible eating patterns

If the above goals are not achieved, usually admit to hospital

Usually admit to hospital

Provide programme to help patient:

* increase weight by 1–1.5 kg a week
* cease weight-losing behaviour
* learn sensible eating patterns
* exercise appropriately for body weight

Throughout programme provide:

* supportive psychotherapy
* cognitive and behaviour therapy
* help for other perceived problems (marital, family, medical)
* help in learning sensible eating patterns appropriate to life style and age
* help in developing sensible exercise patterns
* confidence in ability to eat sensibly

Later provide help for patient:

* to stabilise weight in desirable range
* to continue to avoid dangerous weight-losing methods
* to decrease preoccupation with weight and food

Overall aim is to help:

* to live a normal life
* to be able to cope with life

8

Bulimia nervosa

I think that I look forward to a binge-eating session. Exactly what I am thinking is vague, but on reflection it is: 'Oh good, I won't have to think about dieting any more—what a relief'. If anything happens which delays the start of the binge I become quite angry and rather rude to the person who caused the delay. This anger is not warranted and is totally inappropriate—it could be likened to a temper tantrum.

Bulimia nervosa was considered to be a part of anorexia nervosa until recently, as it was observed that about 40 per cent of anorexia nervosa patients episodically lost control of their eating behaviour and binge-ate. Bulimia nervosa is now accepted as a separate illness, but many of the features are similar in both illnesses, and some bulimic patients develop anorexia nervosa. The prevalence of bulimia nervosa in the community amongst adolescent and young adult women is unknown. Earlier estimates based on looser criteria gave an incidence of between 3 and 7 per cent, but more recent estimates based on the stricter criteria proposed by the American Psychiatric Association (page 22) indicate that the prevalence is 1 to 2 per cent. The true prevalence may be higher as only those women who seek medical help are identifiable. Even these women may not be diagnosed as bulimic. Most do not tell their doctor about their eating habit and, as a result, are investigated for gastro-intestinal problems, such as a spastic colon, or gynaecological problems, such as infertility and menstrual disturbances, or are thought to be depressed and are given antidepressants. In the past the majority of binge-eaters only received help because of an excessive weight gain (or a weight loss) or because of an attempt at suicide, but now, because of articles in women's magazines, many women who have bulimia nervosa seek help earlier.

Binge-eating usually starts between the ages of 15 and 24 and follows a period of increased concern about body weight and appearance, during which the woman decides to diet or at least to 'watch' her weight. This is demonstrated by the fact that over 90 per cent of bulimia nervosa patients often say they have been over-eating and have usually tried to avoid gaining weight by strict dieting before they started binge-eating.

Some have attempted to control their weight by sensible dieting which has been associated with a reasonable loss of weight for a period of time. The desired weight loss of other women has not occurred satisfactorily in spite of fasting or adapting 'fad' or 'crazy' diets.

The woman develops an exaggerated concern about her body shape and weight, and this leads to more stringent periods of dieting, with episodes of binge-eating when the control over food intake weakens.

Case history: Jill

When I was 15, I looked at myself and thought: 'I'm too fat, and hate the size of my thighs and bottom.' My weight was then 63 kg (139 lbs, 9 st 13 lbs). So I started to diet taking in only 5040 kJ (1200 kcals), and got my father to buy an exercise bike which I rode for an hour each day. I lost 5 kg (11 lbs) of weight. In the next year I exercised a lot but ate normal meals and didn't gain weight. Then I got hepatitis and was in hospital for six weeks when my weight dropped to 54 kg (119 lbs, 8 st 7 lbs), but it built up to 57 kg (126 lbs, 9 st) in a few months —and that's the weight I think I look best at. So I was happy.

I went to 'Tech' when I was 18 and had a permanent boyfriend. We got on well but I started eating more and exercising less and my weight went up to 60 kg

Fig. 13. Bulimia nervosa.

(132 lbs, 9 st 6 lbs). He said I was getting fat and so did May, a girl in the class who was really fat. I don't know if it was what they said, but about then I began to be very aware of women's bodies, and how much they varied in shape. I began to be quite obsessed with body shape and how it was often out of proportion and ugly and I began to diet to get my body into a better shape. It didn't do much good because my body remained the same shape and I didn't lose any weight although I tried for a year. I think I became convinced that I couldn't eat as much as other people because if I did I would get really fat like May.

Then my boyfriend and I split up and I was sure it was because I was fat. I started taking slimming pills—I suppose I took more than 20 of them some days. They didn't work either, so I tried I don't remember how many diets. I tried staying awake all night because I'd read that mental activity helped lose weight. I went to a doctor who gave injections to dissolve fat, but that didn't work either. I tried wearing plastic to lose weight. I tried hypnotherapy. And once, when I had 'flu I stood under a cold shower and then went outside in winter for two hours to try and catch pneumonia. I even stopped taking vitamin tablets because I thought that there might be calories in the capsules. Nothing worked for me, and my weight stayed between 63 and 66 kg (139–145 lbs, 9 st 13 lbs–10 st 5 lbs). It was very discouraging.

I felt the only way that I could really lose weight would be to starve. And I did, but I got so hungry that when I had fasted for two or three weeks, only drinking fluids, I would binge-eat. I used to go out late at night and buy food or if I could, steal it. I tried to induce vomiting after the binge by sticking my fingers down my throat but I couldn't manage it so I started taking quantities of laxatives, and when, after a binge my ankles were swollen, I would get diuretic tablets from the doctor. My eating was really out of my control.

In fact I saw several doctors but none of them seemed to think there was anything wrong with me. So one day I took a large quantity of aspirin—I can't remember how many—to try to draw attention that I needed help—I really did need help!

Three years later she wrote to the clinic:

Looking back I think that the reason I started binge-eating was because of my obsession with dieting which stemmed from the fact I didn't realize in the first place that I wasn't overweight but that I had inherited fatter legs and thighs than the average person.

The onset of bulimia nervosa may also be associated with stressful life events, which are not related to the woman's concern about body image or weight. A domestic argument, illness or death in the immediate family, the stress of examinations, a change in job, breakdown of a relationship, divorce, or pregnancy may precipitate the first eating-binge. The age of the woman has a bearing on which of the life events will precipitate binge-eating. Family problems or failure to achieve independence from parents are more common precipitants if the woman is teen-aged, while, above the age of 20, marital and relationship difficulties are more common. Many women who have bulimia nervosa have a normal personality and no detectable psychopathology but some patients have a personality disorder which results in the woman having difficulties in every day living. It is unclear whether the personality characteristics of binge-eaters have any relevance to their illness, as they occur among women who do not binge-eat.

It is important to be aware that the life events or problems in day-to-day living, which were associated with the onset of binge-eating, may be different from those which occur during the continuation of the disorder. These facts may have a bearing on the treatment adopted.

Binge-eating and depression

There has been much controversy among physicians who treat bulimic patients as to whether bulimia nervosa is caused by depression and will respond to antidepressant drugs, or whether the fear of weight gain, the physical effects of binge-eating, and the use of dangerous methods of weight control, increase the anxiety and guilt of binge-eating and cause the depression.

There is some evidence that if binge-eaters are prescribed antidepressant drugs they binge less frequently, but after 4 months of treatment a relapse occurs. It is interesting that the antidepressant drugs were equally effective if the binge-eater was not depressed, which suggests that the action of the drugs was on the centre in the brain which 'controls' eating!

A recent study supports the view that the person's distorted attitudes to eating and to body image lead to depression rather than that depression leads to bulimia nervosa. This concept receives further support from a study of teenage women in the USA in 1990 in which it was found that twice as many women were depressed compared with men of the same age. The authors reported that the adolescent girls' preoccupation with their body shape and weight accounted for the difference.

The eating binge

It is easy to convince yourself on the day after each binge that that was the last one, and as of today you are never going to binge again. Unfortunately the nausea and feeling of self-revulsion disappears after a few

days, and before you know it, the idea of escape into a session of eating
unlimited amounts of anything that takes your fancy gets hold of you
again. This can be caused by boredom, anxiety, or just a desire to relax or
escape for a while.

Most binge-eaters are secretive about their behaviour. Many prepare
secretively for the binge or plan for it by hoarding food beforehand.
During the binge, as well as 'raiding the fridge', the woman usually
prepares simple meals for herself, but some women prepare and cook
elaborate dishes such as biscuits, cakes, and casseroles. Some women
buy food especially to eat during episodes of binge-eating. About half eat
most of their food during a binge in cafés or milk-bars, or go from shop
to shop buying food and eating it immediately.

Most bulimia nervosa patients gulp their food quickly during an
eating-binge, some stuffing food frantically into their mouth, often
making a considerable mess, leaving empty, open cans around. Other
women are careful to make no mess so that they may avoid being found
out. The rate of eating during an eating binge varies between individuals
and between binges. If the woman knows that she will not be disturbed,
she will eat more slowly, particularly if she knows she can induce vomiting without being discovered. In general the rate at which she eats
becomes slower as the binge-eating episode proceeds.

The binge may start at any time of the day and end as suddenly, but
about one-third of binge-eaters have specific times, such as weekends,
when they begin to binge-eat.

The amount of food eaten during an eating-binge varies considerably,
and ranges from 3- to 30-times the amount of food usually eaten in one
day. The 'pickers' eat less than the 'stuffers', many stuffers eating over
ten-times the amount of food that they would eat each day when not
bingeing. This can provide a large amount of energy, exceeding more
than 83 700 kJ (20 000 kcal) during days of 'bad binge-eating'. Those
who eat large quantities of food are more likely to reach higher body
weights, to use slimming tablets and diuretics, to prepare food for a
binge, to eat all the food that is available, to eat inappropriate foods, to
have nocturnal binges, and to binge anywhere. The 'stuffers' are more
likely to use and abuse alcohol or marijuana and may make an attempt at
suicide following the episode of binge-eating.

Many binge-eaters claim they go on eating until they have eaten all
the food available. But when this claim is analysed it is found that they

are usually referring only to what they describe as 'binge' or 'bad' foods. They define these as foods they do not allow themselves to eat at other times, for example, cakes and ice-cream, peanuts, or biscuits. Only a few actually eat everything in the cupboards and fridge. By the time that most bulimia patients seek treatment, they either induce vomiting, or take purgatives, or both. This behaviour may take place during the binge or immediately the binge ends.

The binge-eating episode ends for a variety of reasons. Some binge-eaters say simply that they 'ran out of steam'. Others stop because they feel discomfort being nauseated or full. Others because they can no longer continue to binge secretively.

After the binge, most binge-eaters promise themselves that they will keep to their strict diet or will fast and will not repeat the binge. A few fall asleep, but most take up their usual activities as if the binge had never happened.

Once binge-eating had been recognized by other people, most binge-eaters admit to it and some of them occasionally indulge in binge-eating in front of family members or close friends. A few binge-eaters use this in a manipulative way against parents or husband, implying: 'look what you have made me do'. Others go to great lengths to disguise their behaviour for long periods and are successful for many years. When discovered, most patients will admit to binge-eating and nowadays will usually admit to self-induced vomiting, if they use this method to control their weight. This is a recent change, probably resulting from the availability of information in non-medical publications about bulimia nervosa.

It is difficult to be certain what binge-eaters mean by the length of an episode of binge-eating, as they describe episodes ranging from 15 minutes to three weeks in duration. Some women, especially those who have only recently developed abnormal eating patterns, see their binge-eating as occurring in separate episodes, up to six in one day. Others, often those with long histories of binge-eating, describe episodes lasting for 'days or weeks'. By this, they mean that the urge to binge-eat is continuous and is present when they go to sleep and on waking, although it is obvious that they do not binge continually. Other women with a long history of binge-eating continue to perceive their bingeing as occurring in discrete episodes, often more than 20 episodes a day, each being terminated by self-induced vomiting.

The frequency with which bulimia victims indulge in binge-eating varies considerably. Episodes of binge-eating occur two or three times a week or more often. Some women who are thought to have bulimia nervosa say that they only binge twice a month. These women do not have bulimia nervosa, as a diagnosis of bulimia nervosa can only be made if the woman binge-eats more than twice a week and has done this for at least three months. However they may have an atypical eating disorder.

A physiological reason for binge-eating has been suggested. Normally when a person has eaten a normal amount of food, messages from her brain 'turn off' her desire to eat more. As most bulimia patients starve or diet strictly between eating binges, they are in a 'food-deprived state' and changes in brain chemistry occur. One possible mechanism is discussed on page 129. When a person in a food-deprived state starts eating, the brain messages which normally 'turn off' appetite fail to work so that the person continues eating and overeats, commencing an eating binge.

Food preference in bulimia nervosa

Each of the binge-eaters we have heard about or have studied include food in their binges which they do not allow themselves to eat at other times, calling them 'junk food', 'fattening food', or 'bad food'. Food eaten during a binge is sometimes selected because it is easy to 'stuff down' at the beginning of a binge, and easy to vomit up. Some of our binge-eaters said that their binges consisted mainly of soft, milky, or fluid foods, whereas others said they used such foods merely as a means to assist vomiting, and ate them towards the end of the binge.

The amount, type, and nutritional content of food eaten during a binge varies widely both within and between individuals. Contrary to most binge-eaters' impressions that the food eaten during binges is exceptionally high in carbohydrates, analysis of records of food actually consumed in a binge revealed that they were just as likely to contain excessive amounts of fat or protein. A few patients become vegetarian in order to control their weight and change from binges of food which are high in fat content to binges of fresh vegetables, on occasions, for example, eating 2-3 kg (4½-7 lbs) of raw carrots in a day. The amount, type, and nutritional content of food eaten during a binge may be entirely dependent on what is available in the home. Some women will eat anything that is available, including tinned food, baby foods, frozen food, and scraps from rubbish bins (Table 8).

Precipitants of an eating-binge

There seem to be a number of factors which may precipitate an eating binge in a susceptible person. Most women say that before starting a binge they are unduly tense. Three-quarters say that loneliness or boredom precipitated a binge or that constant thoughts of food and a craving to eat, which they were eventually unable to control, were factors. Although many women diet rigidly between binges, only one-third say that hunger precipitates the binge.

Table 8. Food eaten during a 'bad' binge lasting 8 hours (as reported by a patient)

3 loaves, 5 lb potatoes (chips), 1 jar honey,
1 jar anchovies (on bread), 1 lb rolled oats;
2 lb flour (as pancakes), 1 lb macaroni,
2 instant puddings, 4 oz nuts, 2 lb sugar,
1 large pkt Rice Bubbles

1½ lb margarine, 1 pint oil (for cooking), 4 pints milk powder, 1 tin condensed milk (in porridge on bread or in drink), 4 lb ice-cream

1 lb sausages, (or meat rissoles), 1½ lb onions

12 eggs (in milk-shake, scrambled eggs)

1 lb liquorice (liquorice allsorts), 2 family-size blocks chocolate, 1 lb dried figs, 2 pkts sweets, 6 'health bars', assorted cream cakes (up to 12) eaten while shopping, 1 lb sultanas (on bread or in porridge)

left-overs found in fridge, 1 bottle orange cordial

This amount of food gives a total of:

Energy	226 070 kJ (54 000 kcals)
Protein	1071 g
Fat	1964 g
Carbohydrate	14 834 g

A scenario might be that as the women are constantly concerned about their body image and keep to a diet to reduce their perceived ugly shape, an episode of loneliness, unhappiness, or boredom triggers thoughts of the pleasure of the taste of food, and this leads to an eating binge.

Strategies used by bulimia nervosa patients to control weight

Women who have bulimia nervosa are aware that obesity is inevitable if they continue to binge-eat and do not take measures to control their weight. Their fear of fatness is as great as their love of food. Faced with this dilemma, two strategies are available to them. The first is to reduce the amount of energy absorbed from the food they eat by inducing vomiting during and after binge-eating and between binges. The second method is to diet strictly between binges. Some women choose to vomit as a strategy, others choose to diet. In addition to these primary measures, many binge-eaters in both groups use other methods of weight control, most of which are potentially dangerous. Between 75 and 90 per cent of binge-eaters abuse laxatives during a binge, at the end of a binge, or between binges. The reasons are twofold. First, purgation clears out the mass of 'bad' binge-food and the patient believes that it will prevent the energy being absorbed and converted into fat. Second, the use of purgatives relieves the fullness of abdominal discomfort and bloating which occurs after binge-eating. The quantities of purgatives taken varies from double the recommended dose, taken immediately after an eating binge, to 30 tablets, or 'handfuls' of laxative tablets every day. The prolonged regular use of laxatives to control weight gain amongst bulimia nervosa patients is declining in popularity as women are learning how ineffective they are in controlling body weight.

About 60 per cent of binge-eaters take commercial slimming 'pills', which contain some form of laxative, and a number take appetite-suppressing medications which may have an addictive property.

About 40 per cent of binge-eaters take large quantities of diuretic tablets, as they believe that the tablets will enable them to lose weight. Some women are aware that only fluid is lost, others believe that diuretics in some way 'dissolve' fat. And 10 per cent of binge-eaters abuse alcohol or drugs.

Case history: Karen

I find it easy to pinpoint the beginning of my illness. It began with an experience concerning one of my fifteenth birthday presents: a box of chocolates. I was at an age where pressures for social acceptance were, to me, immense, and pencil thinness, to me, was a prerequisite for social acceptance and self-confidence. I ate some of my birthday chocolates and was offered a suggestion by my mother; 'If you don't want to get fat, stick your fingers down your throat'.

Maybe this statement has more relevance than I'd previously thought. Mum's simple statement triggered off every emotional fear within me: 'I'll be fat—socially unacceptable—ugly—have no self-confidence—no self-esteem. . .' The fears were inexpressibly greater than I can even imagine now. My future, with those chocolates in me, appeared what can be plain and simply described as 'black'. My mother's suggestion seemed the only exit from the 'black future' I had prescribed for myself.

Naively I took this exit, which turned out not to be an exit at all but an entrance into hell. If only I'd known!

To induce vomiting was a revolting experience to me, but the fear of the 'black future' provided no alternative at all. Physical weakness and psychological euphoria followed my regurgitation. No matter how painful, or revolting, I'd found the key to freedom from that dreaded 'black future'.

I left school on my fifteenth birthday and found an increase in life's pressures. Coping became difficult, but I still possessed my 'key' to confidence and acceptance. I made a habit of vomiting after every evening meal and, as the months progressed, I gradually lost weight, believing that I was becoming more attractive all the while. The fact that my food output by means of regurgitation was almost equal to my food intake allowed me to indulge for longer periods of time in my means of relief from life's pressures—eating—without gaining weight.

I became increasingly aware of my increasing ability to relieve life's pressure through the intake of food. Although the induction of vomiting continued to be traumatic, the relief beforehand, and the euphoria afterwards, were, to me, of no comparison to it. The vomiting became more frequent as the food intake rose and I accompanied my physically strenuous job with all the exercise I could muster. Some nights I could not sleep due to the immense guilt of either not having done enough exercise or having allowed too much food to digest.

By the age of 16 I found myself unable to cope not only with problems, but with spare time. Anxiety seemed to rule my existence and I could not relax without food. If, even then, I was relaxing, I'm unsure.

I felt revoltingly fat and ugly when I could not see all of my ribs when I looked in the mirror. I took a large daily dose of Epsom salts, along with what progressed to 13 laxative tablets daily.

Fortunately, my weight only regressed to just below 51 kg (112 lbs, 8 st) at its lowest. But it took its toll of my life. For breakfast I would eat 8-10 slices of toast plus cereal. Then I would do the dishes, eating everyone's scraps in an anxious, embarrassed, hidden hurry. I would then disappear inconspicuously to the toilet, and bring up my breakfast. My nose often bled, as did my stomach, and ten minutes later (to the dot) I would become very weak, dizzy, and pale.

I suffered malnutrition to the extent that my menstrual periods ceased for six or seven months. My god, I accepted such as being normal!!

During the following year, I began to realize that I was too thin so I fought my conscience and established my weight at about 57 kg (126 lbs, 9 st).

My eating, cunning and patient as it was, had increased during this time, and I was spending about $A10 [£7] per day on food outside the house. This was quite substantial to me, for I was earning only $A80 [£56] per week. Fortunately I didn't have to pay board.

It was about this time that my boyfriend became too heavy to pursue his career as a jockey. I worried about his future, I worried about myself, I worried about everything and my only relief was food.

Being immature and mixed up, I acted strangely and desperately. My boyfriend had become part of a new group of friends who were heavily involved with drugs of every description—from heroin, to magic mushrooms, to petrol and glue sniffing. This was beyond my capacity to cope. My 'other half' was dying and I was dying with him.

I knew subconsciously that I couldn't go on with him, nor could I go on without him. Without directly breaking up our relationship I acted in a manner which drove him and me 'up the wall'. I was subconsciously hoping that he'd break off our relationship and therefore I'd have it easier. It didn't work that way. He clung on, as I did. My eating worsened, my mind and soul weakened. He got deeper into the drug scene, and I began to follow, but, thank god, he loved me enough to keep me out of that 'black hole'. I suppose I'd have gotten in elsewhere if I'd really wanted to, but although I got drunk a couple of times and tried a few drugs, they did nothing for me. Food was my relief—my drug!

I isolated myself with food as often as possible. My crazy desperate behaviour dared, and received, the punishment it deserved. And one desperate day when I'd driven my boyfriend so hard he hit me and threw me down in the middle of the road, (I was trying to stop him going to the pub). I returned to his house, alone and desperate. There was no food in the house, I had no money, and I felt that I could take no more of the torture I felt the world was inflicting upon me. I took a loaded shot-gun from the wall, and placed the end of the barrel in my mouth. I mustn't have wanted to die, because I received a sensation of strength which took away my need to pull the trigger. Although I didn't want to die, the desperation remained. I screamed and bashed the wall and cried for what must have been about an hour. After this I felt terribly weak. I returned to work but wouldn't speak to my boss, nor later to my family. They had no idea—nor did I want them to. I'd constructed an impermeable barrier around myself. I couldn't cope outside of it.

The next day I penetrated my barrier and began to feel my way into the world again, like a child's first adventure into a garden. I felt I had a new lease of life, when crash, down fell my depression and desperation, taking on a new tighter grip of me. I desperately ate my way through the day, resenting everyone and everything, playing sad music and feeling sorry for myself (although I didn't recognise self-pity then), and topping off the mountain of hate I had constructed against the world; or was it myself? I rather believe the latter.

I tried to escape. I went to Scotland and ate my way through my short stay there. I returned home and couldn't cope with a single day. To my parent's horror and disappointment, I quickly packed and moved. The torture followed me, pouncing on me which ever way I turned. I spent my time obliviously eating my way through each day. Trying to live, but to no avail. At weekends I'd try to get home simply for the sake of the available food. I'd eat Mum out of house and home and the self-hate and guilt built up more and more due to my reasons for going home. It hurt me terribly when my mother confronted me with the fact that she was aware of my attraction to home. I loved my family dearly, but I then felt like a leech, so I went home as little as possible.

I spent my evenings at the local shops, with immense fear of being caught there, and with the guilt and anxiety continually mounting. To be so totally out of control in sobriety seemed so terribly degrading.

I couldn't cope with this life, so after five-and-a-half years of bingeing and vomiting I told my sister what I was doing. She arranged for me to see a doctor, who laughed at me and said 'What do you want me to do about it? Sew your mouth up?' I was temporarily numbed by this experience. The guilt and embarrassment then came on hot and strong, and I broke down crying in front of him. He then decided that I was crazy so he referred me to a psychiatrist.

She made me feel more acceptable to myself. Nevertheless, my obsession with food continued to increase. I couldn't bear to live with myself, so my psychiatrist arranged for me to be admitted to hospital as I wasn't improving.

If ever I've believed in my own 'God', it's now, for by what to me is a miracle, I've been identified as an addict, and have progressed to 12 days in a row without over-eating or vomiting. I hadn't succeeded through one single day in over a year before this, and how I'd tried!!

With the aid of the addiction program, and Alcoholics Anonymous philosophies, I've learnt more about myself and how to cope with life in the past 12 days than I have in the 20 years preceding. I'm gaining confidence, hope and see life as I've only dreamed of seeing it. I have a long way to go to recovery and I accept this. I've told the truth to my family and close friends, who have accepted it well. I'm truly getting there, and I won't give in for I've too much to lose. I've now had a taste of how enjoyable and exciting life can be; so hopefully I will be able to stay in the life I love so much, and hopefully maintain self-control for the rest of my life over my eating and vomiting.

How do binge-eaters try to resist bingeing?

Nearly every binge-eater has attempted, at times, to resist the urge to binge. The methods chosen to resist the urge to binge-eat vary considerably. Some women feel a reduced urge if they keep no food in the house, buying only what is needed each day; others avoid cooking or going into the kitchen. Still others spend a long time chewing a mouthful of food to prevent themselves stuffing more and more food into their mouths. Other women avoid eating with the family or going out to social gatherings where food is served. A few women take more positive action by locking themselves in the bathroom, driving into the country where no food is available, or keeping no money in their purse. Still others try to divert their thoughts from food, planning to be completely occupied at all times, by knitting obsessionally, telephoning friends, or going out to meet people. Another method used by some women is to start doing jigsaw puzzles. After a few days of not binge-eating, the woman may feel very agitated. These feelings usually lead to her going to the kitchen and starting an eating binge. If a large jigsaw puzzle is on a table she may choose to go to the table and put in a few more pieces, rather than going to the kitchen and bingeing. It appears that although she is unable to concentrate on reading or watching television, she may become absorbed by doing the jigsaw puzzle until the agitation passes. Some women undertake work with long periods of overtime, in jobs where no food is available; others try to keep to strict diets, or eat only minute quantities of food at a time and avoid food shops. Other women use exercise as a way of avoiding binge-eating. They spend long hours at the gym, play squash, or tennis, or jog for many miles each day. Some women may try to avoid eating binges by abusing alcohol or other drugs. Other women abuse alcohol or drugs and continue binge-eating and vomiting. A few women who develop a drug or alcohol problem may recover from their eating disorder, but the drug or alcohol problem may persist for years and require treatment. One woman was so desperate she attempted to wire her jaws together by passing the wire through her gums after using a local anaesthetic ointment. Another cut the tips of her fingers so that they would be too sore to induce vomiting, hoping that this would stop her from starting on a binge.

Information about 'resistance behaviours' used by a binge-eater is often helpful in devising treatment.

The physical symptoms and signs associated with bulimia nervosa

Most compulsive eaters describe a number of physical symptoms associated with the binge. In addition, physical symptoms may follow induced vomiting or laxative abuse.

During an episode of binge-eating, most of the women feel 'bloated' or 'full' and some observe that their hands and feet swell. One-third are nauseated or complain of abdominal pain. By the end of the binge, over one-third complain of headache and half of the women complain of tiredness.

About six bulimia nervosa patients in every ten habitually induce vomiting. Initially vomiting is achieved by stuffing the fingers or a spoon into the throat, but later many women can induce vomiting by inducing a strong contraction of the diaphragm and abdominal muscles, to force the contents of the stomach into the oesophagus and then to vomit. In each episode of vomiting many women regurgitate one- to ten-times until they are certain all food has been brought up. Some women use 'markers', beginning a binge with food such as red apple skin, lettuce, or liquorice which they can recognize in the vomit. A number of patients also use 'wash-out techniques': they keep on drinking water and re-gurgitating until there is no residue of food in their stomach, a process which can last up to half an hour. In most cases the vomiting episodes last from 5 to 30 minutes, depending on ease of vomiting and quantity. The women tend to exaggerate the amount of vomit describing the amounts regurgitated in terms of buckets full, ice-cream containers full, or saucepans full. To avoid detection they vomit into disposable con-tainers or plastic bags. In one case the mother of the binge-eater habitu-ally collected the vomited material and used it to fertilize the garden.

Women who habitually induce vomiting may develop enlargement of their face and cheeks due to swelling of their salivary glands. Some women develop calluses on the back of their fingers as a result of inserting them frequently into their mouth to induce vomiting. Some women retain fluid after binge-eating large amounts of food and then inducing vomiting. This is especially disconcerting to a woman who is anxious about gaining weight. Most of the women who habitually induce vomiting have had extensive and expensive dental work to correct the damage to their teeth caused by acid vomit which etches away the tooth enamel. Over half of the women who induce vomiting often, report that sometimes the vomit contains blood.

Of greater danger to the women is that frequent self-induced vomiting over a period of time may result in dehydration and possible disturbances in the electrolytes in the blood, cardiac arrhythmias and changes in the electrocardiogram, renal problems, and occasionally death.

When a woman stops vomiting she may suffer abdominal cramps, bloating, constipation or diarrhoea, and may feel exhausted or become very agitated. These 'withdrawal' symptoms cease after ten days. Three weeks later she is no longer agitated or fatigued and usually says that she feels better than she has done for years.

Over 75 per cent of women have taken laxatives to purge themselves either during or immediately after the binge. In some cases the quantity of laxatives taken is considerable, ranging from twice the recommended dose to 'handfuls'. Many of the women are aware that the diarrhoea following excessive laxative intake may lead to electrolyte disturbances, particularly potassium deficiency, and avoid them by eating potassium-rich foods such as oranges or tomatoes. The use of laxatives is irrational as well as potentially dangerous. Laxatives act mainly on the large bowel inducing it to empty, but this occurs *after* the energy obtained from the food eaten has been absorbed in the small intestines. All that laxatives do is cause the body to lose fluid, not energy. This is followed by rebound water retention so that the person's body weight may be higher after taking laxatives than it was before.

Stopping laxative abuse is also followed by 'withdrawal' symptoms, which are similar to those which follow cessation of self-induced vomiting. These are constipation, abdominal cramps, abdominal bloating, agitation, and feeling 'awful'. A woman needs to be reassured that these symptoms usually occur, are normal, and will cease after ten days.

Half of patients who have bulimia nervosa have taken 'slimming tablets' or diuretics to lose weight, and these women may also abuse the diuretics with an inevitable electrolyte disturbance, particularly a potassium deficiency, unless they take measures to prevent this happening. As many of them are aware of the problems of potassium deficiency, they take potassium supplements or drink orange juice which is rich in potassium. In some cases severe potassium deficiency occurs which requires treatment in hospital.

Diuretics only rid the body of water and electrolytes: they do not have any effect on ridding the body of stored fat. Their regular use may lead to short-term, or long-term, persistent fluid retention when they are discontinued.

Many binge-eaters develop menstrual irregularities, although, in contrast to women who have anorexia nervosa, their body weight is usually in the normal range for age and height or they are slightly overweight. About 40 per cent of women who have bulimia nervosa develop irregular menstruation and, in another 20 per cent, menstruation ceases. Women who cease to menstruate may be found to have high levels of cholesterol in their blood, which may cause concern, but the levels tend to fall when menstruation returns.

The psychological effects of binge-eating

Before starting to binge-eat, most women feel tense and anxious, have palpitations, or begin sweating. During the binge, most binge-eaters feel a sense of freedom; the anxiety or worry they had been experiencing lifts and they no longer have anxious or negative thoughts. If the woman chooses to induce vomiting, she may also reduce tension with the act of vomiting. At the end of the binge, most binge-eaters feel less tense and anxious, but may not like themselves because of what they have done to their bodies. They may feel guilty about inducing vomiting and panic that the binge may induce a weight gain. This in turn may lead to further anxiety and tension, with the result that they may start binge-eating once again. A vicious circle is established (Fig. 14).

If a binge-eater is unable to relieve her anxiety and tension, for example, if the person is interrupted or discovered when binge-eating, her behaviour may change to agitation, anger, or aggression.

It is also apparent that if a woman with bulimia does not recognize the tension and anxiety or has no other ways of coping with them, she easily enters the vicious circle and becomes a frequent binge-eater. As will be seen, a major objective of treatment is to break this vicious circle of eating behaviour.

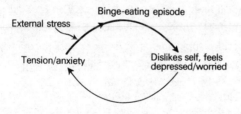

Fig. 14. The psychological circle of binge-eating.

Case history: Penny

I really started binge-eating when I was about 12. Before that I had bought lots of sweets, candies, and lollies, because Mum gave me a lot of pocket money—but all kids do that. Then, when I was about 12, I started dieting and began binge-eating. I remember that I used to eat my pack lunch on the way to school and then scrounge food from the other kids. By the time I was 14, I was a real binge-eater. After a binge I would vomit and after a time I could vomit without putting my fingers down my throat. I still can, but I don't do it. What with study and fixing up bingeing, I didn't have time for friends. But it didn't seem to matter, I just had to binge-eat and I did, and then I vomited so that I wouldn't put on weight.

That went on until I was 20. I had this job—it was so boring and I hated it. One day after an eating-binge, I was so agitated I drank half a bottle of sherry. It worked wonders. It steadied my nerves and I felt better. I started thinking that if I had a drink I wouldn't need to binge-eat. I bought a bottle of whisky and kept it in my wardrobe. When thoughts of food and putting on weight became overwhelming I'd drink some alcohol and they would be less insistent. That's how I stopped bingeing. I went on vomiting—it's easy to do when you know how and my weight dropped from 67 kg (148 lbs, 10st 8 lbs) to 46 kg (101 lbs, 7 st 3 lbs). When I was drinking I was much more relaxed and began to go out with friends.

About this time I realized I was wasting my life so I left the dull job and stopped drinking, except on social occasions when I would drink until I was drunk, or eat all the food I could. I guess the occasions gave me permission to indulge my needs. I started a secretarial course, which was hard work, and one day I began binge-eating again. It was just after my 21st birthday when I had got drunk and had horrified my parents. Soon I was binge-eating three or more times a week. I started vomiting again and took large doses of laxatives. Because I was scared that I would put on weight even after what I was doing, I began to jog and was soon running 6 miles (10 km) a day. It seemed to help. When I was jogging I stopped thinking about food and my weight, which stayed at 54 kg (119 lbs, 8 st 7 lbs; BMI 20.8; 100 per cent of ABW). Because of the vomiting my teeth were going bad, but I couldn't stop vomiting after an eating-binge; it made me feel relaxed. And if I was having problems, or was worried, I'd drop into the pub and have a few quick whiskys. Mind you, I was worried that I might be an alcoholic.

The next year I met Wayne and we married. It was great at first but I still needed to binge, and I did, often every day, and I kept a bottle or two of whisky hidden at home, just in case I needed a drink. When Wayne found out he was furious and I felt it was time I saw a doctor.

The Clinic records show that over the next three years, when Penny was attending regularly, she occasionally binge-ate, and twice returned to her previous behaviour of binge-eating three or more times a week and using alcohol. Her weight is stable at around 55 kg (121 lbs, 8 st 9 lbs), and she leads an active social life. Her employer says she is excellent at her job.

The effect of bulimia nervosa on body weight

Before developing the eating disorder the body weight of most binge-eaters is within the normal range. About 20 per cent are overweight or

obese, and a similar proportion are underweight, often being diagnosed
as having anorexia nervosa. After starting the binge-eating, many of
the women show frequent swings in body weight. These facts indicate
that women of all weights may binge-eat. Binge-eating occurs among
obese women, women of normal body weight, and some anorexia
nervosa patients binge-eat.

Case history: Jane

Jane started dieting at the age of 16 to control her weight. At first she had a small
steady loss in weight. At the age of 17 she began binge-eating and for the next six
years she alternated between binge-eating and strict, almost starvation diets, with
resulting large swings of weight, of up to 19 kg (42 lbs, 3 st). When her weight
was below 55 kg (121 lbs, 8 st 9 lbs), her menstrual periods ceased, to return
when her weight exceeded that weight. On two occasions of about two-weeks'
duration her weight fell to a BMI of 15 (less than 75 per cent ABW), placing her
into the category of anorexia nervosa, as it is defined clinically.

Other binge-eaters control their weight fluctuations to within 3 kg
(6½ lbs), by dieting and exercising excessively between binges, or by
using vomiting and purging to try to prevent absorption of the food eaten
during a binge. The belief held by many women who have bulimia
nervosa that self-induced vomiting, immediately after eating, is a very
efficient way of controlling weight gain as no food is absorbed, is
erroneous. Some food must be absorbed as women who binge-eat a large
amount of food are usually overweight, whilst the weight of women
whose binges are small is usually in the normal range.

The treatment of bulimia nervosa

*The one major element required for recovery from bulimia is a desperate
will to live normally. Normality is the heaven for which I strive. Perhaps
I will have it some day. I certainly haven't given up. This however is not
as simple as it sounds to a binge-eater. It should be so easy to forget about
counting calories and just eat three normal meals every day, but
somehow the reassurance of knowing that you didn't eat more than your
allowed calories is necessary. Without this reassurance, confusion can
result, bringing on a binge. Counting calories doesn't mean dieting or
denying yourself fattening foods—it simply means controlling your
overall food intake and allowing for these fattening extras in your diet. It
can stop the guilt associated with eating high-calorie items, a guilt which
may be the cause of a binge.*

The wide variation in eating behaviours of binge-eaters, the changes which occur in an individual over a period of time, the symptoms associated with binge-eating, and the consequences which may arise indicate that treatment has to be individualized and should be aimed to help the particular individual correct her disordered eating behaviour. Before treatment is offered the history of the eating disorder and physical condition of the patient have to be assessed, so that her specific needs can be taken into account. Treatment is usually directed at changing the woman's eating behaviour, modifying her disturbed attitude to her shape and weight, and at helping her cope with any specific problem she may have. It is hoped that by discussing problems with the woman, by suggesting that she records her feelings and thoughts so that they may be evaluated and discussed, she will be helped to overcome her eating disorder. The concept is that if a person thinks differently, she will behave differently. Psychiatrists call this approach to treatment 'cognitive therapy'. On some occasions family therapy may be required. In other cases relaxation therapy may be useful. If the person has a specific psychiatric problem not related to eating this has to be treated either before, or at the same time as, treatment for bulimia. In such cases specific medications, particularly antidepressants, may be prescribed.

Four general statements can be made about treatment:

1. Admission to hospital and in-patient treatment is usually undesirable in the first instance unless the bulimic woman is in a 'crisis' or has other psychological, psychiatric, or medical problems, such as depression or is suicidal or has a personality disorder which needs treatment in hospital (Table 9). A short stay in hospital may benefit a woman whose life is in chaos, whose place of living is contributing to her problems, or who lives in a country area which prevents her from attending regularly as an out-patient. A short hospital admission may be needed so that the therapist can assess the woman's psychological or medical problems further and devise a programme of treatment appropriate for the woman.

   If out-patient treatment has not been successful over a six- to twelve-month period, admission to hospital may be required to help the woman overcome her disordered eating pattern.

   The aim of in-patient treatment is, first, to provide a supportive environment in which the woman can learn 'normal' eating habits and can cease to use the potentially dangerous methods of weight control, for example, self-induced vomiting and purgative abuse. Second, to provide the patient with a supportive environment to

Table 9. Possible reasons for admitting a patient with bulimia nervosa to hospital

---

If she is in poor physical health because she uses dangerous methods of weight control

If she has medical, psychological, or psychiatric problems which are best treated in hospital (for example, depression, drug addiction, severe biochemical disturbance, personality disorder)

If she is suicidal

If her home environment is preventing changes in her eating behaviour

If her personality is such that out-patient treatment is unlikely to be effective

If she lives in a remote area where out-patient treatment is not available

If no improvement has been obtained as an out-patient, particularly if several attempts have failed

---

enable her to make changes in her life-style and gain insight into her other problems which will aid her recovery, particularly if she is admitted to a specialized Eating Disorders Unit. In these units, a team of skilled health professionals is available to help her overcome her problems. Women whose eating disorder is of long duration, who are severely ill, or who have multiple psychological or physical problems, usually need and benefit from in-patient treatment.

For some women, hospital admission appears to be disadvantageous rather than beneficial. Some in-patients take on the role of a psychiatric patient (as many admissions are to psychiatric units); they use manipulative behaviour, such as suicide threats, to gain repeated hospital admissions when facing personal, work, or other challenges; they use their 'illness' to avoid facing up to the usual problems that women of their particular age meet with; and they avoid responsibility for changing their own behaviour, expecting the hospital staff to take on this responsibility. Often within a few weeks of discharge from hospital the woman is binge-eating again. If the patient is able to contact the skilled staff working in a specialized Eating Disorder Unit, she can seek their help to avoid falling into this pattern of behaviour.

2. If a stressful life event is expected, such as an examination or the challenge of a new job, or if an interpersonal relationship ends, the woman must be warned that she may revert to binge-eating and the therapist should be available to talk with her and help her get through the crisis.

3. Binge-eaters should not take part-time jobs which are associated with food, such as waitressing, unless this is unavoidable, as association with food preparation or serving it is likely to provoke an episode of bulimia and to retard or prevent recovery.

4. Until the woman has been free from bulimia nervosa for six months, holidays or trips overseas should be avoided. In an unfamiliar environment, with a loss of routine and frequent new experiences, it is common for binge-eaters to feel a loss of control of their body weight and to revert to a pattern of binge-eating, self-induced vomiting, and purgation. A few bulimia nervosa patients resort to a starvation diet when on holiday because they fear that in the new environment they will lose control of their eating habits. If they do lose control, their weight loss can be extreme and they need to return home.

Binge-eaters can be extremely demanding of time, and they can be manipulative and are not always truthful, as they are usually desperate for help and want the therapist to like them. Most realize that their behaviour is abnormal so it is not surprising that they are not always truthful. However, they have a great number of assets which makes working with them rewarding for the therapist. Even though not always appropriate, the resources they have developed, such as their resistance behaviour and their desire to get better, mean that progress can be made once the therapist has formed a good relationship with the woman.

The treatment of bulimia nervosa, as with other eating disorders, is to alter the eating behaviour and to help the woman maintain her weight in the desirable range.

This is done by sessions of talking with a therapist during which the following matters are discussed and the woman learns:

● to acquire new attitudes to food, eating, body weight and shape;
● to keep her weight within the normal range (BMI 19–24.9);
● to eat some food at least three times a day;

- to avoid inappropriate methods of losing weight;
- to recognize when she is in a 'bad mood', and to learn to have insight into her mood changes;
- to recognize what precipitates binge-eating; and
- to find ways of coping with her problems, other than resorting to binge-eating.

Several types of therapy are used to try to help the woman achieve these aims. Those most often suggested are supportive psychotherapy, behaviour therapy, and cognitive therapy. Supportive psychotherapy is used to help the woman get through a time-limited crisis. In behaviour and cognitive therapies, techniques are used to try to help the patient change her disordered ways of thinking about her body shape and weight, food, and eating, so that she learns to eat normally (see page 127). The technique used in these treatments is for the therapist to encourage the patient to talk, and to listen carefully to what she says. Simple explanations and advice are provided for issues which have been ventilated, reassurance is given when appropriate, and the woman is encouraged to take responsibility for her behaviour. She is helped to solve her own problems and to make sure that she does not become dependent on her therapist.

Counselling and crisis intervention may be useful. Family and marital (couple) therapy may be required if indicated. Some patients choose group therapy and others choose to attend self-help treatment sessions. Different therapies may be needed, at different times during a course of treatment, to help a woman who has a long history of bulimia nervosa.

These treatments seek to help the woman achieve the listed aims whether she is living in the community or is an in-patient in an Eating Disorders Unit. The effect of treatment varies, some women are cured of their eating disorder, while in others the degree of disordered eating is decreased and the woman feels better for most of the time, but has occasional episodes of binge-eating.

Case history: Pat

I still have binges now—but they are shorter, they cause me less remorse and guilt, and I consume less food during them than before. I simply can't fit the *volume* of food in I could before. I am fuller sooner. They also relieve my anxious feelings better. I have the binge and I feel relieved. I can even sit and watch television for the rest of the night without continuing to eat, because I am *satisfied*.

When I was caught up in it before, the night would dissolve into an endless foray in and out of the kitchen. I might stop for 1–2 hours (when absolutely full) but restart eating later. Now, I usually stop and that's it—no more. (Although not always—I still experience a few binges like before and feel sick in bed afterwards.)

If I want to, I can stop the binge before it starts, or even *at* a point during it. But I have to say to myself: 'Why are you doing this? What's the matter? What are you trying to say to yourself?' or 'What are you unhappy about?'

Often the answer comes easily—'I'm unhappy about Bill, I miss him' or 'I had a fight with Kevin and he boxed me into a corner again' or 'I'm hassled. There are too many things to do and I don't know if I can do them all in time' or 'My mother-in-law was here today and she annoys me. She seems to take over *our* house (even though I know she doesn't) and when she's here everything revolves around her' (she's a semi-invalid).

Sometimes I don't know why I'm bingeing (unlike before when I *never* knew why I was bingeing). And then I can't stop the binge.

Now the binges don't affect my weight that much. Firstly, they mean less food intake. Secondly, I can make up by eating sparingly the next day (and I usually am *not* hungry for a while). Thirdly, I can run or play squash to adjust my weight and enjoy the exercise.

How strange to feel 'satisfied' and happy with your life! It is the most superb feeling, to feel good about yourself!

I am pleased with my body and what it can do for me (in terms of sport or sex). It is not as skinny as I had wanted nor is it a model's figure. But it suits me and two men have lately confirmed that, saying things I would never have thought possible, like 'you have a little bottom' or 'I like your legs'.

I have treated myself to the luxury of new fashionable trendy clothes—a joy from the days when I dreaded trying on jeans because even size 14 (UK size 36, European size 42) never fitted me. In fact, many of the clothes from previous seasons look dowdy and very boring now—they represented a me who was afraid to show any of her body, who wore discreet plain clothes so as not to 'show off' and who never looked sexy because a fat person had no *right* to be sexual.

I know my body attracts men. I can feel the 'vibrations' or I can feel them watching me sometimes. This confirms my feelings of self-confidence in myself but also perhaps suggests that the new-found sexuality is showing. I feel a 'complete' person—all the pieces are there fitting together correctly—including the sexual part of me—and I guess it shows.

Binges for me are also a way to relax. I always keep little activities to do around the house so I am 'busy' and occupied away from food. But if I am tired or don't want to do them, then sometimes I'm stuck. I want to unwind and food is a good way. It involves little mental effort, it calms the nervous feeling in my stomach, and it takes my mind away from work or troubles.

Changing attitudes to food, shape, and weight

In the back of my mind, I still feel that—should events one day go bad in my life—I could return to the bingeing as before. If there was too much pressure, worries, or if I couldn't cope with problems, food is the crutch to keep me going. It would have to be very bad, but I also think I would seek help from my counsellors to keep me from turning entirely to food. I'm not sure—it exists as a possibility. Certainly, if I was bored, unhappy with my life-style (for example, stuck in a little house with a baby and no friends or money to buy things) or doing things I did not really want to do—food or eating might become the only interesting facet of life (as they were once to me). But I hope not. And I think—I really think—I'll make it without food in the long run.

Women who binge-eat, like patients with other eating disorders, are preoccupied with food, shape, and weight. They have to be encouraged to stop keeping food records, weighing themselves frequently, constantly counting calories (kilojoules), cooking for others, and reading recipes. Each of these behaviours usually lead bulimia nervosa patients to gain weight in the long term. It may be helpful at some stage in counselling if the woman marks the days when she binge-eats on a calendar or, preferably, keeps the Eating Behaviour and Mood Diary which we described on page 56. The two findings which often arise from these records are that the incidence of episodes of binge-eating may decrease, but not be recognized by the patient, and that the frequency of binge-eating may be increased premenstrually and during early menstruation. Patients find it reassuring to know these facts.

Binge-eaters should be encouraged to eat out socially and increase other social activities. Most of them have withdrawn from social occasions because of the presence of food or because of feelings of social unease, not related to food. They need help to find out what social eating is and to learn to incorporate it into their life-style. The fewer diet restrictions there are the easier this is. It also means giving up the distinction between 'good foods' and 'bad foods'.

What some women think of as 'bad' and 'good' foods is shown in Table 10. This table shows that many of the 'good' foods are those recommended by Expert Committees concerned about preventing heart disease, diabetes, and obesity. However, many eating disorder patients' ideas about foods are not accurate and the likelihood of a woman being able to resist eating all of the foods on the 'bad' list over a long period of time is very small. Learning to eat all foods in moderation at meal times or on social occasions, rather than only during binge-eating, is an important action for women who are recovering from bulimia nervosa to learn.

The main purpose of changing the woman's attitudes to food, shape, and eating is to persuade her to learn to eat normally. Many patients have forgotten what normal eating is, and will be helped if they can identify some of its criteria, which are shown in Table 11.

Table 10. Eating disordered women's perceptions of 'bad' and 'good' foods

'Bad' foods	'Good' foods
Energy dense foods	Foods with no or low carbohydrate content
Takeaway ('junk') foods (including hamburgers)	Foods containing a low fat content
Snack foods	Vegetables—but not potatoes
Fatty foods	Fruit, including dried fruit
Dairy products (including milk and cheese but not yoghurt)	Chicken and fish, but not red meat
Bread and biscuits but not diet biscuits	High fibre foods
Sweets, lollies, candies, ice cream	Anything bought in a health food shop, including honey

Control of weight

As most bulimia nervosa patients have experienced large swings in body weight during the years of binge-eating, part of the treatment is to help the woman learn, often for the first time, how to stabilize her body weight and maintain it within the 'desirable' range. But first the woman and the therapist have to agree upon a sensible weight, which the patient will seek to maintain. This is usually only a problem with patients who

Table 11. Normal eating

Normal eating is:

- eating something at least three times a day;
- eating more than you feel you need to eat on some occasions (overeating);
- eating less than you need on some occasions (undereating);
- eating more of the foods that you enjoy the taste of, when you choose to;
- eating less of the foods you like, as you know you can eat them in the future;
- eating or not eating on occasions because you feel unhappy, 'bad', or tense;
- eating both 'good' and 'bad' foods, in other words a variety of foods, without feeling guilty;
- eating in a flexible way so that it does not interfere with your work, study, or social life;
- eating sufficient food and a variety of foods, often enough to prevent a desire to binge-eat;
- eating, when out socially, in a similar manner to the other people in the group;
- eating at 'fast food' outlets occasionally as a treat to yourself;
- being aware that eating is not the most important thing in life but it is important for good health.

Normal eating is:

- *not* counting calories (kilojoules), weighing food, or following a strict diet;
- *not* eating low calorie (kilojoule) foods, for example, diet biscuits rather than bread;
- *not* eating to lose weight but knowing that you can 'watch your weight' if you want to;
- *not* assuming that you can control the amount and type of food your body needs better than your body can;
- *not* having to weigh yourself for reassurance;
- *not* playing games with yourself to prevent eating certain foods, for example, saying to yourself 'dairy products make me feel nauseous'.

---

have previously been at very low weights, as they may wish to remain or achieve low body weights which are difficult to maintain, unless the woman is preoccupied with food and dieting, which hinders progress to recovery. It is interesting that many patients who have been at high body weights often select as their desired weight one which is still above the normal range, for example, a BMI in the ranges 25–29. The woman should understand that she is not expected to maintain a constant weight, as fluctuations of 0.5–1.5 kg (1–3 lbs) are normal and are due to daily fluctuations in water balance and contents of the intestinal tract. Unless the woman is aware of this, she may respond to an increase of 0.5 kg (1.1 lbs) with panic, and this may precipitate an episode of binge-eating. On the other hand she may respond to a small loss of weight by thinking that she can eat more and this may start an episode of binge-eating. For these reasons a woman who has bulimia nervosa should stop weighing herself or at least avoid weighing herself more frequently than once a week, as this may precipitate feelings of panic, inadequacy, or failure.

A binge-eater has to learn to control her disordered eating behaviour before trying to reduce her weight, as any serious attempt at dieting will usually result in binge-eating episodes. This requires frequent discussions with her therapist, and often with a dietitian.

The object of these sessions is to help the woman learn to eat the appropriate amount of food required to maintain her weight. To help her resist binge-eating, the food should be divided so that she eats at least three-times each day. To help her achieve this objective dietetic counselling may be helpful, as many patients no longer know how much they can eat in order to maintain weight. When patients describe the amount of food they feel they can eat, they do not take account of their binge-eating. For example, many patients are convinced that if they eat more than 5040 kJ (1200 kcal) a day they will put on weight, and they claim that they have to keep themselves on a reducing diet when not binge-eating. A skilful dietitian can help a woman learn normal eating behaviour without increasing her need to focus on food and become more preoccupied with food, eating, and weight control. It may take some time for patients to have enough confidence to accept that when they cease binge-eating, self-induced vomiting, and purgation they will be able to eat more at meals without weight gain.

In-patient treatment may be necessary for some patients to feel safe and confident that they can learn normal eating behaviour and can cease inappropriate weight-losing behaviours.

Avoiding inappropriate weight-losing behaviour

Although many binge-eaters are aware that 'starvation diets', self-induced vomiting, and laxative and diuretic abuse are potentially dangerous, their knowledge is often inaccurate. Treatment of binge-eating includes discussion of the use the woman has made of weight-losing methods and her willingness to reduce their use. Many women who binge-eat are willing, at least initially, to try to change their behaviour, and are reassured when they learn about the effects which may occur. Most are unaware that they may gain weight temporarily when they cease the behaviour, as they retain fluid in their body. Most do not know that after ceasing to use the behaviour, constipation may persist for some time, as well as a feeling of abdominal fullness and cramps. As these women are preoccupied with body weight and abdominal fullness, such symptoms make them anxious, which may precipitate self-induced vomiting and purgation, starvation or binge-eating. It is often helpful for her to think of the symptoms as 'withdrawal symptoms' which she will have to suffer for a period of time. After ten days of avoiding the behaviours mentioned, most patients usually feel comfortable; and after three weeks they usually report feeling better than they ever have, especially with respect to fatigue. Unfortunately it takes most patients some time to have the confidence to stop their behaviour completely, because they fear a rapid weight increase and loss of control of eating. It is difficult for them to be able to feel that their binge-eating will lessen if this behaviour stops and in-patient treatment may be needed for some women to achieve this objective.

Recognition of negative (dysphoric) moods

Patients describe anxiety, tension, and unpleasant moods prior to binge-eating. In most, the negative mood is relieved during or after the binge. A theory has been advanced which seeks to explain why the binge relieves the negative mood (see page 34). The theory relies on the belief that the brain level of a hormone called serotonin is low in people who are irritable, depressed, or anxious, in other words, those who have a dysphoric mood. If such a person eats a carbohydrate-rich meal or binges on carbohydrate-rich foods, the level of a substance called tryptophan in her blood is raised. The higher blood level of tryptophan permits some of the tryptophan to cross from the blood into the brain where it stimulates the synthesis and release of serotonin. This raises the level of serotonin in the brain and relieves the dysphoric mood, making the woman feel relaxed and drowsy. However the relief only lasts for a time, after which the dysphoric mood returns, and is relieved by eating another carbohydrate-rich meal or a binge. Recognition by the patient of the association between unpleasant moods, especially anxiety, and relief from them by binge-eating assists her to find other more appropriate ways of coping with tension. Relaxation therapy can help, if only to enable patients to recognize their anxiety. Many patients find relaxation difficult at any time and almost impossible prior to a binge when they are most agitated and tense.

If the theory of lack of brain serotonin is true, drugs which increase brain serotonin may help some bulimic women reduce or stop bingeing. Experiments using tryptophan have shown some success. Women with bulimia nervosa felt better and decreased their binge-eating and overeating. Two drugs, dexfenfluramine and fluoxetine, which appear to increase brain serotonin levels are currently under investigation. The results of the studies are awaited. As these chemical agents have only small effects it is obvious that a physiological explanation for bulimia nervosa is only part of the aetiology of the disorder.

As the frequency of binge-eating decreases, the woman can discuss her need to eat in the face of tension or stress. Once she understands herself a little better, she can reorganize her life-style to minimize eating due to tension or stress, for example, when examinations are approaching, by working more consistently without a last-minute cram or by studying in a place which does not have easy access to food; by learning to have confidence to ask questions of, or help from, lecturers and tutors rather than worrying about what she does not know; or by arranging activities so she does not spend all day feeling she should study and eating as an excuse not to start. Some women, particularly those with a long history of bulimia nervosa, will explain that they 'binge' only so that they can induce vomiting. They become 'addicted' to vomiting to reduce tension.

The recognition of precipitants

The patient and the therapist explore and discuss those factors, such as marital and family stress (which we have mentioned on page 120), loneliness, tenseness, and boredom, which have precipitated binge-eating in the past and currently. Recognition of precipitants to binge-eating assists patients to reorganize their life-style either to avoid these situations or to find other ways of coping at these times. It is interesting that as patients improve they recognize hunger as a precipitant but also explain that previously they had trouble recognizing accurate cues for hunger and satiation.

Encouragement of resistance behaviour

As was mentioned earlier, most binge-eaters have tried to resist binge-eating at some time or other. The methods they have used are many and various, and exploration of these with the therapist can give the patient insight into the problem. Some of the less-extreme behaviours can be used successfully at times by patients and can be included in treatment programmes. Reorganization of life-style so that patients are occupied at the times they are most likely to binge-eat is useful, for example, attending a gym on the way home from work and before dinner, or washing hair and knitting when at home at night. Patients need a number of these interests, as they tend to become less effective over time, and the patient must enjoy the chosen occupation. Sensible exercise can be promoted for most bulimia nervosa sufferers, but the exercise needs to be controlled as some patients are at risk of developing an exercise disorder (see page 60) which may replace or co-exist with the eating disorder. The chosen exercise regimen must be perceived by the woman as enjoyable. For example, if the woman hates jogging or bike-riding, there is no point in suggesting that she jogs or cycles. Taking up interests also helps patients to feel better about themselves and feel more like other people.

Treatment of the physical symptoms

Most bulimia patients require little medical treatment for their physical symptoms. When treatment is needed it is usually because the woman has developed a potassium or a vitamin deficiency because of 'starvation diets', or self-induced vomiting, or abuse of slimming tablets, laxatives, or diuretics. In a few cases, treatment is needed because of a suicide attempt.

The symptoms of physical discomfort described by patients during or after binge-eating are: swelling of hands and feet, abdominal fullness, fatigue, headache, nausea, and abdominal pain. The swelling of hands and feet appears to be associated with the amount of food eaten and this symptom may be used by patients to obtain prescriptions from doctors for diuretics. The presence of the other symptoms appears to be associated more with the presence or absence of induced vomiting.

Management of gynaecological problems

Many bulimia nervosa victims have disordered menstruation. Their menstrual periods either cease or occur only infrequently. In the past these young women have been subjected to endocrine investigations because of the menstrual disorder. Following the investigation they have been prescribed hormonal tablets to restore their menstrual function. The treatments have usually failed. Investigation and treatment of menstrual disturbances is rarely needed, as the menstrual pattern will return to normal once binge-eating, starvation, vomiting, excessive exercise, and abuse of laxatives and diuretics have ceased. However, if the woman is at low body weight and has not menstruated for some months, oral contraceptives should be prescribed, as these will protect her bones from becoming brittle. In such patients the lack of menstruation is associated with the woman's low body weight. In most bulimia nervosa patients, lack of menstruation seems to be associated with the eating and the weight-losing methods rather than low body weight, as the woman's weight is in the normal range.

If the woman is sexually active, oral contraceptives will also prevent her from unexpectedly becoming pregnant, as pregnancy may occur occasionally even if the woman has not started menstruating again.

During the period of recovery from bulimia nervosa, many women need reassurance that they will not have become sterile as a result of their infrequent or absent ovulation and menstruation.

Bulimia nervosa patients should avoid becoming pregnant until the woman binge-eats less often than once a week. This advice is particularly important if the woman frequently abuses laxatives or diuretics, as the abuse of these drugs may affect the growth of the fetus.

Some bulimia nervosa patients (and some women with an atypical eating disorder) who desire to become pregnant may have difficulty in achieving a pregnancy, particularly if the woman maintains a low body weight, and require ovulation-induction drugs ('fertility pills or injections'). The problems are similar to those described for anorexia nervosa patients on page 83, and the cause is a persistent lack of ovulation.

If the woman does become pregnant, she may develop some of the problems described as occurring to some pregnant women who have or have had anorexia nervosa (page 83). For these reasons, a woman who has not recovered from bulimia nervosa should think carefully before she embarks on a pregnancy.

If she still has bulimia nervosa after the birth of her baby, further problems may occur. Research has revealed that many bulimic mothers have difficulty in forming a good relationship with their child. Most of the women prefer not to breast-feed, thinking that it will affect their appearance adversely.

In order not to be disturbed during an eating binge, they may lock the child in a room and ignore its cries. They tend to be over anxious about their child's weight and appearance, which in turn affects how the child is fed.

Family relationships, social, and other problems

Many bulimia nervosa patients have problems relating to their age and their life-style which they have been unable to discuss with others. When they feel confident in their therapist they are able to start talking about these problems. In adolescent women a struggle may be going on between the woman and her parents, over her independence and the parents' need for a dependent child. Other bulimia nervosa patients are ill at ease in social situations, have a low self-esteem, and are uncertain of the direction of their life. They may find it difficult to relate to others. These problems have been discussed in relation to women who have anorexia nervosa (page 96).

During treatment, women report changes in their binge-eating behaviour. Some women say that they no longer binge-eat, only overeat, while others say that the feelings associated with a binge still occur from time to time but the amount of food eaten is small and the frequency is reduced. These patients have a good chance of ceasing to have bulimia nervosa.

A few patients simply decide to stop fighting binge-eating. They buy and prepare food to binge upon each day. In other words they stop the out of control nature of eating during a binge by being prepared and knowing when they will overeat. These patients have a poor outcome, as their eating behaviour continues to interfere with their social life, relationships, and career.

Support groups for parents and partners are also important, particularly soon after the problem has been discovered or while the woman is being treated in hospital. It is reassuring for parents and partners to know that other people have a daughter or a partner who has similar problems and to be able to share and talk through their fears and hopes.

Treatment in hospital

In-patient treatment has the advantage of being able to achieve a lot in a short period of time. The woman has the opportunity to take part in other treatments, such as small-group therapy, social skills and assertiveness training, psychodrama, and anxiety management.

Women who are admitted tend to have had the disorder for a long period of time and to have severe symptoms, which may be a reason why in-patient treatment seems to be no more successful than out-patient treatment. It has to be said that many women who require admission report feelings of confusion, anger, tension and, often, depression during the first few weeks after admission.

In the Eating Disorders Unit with which we are associated, the treatment programme is intensive and involves the patient being in contact with a range of people from different disciplines in health. Each patient has her own special nurse who co-ordinates the programme and acts as an advocate for the patient between the formal sessions with her psychiatrist or psychologist.

The problems that women experience are graphically illustrated by the extracts from the diary of a 19-year-old patient who was popular and who had been outstanding in her studies before she acknowledged the need for treatment. The following extracts from her diary are recorded week by week.

Week one

First, I must accept the fact that it is my problem and, even if it isn't all my fault, I am the one who has to do the work to cure it . . . and not play games . . .

I need to give some time to myself to think about my problem. I have to stop trying to keep busy to stop trying to take my mind off the problems and to stop the loneliness . . .

I'm thinking about packing up and leaving and sorting it out at home instead of here . . .

I want to know more about my problem:

—why has it happened?

—what happens to me?

—what I need to get better . . . ?

I wish there were some rules to follow to get better, it's so hard because it is not a physical problem: it's emotional and psychological . . .

The one cause or associated problem is my fear of being alone, which I find hard to understand and which is pretty paradoxical. I'm afraid of being left alone at home or out because I know that I'll lose control and binge-eat. On the other hand, when I'm feeling like binge-eating, I get irritated when somebody is with me because they are preventing me from starting the binge. That is the paradox I'm beginning to understand . . .

The anxieties that started me binge-eating have long since passed I think. Now the bingeing is habitual and creates anxieties instead of the anxieties creating the binge. The anxieties that are created by the loss of control, and the binge, and the low self-esteem that goes with it, cause the bingeing behaviour. I'm not sure how to correct this but think that it has some relevance—there's more to it as well I'm sure . . .

End of week one

God, where do I start? I'm really so confused . . . there's so much to grasp at once.

I'm constantly trying to please people and to do what I believe they expect of me and *I have stopped being myself* because of it. Always being ready to listen to and to help others. Always being *selfless* is partly a cause of this problem.

Week two

I've been very moody and restless since Wednesday. Woke up OK today but since breakfast I've been really angry. Stuffed myself with AllBran and feel revolting and fat. Just want to throw it up—now I know that anger leads to purging: anger, self disgust, revulsion and hatred . . .

End week two

Still angry and frustrated and confused. All day I felt dreadful . . . felt fat and ugly and dreadfully alone and empty. I cried, being so angry and frustrated and not understanding what was going on. I was ultra-upset after my appointment with the dietician. She made it clear to me just how I've been stuffing myself around by cutting back on my diet plan. Losing 750 g while cutting back—which is pretty easy to do in here because you don't build up much appetite—is stupid. To cut back while being in here is stupid because the minute I go out I'll cut back, deny myself things and then binge and vomit and be back to square one. It's just so futile! All I want to do is lose weight and get over this eating disorder. I have to *stop cutting back*, which means stop losing weight . . .

End week three

I want to go home. But I know that's running away. But it won't really be running away. I'll be running away from *this environment to another environ-ment*, but the *feelings* won't change. *I can run away as far as possible, but I can't run away from how I'm feeling*.

Week four

Oh, what a day! YUCK . . . YUCK . . . YUCK . . . ! [later] The *best thing* I did for myself tonight was to stop myself from bingeing and *I feel so good* about it.

On my way to bed I stuffed my pockets with about 15 biscuits, but after eating four (*I think I was so off the planet with mixed emotions I'm really unsure*) I came back to my room and my positive—very positive *new mind* defeated the bingeing.

I thought '*Be nice to yourself—do something good for yourself for a change*', and I picked up all the biscuits and took them and got rid of them. I felt so *powerful*. I jumped for joy and happiness about myself . . .

End week four

Some nights when I have the urge to binge I don't go near the kitchen, I feel strong and those times are positive. But tonight's defeat of the Bulimic Binge Devil was even stronger. Stronger because I'd taken the first step and there was *no chance* of being caught.

I'm so *pleased*, because that's the hardest thing I've done for a long time. And the best thing was that *I did it for myself. For nobody else but me and I did it for me*

because
I
deserve
to
beat
it.

Week five

Went home on Friday. Aaaaaaarghhhh! I'm going up and down like a yo-yo. It's unbelievable. I did vomit and then felt so *guilty*, mainly for Mum but also for myself.

End of week five

This morning I woke up with a new attitude. I realized last night that going home without taking responsibility just wasn't the answer. Responsibility for my own dilemma was the key to beating it. I made some decisions . . .

Spoke to my doctor which annoyed me because she emphasized the importance of getting on with it.

I can't FANTASIZE . . .

I must do it.

The response to treatment

The binges still occur but I would define them now as 'over-eating'. My weight has gone up 3 kg (6½ lbs) but it doesn't bother me. I don't weigh

Table 12. Binge-eater's needs

Be motivated to recover

To learn that dieting is unnecessary

To learn that most foods can be eaten in moderate
quantities without a dramatic change in weight

To eat at least three meals a day

To discontinue vomiting and purging

To understand that urges to binge-eat certain
foods may persist for many months

To meet with the therapist each week or every
2 weeks to plan for the next period

To stop dividing foods into 'good' and 'bad' foods

---

*myself anymore, at least not often. I don't try to stick to a diet as it would
just emphasize food once again (but I'm sure that I will always count
calories in my mind—but only in hundreds). I feel happy and try to eat
normally whenever possible.*

A good response to treatment is: (1) that the woman ceases to binge eat,
or binge eats small amounts of food less than once a month; (2) that she
ceases to use potentially dangerous methods of weight control, such as
self-induced vomiting, purgative abuse, slimming tablet abuse, and
diuretic abuse; (3) that she is able to stabilize her weight; (4) that she eats
regular meals with no oscillation between over-eating and starvation;
(5) that she is able to interact with others of both sexes in social
situations.

An intermediate response is that the patient shows; (1) a decreased
frequency of binge-eating; (2) a decreased use of potentially dangerous
methods of weight control; (3) stabilization of weight; (4) eats meals
regularly; (5) develops improved social interactions; and (6) feels she has
more control over her eating behaviour.

Case history: Yvonne

It's good to feel 'normal' about eating and my weight now. I eat whatever I feel
like, including cakes, an occasional chocolate, honey, bread, puddings, rich

savoury dishes like quiche or pies. I eat when I want to, but I have found that I enjoy food most when I *am* hungry and can sit, eat leisurely, and savour it. I have also found that my stomach will signal when it's full (although it's too easy to miss the signal at times) and I usually stop eating then. It's like regular people who eat when they're hungry and stop when they're full.

My appetite varies tremendously. Sometimes I will be hungry in the morning and eat breakfast, followed by something at 10.00 or 11.00 a.m., and then a bite at lunch. Other times, if I've had a big meal the previous night, a cup of tea takes me through till 12.00.

It amazes me how little food I need to satisfy my hunger at that moment. However, if I discover myself constantly in the kitchen searching for 'something' simply to put in my mouth, I realize I am bored or uptight and am seeking a pacifier. Then, I ask myself '*Exactly what* food appeals particularly?' Often the answer comes back 'Well, nothing really' or 'I don't know' and then (if I feel like it) I will say to myself 'You're not hungry really; you're just looking for a diversion' and go away to find something else to do.

My weight varies in cycles (this being deduced, not from the tyranny of the bathroom scales, but from the looseness of the clothes around my waist and bottom and the actual look of my stomach and lower chest—slight rolls being apparent at the heavier weight).

My weight does not worry me, nor do I try to control it by strict dieting. If I feel 'heavy', I will eat less food and drink less, watch carefully for that point of stomach fullness, and exercise more (running, dancing, gym classes, tennis).

There are cycles of heaviness when I feel heavy and have been over-eating and even non-aggressive binges. It's nice to know the connection between weight and eating. I know I am eating more and I feel my weight going up—not like before when I always seemed 'fat' regardless of how much or how little I ate.

Then there are slim cycles when I feel slimmer, trimmer, and eat less (no sweets or dessert after dinner, no wine, no lunches out, no picking) but this just happens and I do not control it or feel guilty about eating less or more. . . .

Recently, under much pressure of work and relationships, I started experiencing a 'knot' in my stomach, thinking it may be the start of an ulcer!

It immediately reminded me of my binge-days when I often had this knot and thought it was stomach (i.e. physiological) hunger. Then, I would eat to relieve the 'hunger'. Food soothed away the pain and did, in fact, make me feel 'better', no longer being plagued by a gnawing in the stomach. However, when I ate food or drank milk to relieve the knot, it relieved it temporarily but then left me in 5 minutes again feeling the same. It was a tension build-up and I learnt I could relieve it by deep breaths (trying to relax) or walking around and stretching. It went away after a couple of weeks.

About 40 per cent of bulimia nervosa patients, followed for a period of five years, show a good outcome to treatment, 40 per cent show an intermediate outcome, and 20 per cent show no improvement. In reported outcome studies it is important to check that the patients have not substituted their eating disorder with an exercise disorder or an alcohol disorder.

A good outcome is more likely if the woman is less than 20 years old when she seeks help and if she has been binge-eating for less than five years. In other words, if the young woman, or her immediate family, had a greater understanding of bulimia nervosa, she would seek help earlier and could expect a more rapid cure. The more difficult problem to overcome is the delay of binge-eaters in presenting for treatment. In part, this results from the patient's secrecy about her eating behaviour and her belief that if she really wanted to stop her eating behaviour she could do so. She may only accept that she has an eating problem after she has tried to stop, or has been placed in a situation where she has not been able to continue her eating behaviour without being discovered. In the last five years, family doctors have become more aware of bulimia nervosa and are helping their patients to obtain treatment. Unfortunately, this depends on the woman admitting her bulimia nervosa behaviours to the doctor. Many women do not and are extensively investigated for their menstrual problems (often including gynaecological operations), or are diagnosed as having an 'irritable colon', or are prescribed anti-depressants, which they usually do not take.

Relapses to binge-eating are not uncommon and are usually precipitated by a new life stress such as an impending examination, a change of job, illness, marriage, divorce, abortion, or the birth of a dead or deformed baby. It is of help to an ex-bulimia nervosa patient to know that she can seek help from a therapist whom she knows and with whom she feels comfortable should a relapse occur.

Summary of treatment of bulimia nervosa

Treat as out-patient or as in-patient

Help patient to:
* stop trying to lose weight
* stabilize weight in desirable range
* stop using weight-losing behaviour
* learn sensible normal eating patterns, appropriate to life-style
* eat food at least 3 times a day
* decrease preoccupation with weight and food

↓

Throughout programme provide:
* supportive psychotherapy
* cognitive and behaviour therapy
* help for other perceived problems

↓

Once binge-eating and weight-losing behaviours have ceased, if the woman is still overweight and wishes to lose weight, sensible dieting may be attempted. However, dieting is usually not necessary as a slow persistent weight loss occurs over a period of months or years.

↓

Overall aim is to help patient to:
* live a normal life
* be able to cope with life

9

Obesity

My other good news is that my weight isn't such a worry any more. I am still overweight, but I certainly don't feel the grotesque elephant I used to feel. I'm 72 kg (159 lbs, 11 st 5 lbs) at the moment which is low for me, and I haven't put on any weight for about seven months. I'm not really dieting I guess . . . just eating pretty sensibly and that seems to be enough to keep my weight stable. I know its a slow and black way to lose weight, but this way my eating doesn't dominate my thoughts so much. I really do hope to get down to about 63 kg (140 lbs, 10 st) by Christmas and at that weight I'd like to think I'll be slim and satisfied with myself.

Obesity occurs when, over a period of time, the net energy intake exceeds the net energy expenditure. The term net energy intake is necessary because it has been observed that when a person increases the amount of energy ingested an increase in energy output occurs, and the excess energy available for storage in the body is less than 100 per cent of that ingested. The excess energy is stored in two main places in the body. The first place is obvious when you look at an obese person, that is, the energy is stored in adipose tissue. Adipose tissue consists of about 80 per cent fat, 18 per cent water, and 2 per cent protein. 1 kg (2.2 lbs) of adipose tissue has an energy content of 30 000 kJ (7 150 kcals). The second storage area for energy is called the 'glycogen-water pool'. Glycogen is a substance found in muscle, and each gramme of glycogen is bound to 3.5 g of water. The combination of glycogen and water makes the glycogen-water pool. The exact size of the glycogen-water pool is difficult to measure, but it is thought to weigh between 3.5 kg (7½ lbs) in a non-obese person and up to 5.5 kg (12 lbs) in an obese person. One kilogramme of the pool contains about 4 200 kJ (1000 kcals) of energy, which is released [together with 3.5 kg (7½ lbs) of water] when energy is required and none is provided by food or drink. Only when the glycogen-water pool is almost depleted of energy is adipose tissue burned up to release energy.

Obesity is defined in several ways, one being when the Body Mass Index is 30 or more (see page 18). The level of 30 has been chosen because

Fig. 15. Obesity.

statistics from life assurance companies indicate that above that level a significant increase in morbidity and mortality occurs compared with lower BMI. The level is rather higher than that derived from life insurance 'desirable' or 'ideal' weight-for-height tables. These tables were obtained after one particular company, the Metropolitan Life Insurance Company, had analysed the height and weight data of a large number of men and women and had found that 'desirable' or 'ideal' weights fell within a range for men and women. By desirable, they meant that people within this range of weight were at the lowest risk of developing illness or dying prematurely. When the 'desirable' range is related to the BMI the boundaries of the range of 19 to 24.9 fit approximately. People whose weight range lies in the BMI range of 25 to 29.9 are overweight and have an increased risk of developing some chronic illnesses such as musculoskeletal and cardiovascular disorders, but no increased chance of dying compared with people whose weight is in the normal range. They also have an increased chance of putting on more weight so that they become obese.

When a person's BMI is 30 or more she has an increased risk of dying from heart disease or diabetes, amongst other illnesses. This is the reason for choosing a BMI of 30 or more to define obesity.

How many people in a country are obese is not easy to determine. A study made in the USA in the early 1970s, using skin-fold thickness at two body sites (mid-biceps and sub-scapular) as an index of obesity, found that 5 per cent of American men aged 20 to 70 were 'severely obese'. In other words, 7 million American men aged 20 or more were severely obese. Severe obesity was defined in the study as being 23 kg (50 lbs) over the desirable weight for age and height in the case of men and 30 kg (99 lbs) above the desirable weight in the case of women. This equates approximately to a BMI of 35 or more.

If the person's BMI is 40 or more, the person is defined as being *morbidly obese* and has a greatly increased risk of dying. The prevalence in the community of morbid obesity is much less than that of obesity. A rough estimate is that one adult in every 2000 in Western developed countries is morbidly obese.

In Australia a national survey conducted by the National Heart Foundation in 1989 found that 11 per cent of women and 9 per cent of men aged 20–69 were obese as defined by a BMI of 30 or more. In the United Kingdom a survey made in 1990 showed that 10.7 per cent of adults were obese.

The prevalence of overweight and obesity in a community increases with age. Information from several developed countries shows that about 12 per cent of children between the ages of 8 and 11 are overweight and between 2 and 5 per cent are obese. Amongst teenagers aged 14–19, between 11 and 19 per cent are overweight and between 2 and 5 per cent are obese. If a girl is obese in early adolescence (between the ages of 11 and 15) she has one chance in three of being or becoming obese by the age of 35. However, teenaged obesity accounts for no more than 10 per cent of all cases of adult obesity. Most adult obesity results from a steady, inexorable weight gain from the mid-20s onwards.

In Western countries the prevalence of obesity peaks between the ages of 55 and 65, when about 24 per cent of women and 17 per cent of men are obese (Fig. 16). People whose parents were manual workers and who are manual workers themselves are twice as likeley to become obese in their late 30s compared with non-manual or professional workers. Among women, three groups are more likely to become obese: women of lower social classes, women who do not marry, and women who have three or more pregnancies.

The increased prevalence of obesity with increasing age is in part due to the continuing ingestion of more energy each day than is expended; in part due to a reduction in the amount of energy the body needs for its

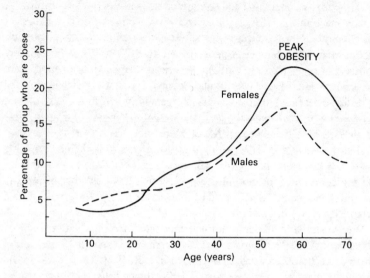

Fig. 16. The prevalence of obesity related to the age of the person.

basic functions as age advances; and in part due to a reduction in the amount of exercise taken as a person grows older.

In an affluent society where a wide variety of foods and drinks are available, and where advertising, particularly on television, plays a large part in food choices, most people tend to eat more than they need for their body functions and thus ingest spare energy. This extra energy is converted into fat. Among people whose weight is in the normal weight range (BMI 19 to 24.9), an average weight gain of 3 kg (6½ lbs) occurs between the ages of 25 and 45. The range of increase in weight usually lies between 2 and 7 kg (4½ and 15½ lbs) and rarely exceeds 10 kg (22 lbs). If the person has gained more than this amount there is a reason.

Causes of obesity

Why do some people gain weight faster than normal as they grow older, tending to become severely obese in middle age? It is easier to start answering this question by listing factors which are no longer thought to be important in the case of most obese people, although one or more may operate in individuals:

- there is no increased absorption of food from the gut of obese individuals;
- there is no increase in thyroid deficiency among obese people;
- obese people do not appear to have a greater 'addiction' for sweet foods containing more carbohydrate than thin people;
- the evidence that obese people choose a diet with a higher energy content than do thin people is not impressive. Further, in an experiment in which obese individuals were given two foods of similar appearance, one of which contained a high-energy content and the other a low-energy content, they were unable to detect any difference in the two foods;
- there is no conclusive evidence that obese people are less active than thin people.

When these hypotheses are excluded, the reasons why people become obese continue to be obscure. A genetic origin for some forms of adult obesity has been postulated, in other words, the theory is that a *tendency* to obesity may be inherited. One way of confirming this theory is to follow the progress of twins for a number of years. An American study reported in 1986 showed that the degree of fatness of nearly 2000 identical twins followed for 25 years was very close whilst that of 2000 fraternal twins was not so close. This suggested that heredity played a bigger part in obesity than environment, although both were important. Another way of determining if obesity is inherited is to see if body weight, and more particularly the BMI, of adopted children (when adults) related more closely to that of their biological parents than that of the adopting parents. A study made in Denmark in 1986 confirmed that the BMI of adopted children (when adults) related more closely to that of their biological parents, again suggesting that the tendency to obesity may be inherited. A third important study was also made in Denmark recently. The researchers were able to trace 57 people who had been adopted in childhood and to compare their weight and Body Mass Index with that of brothers or sisters who had not been adopted. The adoptees and their siblings when adult had very similar BMIs, in other words the fatter the adoptee the fatter was his or her sibling likely to be.

The conclusion of these three studies is that a tendency to fatness is inherited, and this genetic factor may be as important as the environmental factor of overeating. A genetic reason for obesity does not explain why fat people are fat. It has been suggested that what may happen is that the fatness gene or genes, programmes some people to use the energy they absorb from food for their needs more efficiently than thin people. This means that people who will become, or who are, obese use less energy for any given activity, including their resting metabolism, than thin people and the excess of energy obtained from food intake is converted into fat and stored. It is important to note that for all but the most active people sedentary activities (which includes the body's resting metabolism) account for most of the daily energy expenditure. Recent studies show that obese people are genetically programmed to be more efficient in handling this proportion of their energy expenditure, although they use the same proportion of energy for exercise as lean people.

These findings receive additional support from research made by a group of British scientists. They found that healthy, sedentary obese men had inherited a lower proportion of a type of muscle fibre (slow muscle fibre) in their body than sedentary lean men. In their study, the men with a low proportion of slow muscle fibres burned less fat during work, in other words handled energy expenditure more efficiently, and consequently gained weight more readily.

Although attractive, this theory may not be correct. The development of a method of measuring energy expenditure using 'double-labelled water' and new instruments have permitted scientists to measure energy expenditure accurately in people living a normal life and not in the artificial environment of a laboratory. Using this technique, scientists in Britain have shown that a group of women who became fat during pregnancy, and remained fat after the birth, had a higher resting metabolic rate (see page 156) than a group of lean women, and expended a quarter more energy (not less) each day than the lean women.

Another theory is based on the observation that an obese person has a larger number of fat cells in his or her body than a thin person. Until recently it was believed that fat cells only multiplied in the body until puberty. After puberty, if a person absorbed more energy from food than was expended by metabolic processes or by exercise, the excess energy was converted into fat and was stored in the existing fat cells which increased in size. It is now known that when faced with the challenge of fat to be stored at any age, the fat cells first increase in size and, when a critical size is reached, divide to form new fat cells. Once formed the fat cells never disappear. If a person continually eats more energy than she uses up, in every period that weight is gained an irreversible increase in the number of fat cells occurs, which in turn are able to store more energy in the form of fat, and the person becomes increasingly obese. It appears that obese people have bigger fat cells than lean people, and very obese people have more and bigger fat cells. If the theory is true, obesity should be prevented from childhood by establishing sensible eating habits so that the person avoids becoming obese. Once a person has become obese, particularly if severely obese, it is difficult for her to lose weight because of the large number of 'hungry' fat cells which 'demand' to be filled. In some way, messages reach her brain stimulating her to eat more. However, if the person has avoided becoming fat or is only slightly obese, fewer fat cells will have been produced and weight reduction is easier. Unfortunately, these descriptive observations, if true, do not help to identify what messages, biochemical or electrical, induce the person to adopt a disturbed eating habit.

There are several ways in which people become obese. The first way affects those people who have a strong genetic trait for obesity. People in this group are likely to have been fat for most of their lives and have fat relatives. Their fatness usually starts in infancy, as a group of French researchers found. The research team followed up fat infants for 20 years, defining fatness by using the Body Mass Index. They found that 41 per cent of those infants who were obese at the age of one, were obese when they became adults. Most of these infants did not increase their adiposity after the age of one until they were about six years old. At that age a second phase of increasing fatness occurred amongst some of the children and, if it did occur, one child in two would be fat when he or she reached adulthood.

People who have a strong genetic trait for fatness do not have spurts of getting fatter after the age of six or thereabouts. Instead they grow at the same rate as their peers, but at a higher level. They are not slothful, being as active as other people in their age group and they are socially well adjusted, but many of their relatives are fat. They accept their body shape and image well and find it difficult or impossible to lose weight. This group only forms a minority of obese people.

Most fat people have a much weaker genetic cause for their obesity. Their increasing fatness may start in adolescence, or it may start in adult life, particularly in middle age. These people can be separated, to some degree, into two groups. The first group is made up of people who enjoy eating and become fat because they eat too much, in other words their obesity is nutritional. The second group is made up of people who have an eating disorder. They get the habit of overeating to cope with a psychological problem. It is difficult to separate these two groups and probably many obese people fit into both groups.

An example of the first group is described by British researchers who asked nine fat and thirteen lean women to keep a record of the amount and type of food they ate over two periods of seven days. The researchers found that the fat women recorded eating less than the lean women. As the only explanation was that the fat women were eating more than they said they ate or they would not have been so fat, the scientists concluded that the fat women had underestimated their food intake and were unable to admit to themselves that their actual food intake was higher than they believed it to be. This belief has been confirmed in a study using the 'double-labelled water' technique. The researchers found that two-thirds of the people they studied habitually underestimated the amount of food which they ate.

It is known that many obese people snack between meals and indulge in 'picking' behaviour, eating chocolates, cakes, and sweets at varying times during the day. They enjoy a few glasses of beer, or raid the refrigerator for soft drinks. They eat not because they are hungry but because they find eating pleasurable. They do not perceive the snack as food, and having eaten it, forget that they have eaten or drunk anything.

If these findings are correct, the occurrence of obesity in some families may be as much due to eating behaviours as to genetic factors. Fat parents may have fat children because the family enjoys food and are big eaters: food and eating are perceived as socially pleasurable and desirable. It is possible that these fat people are less easily satiated by food, in other words they feel 'full' more slowly. This could be the genetic reason for their obesity but unfortunately what makes a person feel 'full' after eating a particular amount of food is unknown, so it must remain a theory.

In Chapter 3 we gave some reasons why some adolescent women become overweight or obese. We suggested it was because they fail to reduce their energy intake after their growth spurt (and consequently their need for extra energy) has 'peaked' at about the age of 14. Women in families who enjoy eating are more likely to fail to reduce their food intake and become fat.

Some people who become obese do so for the same reasons as the overeaters but, as well, they tend to overeat or binge-eat when faced with a psychological or emotional problem. Their excessive eating may be precipitated by a disruption to their life or by an illness. They tend to be slothful, often dependent on others, and sensitive to criticism. They cope with stress, disappointment, a life-crisis, or depression by overeating. If overeating becomes a habit, because the pleasure of food blots out the pain of the problem, the person will gain weight inexorably. In both of these groups, habit and learned behaviour may be important in regulating food intake.

In summary, the reasons why fat people become and remain fat are poorly understood, but over the years fat people must ingest more energy than they expend. For example, if a person ate 1260 kJ (300 kcals) more energy each day than she expended, and if the net gain of this energy was 420 kJ (100 kcals) (after allowing for the increased energy loss due to increased heat production), a net gain of 1533 kJ (36 500 kcals), which is equal to 4 kg (9 lbs) of fat, would occur each year. Recently there is increasing evidence, in man, that behavioural factors in eating control are important in the regulation of body weight.

Obesity, like many other human characteristics, is due in varying degrees in different people to a mix of genetic factors and behavioural factors. Heredity provides a tendency to obesity; eating behaviours either encourage or control that tendency. This means that learning to control eating behaviour is crucial if obesity is to be avoided.

Childhood obesity

Why some children become obese in childhood is not understood. It is likely that several factors operate. These include a genetic predisposition to obesity, cultural attitudes to feeding children, family eating behaviour, and emotional factors in certain cases. Obese children are disadvantaged children. From an early age obese children are seen as being lazy or as lacking self-control or as undesirable by adults and, more seriously because of the greater psychological impact on the child, by their peers. They are mocked, laughed at, and sometimes castigated by lean people of all ages. In spite of being vulnerable to criticism most obese children manage to cope without becoming psychologically disturbed. This is fortunate because treatment of obesity children is generally unsatisfactory. The surgical methods of weight reduction available for carefully selected adults (see page 176) are unjustified for children and probably dangerous. Most programmes for obese children seek to reduce the weight gain rather than obtain a loss in weight. This is realistic as the latter approach usually fails. Weight-gain reduction is achieved by inducing the family and the child to change their food habits and to eat a diet in which the fat and sugar content has been reduced appropriately. As well as this, physical activity is emphasised.

Care must be taken when dealing with obese children to avoid 'victim blaming'. Earlier studies which showed that four out of every five children who were fat at the age of six would become fat adults have not been substantiated. It is now thought that one obese child in every two will continue to be obese and become an obese adult.

Obesity as a health hazard

The fact that a proportion of the population is obese and a smaller proportion is morbidly obese would be of little consequence if obesity was harmless to health. Unfortunately it is not, as was shown recently by a study group of the British Medical Research Council who stated:

We are unanimous in our belief that obesity is a hazard to health and a detriment to well-being. It is common enough to constitute one of the most important medical and public health problems of our time, whether we judge importance by a shorter expectation of life, increased morbidity, or cost to the community in terms of both money and anxiety.

The effect of obesity on health has been investigated by many researchers, and is shown in Fig. 17.

It can be seen that a severely obese person has a three-times greater chance of dying than a person of 'average' weight and, the more obese the person becomes, the greater is the mortality. Obese people tend to die young: obesity shortens a person's life.

In 1825 an obese man wrote a letter to his doctor:

Sir, I have followed your prescription as if my life depended upon it, and I have ascertained that during this month I have lost 3 pounds or a little more. But in order to reach this result I have been obliged to do such violence to all my tastes and all my habits—in a word I have suffered so much—that while giving you my best thanks for your kind directions, I renounce the advantages of them and throw myself for the future entirely into the hands of Providence.

Many obese people would agree and would argue that the misery of keeping to a strict diet, which does violence to tastes and habits, is not worth it, although it reduces the chance of dying prematurely. That is the person's choice; but obesity may not make life worth living. Obesity also increases a person's chance of becoming ill, and fat people are more

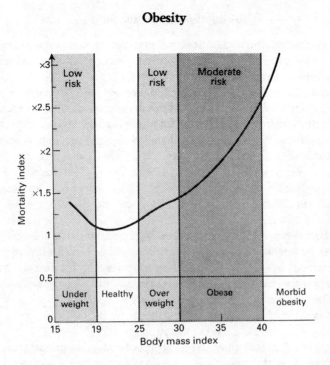

Fig. 17. The increasing risk of dying with increasing body weight. If the person's BMI is 37 he or she has twice the risk of dying compared with a person whose weight is in the normal BMI range. If his or her BMI is over 40 the risk is three times that of a person whose BMI is 20–25.

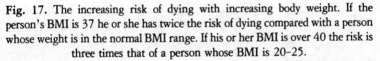

likely to have a disabling disease than people of average weight. In other words obesity increases morbidity:

- diabetes is five-times more common among obese people, and is often cured when the person loses weight;
- gall-bladder disease is more common in obese people and is more difficult to treat;
- obese women have twice the risk of developing bowel or rectal cancer;
- osteoarthritis, especially of hips, knees, and back, is more common in obese people; weight loss will not alter the disease, but is more effective than drugs in relieving the pain;
- shortness of breath is usual among morbidly obese people: it is relieved when weight is lost;

- hypertension (high blood pressure) is more common in obese people, and weight reduction is associated with a reduction in the level of the blood pressure;
- stroke is twice as common in obese people;
- coronary heart disease is more common in obese men, under the age of 40; after that age the risk increases in both sexes, and obese women may have a disproportionate risk. Several studies have shown that 70 per cent of the 'coronary events' (heart attacks and angina) occurring in women are associated with obesity. This is especially so if the obesity is 'upper-body obesity'. This is identified by measuring the circumference of the woman's waist and comparing it to the circumference of her hips. The higher the waist–hip ratio (that is the circumference of the waist divided by the circumference of the hips) the greater the likelihood that a woman will develop heart disease in the next ten years. If the waist–hip ratio exceeds 0.9 in men and 0.85 in women, the person is at an increased risk of having a heart attack. The reason is thought to be that intra-abdominal fat cells release high concentrations of fatty acids into the blood going through the liver, which increases the level of fats in the blood;
- menstrual irregularities (especially less frequent menstrual periods) increase as the weight increases, doubling in prevalence so that, among severely obese women, one in four has irregular or heavy periods. Obese women are also more likely to be infertile than women in the 'desirable' range of weight, mainly because frequently they fail to ovulate.

These rather negative findings may be converted to positive findings (Table 13). If an obese person loses weight so that her or his BMI falls to lie in the range 19–24.9, she or he has less chance of developing diabetes, hypertension, a stroke, gall-bladder disease, and coronary heart disease than an obese person. And, as well, if the person has osteoarthritis it is likely to be less incapacitating. When an obese woman loses weight her menstrual periods become regular and, if infertile, she is more likely to become pregnant.

The investigation of obesity

The physical examination

Three forms of investigation are required to be made before an obese person is offered treatment. The methods are (1) physical; (2) biochemical; and (3) psychological. These investigations start before treatment and continue while the patient is receiving treatment.

A full medical history and physical examination is made. The medical history includes questions about alcohol, smoking, and drugs. In women a menstrual and a reproductive history is taken. The physical examination, is that normally made for an insurance examination, including an estimation of the resting blood pressure, and an examination of the urine. The opportunity should be taken to evaluate those conditions aggravated by obesity such as osteoarthritis and high blood pressure.

Table 13. The advantages of weight reduction

---

(1) Reduction in blood pressure (both systolic and diastolic) (and consequently fewer strokes)

(2) Improved cardiac function

(3) Improved pulmonary ventilation

(4) Reduction in pain from osteoarthritis and low-back pain

(5) Improved circulation in legs with decrease in venous thrombosis

(6) Reduction in fatigue : increase in energy

(7) Increased self-esteem, increased social gregariousness, better 'body image'

(8) Increased physical activity possible

(9) Improved sexual relationships

Laboratory tests have a limited place in the general physical examination according to British doctors, although American bariatric physicians disagree. Dr Garrow, in Britain, states that most of the tests often carried out, for example, X-rays of the skull (pituitary fossa), plasma insulin levels, glucose tolerance tests, secretion of cortisol and catecholamines, are of little value in evaluating obesity. On the other hand, Dr Bray in the United States analyses blood samples for glucose, blood urea nitrogen, uric acid, alkaline phosphatase, total protein, serum glutamic oxalo-acetic transaminase, lactate dehydrogenase, bilirubin, thyroxine, triglyceride, and cholesterol.

Following the history and general physical examination, several specific investigations may be required to determine the most appropriate treatment and the probable duration of time required for the person to achieve his desired weight, particularly if the person is severely or morbidly obese.

Body composition   The body can be thought of being composed of two main compartments: fatty tissue and lean body mass. The fat compartment consists almost entirely of adipose tissue. The lean body mass consists of mucle, bone, non-bone tissue, and total body water. The total body water is the largest portion of the lean body mass. The body water occurs in all body cells (intracellular water) and the water which surrounds the cells and makes up a major part of the blood. It is possible to measure most of the compartments which make up the body either directly or indirectly.

Obese people have an increased amount of adipose tissue in their body and the greater the degree of obesity the larger is the adipose compartment. Thus, morbidly obese people have a large amount of adipose tissue, and their excess weight is mainly due to fat, but a few retain a large amount of water, which forms a significant component of their excess weight. It is important to differentiate the two types of people by determining their body composition. This can be done clinically and by using laboratory techniques. Both are required to fully establish body composition.

Clinical

The proportion of fat in the body can be inferred by making measurements of the thickness of a fold of skin at four sites on the body.

The following skin-fold thicknesses are measured by picking up a fold of skin and measuring its width with calipers (Fig. 18).

(1) *biceps skin-fold* over the front of upper arm midway between elbow and shoulder;
(2) *triceps skin-fold* over the back of upper arm midway between elbow and shoulder;
(3) *subscapular skin-fold* under lower tip of shoulder blade;
(4) *suprailiac skin-fold* above the crest of hip bone.

The information obtained from the sum of the four skin-fold measurements is used to estimate the fat as a percentage of the body weight by referring to special tables constructed for each sex and age range. The results, when compared with the specific laboratory tests outlined in the next section, show that skin-fold measurement gives a close indication of the percentage of fat in the body.

Laboratory tests In obesity research, laboratory investigations are used to increase our knowledge about body composition and about obesity. One of the measurements of interest to scientists is the amount of fat a person has in her or his body. As we have just mentioned, this may be obtained by measuring skin folds which give a good approximation of body fat and are generally all that is wanted. However, a more exact estimation may be needed. This can be obtained by obtaining the person's body composition, including the proportion of adipose tissue, using a dual energy X-ray absorbiometer (a DEXA) machine. The woman lies on a couch and the whole procedure takes about 20 minutes. The method is safe, less than half the amount of radiation being released than occurs in a chest X-ray, it is non-invasive, relatively cheap, and gives accurate measurements. The DEXA enables scientists to measure the total body mineral density (as well as the bone density of regions such as the spine and the legs), the lean body mass, and the percentage of adipose tissue (fat) in the body. These additional measurements are important to middle-aged women, as a low bone density, for example, indicates that the woman is more likely to develop osteoporosis in later

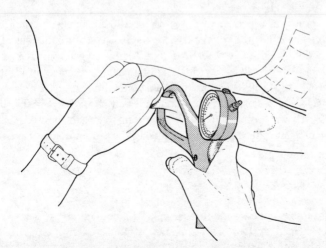

Fig. 18. Measuring skin-fold thickness with calipers.

years, unless she takes action to prevent this happening. The DEXA machine has largely replaced the complicated method of measuring total body water which used to be the yard-stick.

Some research scientists want to measure the resting metabolic rate (RMR) of a person: that is, the amount of energy used for basal body functions. This is done by measuring the woman's total body potassium, by injecting an isotope into her blood and detecting its release using a spectrometer.

Individuals of the same sex, age, body composition, and body weight have different energy requirements for their resting, unconscious functions of breathing, body repair, heat control, intestinal activity, etc., and, in addition, they use energy with different degrees of efficiency for muscular activity. In practice, muscular activity is a less important factor than the RMR in determining a person's energy expenditure. Obese people generally have a higher RMR than lean people, but the energy used by obese individuals differs considerably. This will influence rate of weight loss if an obese person chooses to diet.

The resting metabolic rate can be calculated from the formula:

$$RMR = 99.8 \text{ (body weight in kg} \times 1.155) + \text{(total body} \\ \text{potassium} \times 0.0223) - \text{(age} \times 0.456).$$

The result is expressed as the oxygen uptake in ml/minute. If this figure is multiplied by 7, a rough approximation of the resting energy expenditure (in kilocals) is obtained.

For example, a person whose RMR is 200 ml oxygen/minute uses about 5880 kJ (1400 kcals) a day for the basic resting functions of his body; while a person whose RMR is 270 ml oxygen/min uses about 7940 kJ (1890 kcals) a day. If these two people are given an identical diet providing 4200 kJ (1000 kcals) a day, the first will have a deficit of 1680 kJ (400 kcals) a day, the second a deficit of 3740 kJ (980 kcals) a day. Clearly the former will take twice as long to lose the desired amount of weight as the latter, assuming each takes the same amount of exercise.

The management of obesity

Weight loss is not easy and those people who decide to try to lose weight can be helped by two complementary strategies. The first is to lose weight by eating less and by resisting the urge to eat. Treatment for this strategy seeks to help the person to keep to the chosen weight-reducing programme, and to be motivated to continue to keep to the programme over a period of several months. It also means that she should be aware that she tends to underestimate how much she eats.

The second strategy is to persuade the person to take regular, fairly strenuous exercise in addition to dieting. It is probably helpful to deal with this strategy first and then to discuss how a person may lose weight by using a weight-reducing programme.

Exercise as a means of losing weight

Lack of exercise—sloth—is recognized as a factor which may make obesity worse or hinder weight loss. If someone takes in a certain amount of energy from food it is obvious that the more exercise that she takes each day, the less energy is left to convert into fat. Unfortunately, people have to be very active to use up excess energy (that is, excess to the body's basic needs) obtained from food. For example, a serving of breakfast cereal with milk provides about 700 kJ, an orange 150 kJ, and a slice of bread and butter or margarine about 800 kJ. The amount of time you would have to exercise to use up this energy is shown in Table 14. However, regular exercise, especially if taken after meals, may have a specific action in helping weight to be lost, although this seems to vary from person to person.

Table 14. Energy expenditure in certain physical activities

Energy provided by food (in kJ)	Activity required to burn off the energy in minutes			
	Walking	*Bicycling*	*Swimming*	*Jogging*
400	20	14	14	10
600	30	20	20	15
800	40	28	28	20
1000	60	35	35	30

As an addition to eating wisely, exercise improves physical fitness and helps weight loss. It must be done regularly and exercise which is felt to be enjoyable by the person should be chosen.

Weight-reducing programmes

The reason that we prefer the term 'weight-reducing programme' to a weight-reducing 'diet' is that most diets fail. This is because the woman concentrates on the diet sheet and ignores the other issues which will enable her to lose weight. Many diets have been devised and many have failed to produce either the desired weight loss or permitted the person to maintain the new lower weight permanently. A few strictly controlled diets (such as the milk diet which we mention shortly) help very obese people to start losing weight, and are successful in the short term. But a person who wishes to keep her weight in the normal range, needs a weight-reducing *programme*. During the weight-reducing programme, the woman learns new eating behaviours, which are not seen as 'dieting' but rather as acquiring *normal eating behaviours* (see page 127) which will continue after she has lost the desired amount of weight.

Weight loss is a slow process, and the patient may become despondent about achieving it. The support, information, and encouragement offered by a group such as Weight Watchers or TOPS (Take off Pounds Sensibly), or a psychologist or a physician and a dietician will enhance the patient's motivation, encourage her skills, and offer help in dealing with situations which may trigger the urge to eat excessively. It is also evident that the greater the patient's original weight the longer is the period required to enhance her motivation, and the greater the chance that she will abandon her attempts. In this situation, surgical intervention, in spite of its dangers, may be appropriate, provided that the patient fully understands the implications of surgery and that the long-term 'success' rate has not been clearly defined.

Before the patient embarks on a weight reduction programme it is important for a physician to make sure that the weight loss is medically desirable and psychologically wise. It is even more important for the obese person to accept that an average loss of weight of 0.5–1.0 kg (1–2 lbs) is the maximum usually obtained after the first few weeks [when a weight loss of 2–4 kg (4–8 lbs) a week may occur] and the most appropriate programmes are designed to help the person achieve this small but steady loss of weight. But, as in the treatment of anorexia nervosa or bulimia, a weight reducing programme alone is not enough; motivation to resist the urge to eat and to keep to the programme is essential.

It will be recalled that excess energy is stored in the body in adipose tissue and in the glycogen–water pool. If a person starves in order to lose weight, or at least considerably reduces her energy intake, she extracts energy from the stores in her body to meet the energy needs. The first source of energy comes from the glycogen–water pool. The size of the pool varies. In non-obese people it weighs about 3.5 kg (7¾ lbs). In obese people it weighs about 5.5 kg (12 lbs). It contains about 4000 kJ (1000 kcals) per kilogramme. When energy is released from the stores in the glycogen of the pool, water is also released. For every 1000 kcals of energy released, 3–4 kg (6½–8½ lbs) of water will be lost to the body in breathing, as sweat, or in urine. In the first weeks of a severe reducing diet, or of starvation, a quick weight loss may be expected as the energy in the glycogen–water pool is used up and a large quantity of water is lost to the body. However, the energy in the pool will be depleted within 1 to 4 weeks [when a weight loss of 3–6 kg (6½–13 lbs) will have occurred]. After this time, any further weight loss has to come from 'burning-up' the adipose tissue to release energy. The second component of weight loss is a slow, steady loss. The amount lost weekly will depend on the restriction of the energy intake, but rarely exceeds 0.5–1.0 kg (1–2 lbs) per week.

An obese person who wishes to achieve a weight reduction of 45 kg (99 lbs) has to lose the equivalent of 1 320 000 kJ (315 000 kcals), as each kilogramme of adipose tissue contains 29 300 kJ (7000 kcals). If she takes a diet supplying about 4620 kJ (1100 kcals) a day, which provides an energy deficit of about 4620 kJ (1100 kcals) loss of weight over her energy needs each day, she should achieve this in about 10 months, but the rate of weight loss will depend on her lean body mass and on her metabolic rate. The higher her metabolic rate, the quicker will her weight loss occur, so that the time taken varies and only a range of time can be given to the individual, unless research laboratory facilities are available to calculate her resting metabolic rate.

Case history: Marjorie

It all started about 10 years ago, on my parents' 25th wedding anniversary, when my sister's husband deserted her. We were all living at home and we had endless family discussions, which became very emotional. And at the same time I became increasingly worried about the business ethics of my employers; they were crooked. These two things made be tense and angry all the time. To top it off my boyfriend had a bad accident and became very depressed so he needed my support. I felt that I was everybody's prop and couldn't escape.

I wasn't aware of it at first that my weight began to rise, until I found I needed a size 16 dress instead of a size 12. I tried to diet but the problems remained and food seemed to be the only way I could dull the pain. I got into the habit of looking in the mirror, being depressed at what I saw and eating some more so that I could cope. I dieted and began losing weight, and then I'd give it up and eat enormous amounts and gain weight once more.

My behaviour became destructive to me. I now knew I was using food as an escape from emotional pain and stress. I was really no different from an alcoholic, and I realized I wasn't going to conquer it alone but there was nowhere to go. I was on a roller coaster of eating and dieting and I couldn't get off. I didn't induce vomiting or take laxatives or anything like that. It wasn't as if I had thought of these things and rejected them—I hadn't even thought of them.

I knew I had an eating disorder. I wasn't in control; food was controlling me. I was a fat girl and I wanted to be thin, but I couldn't keep to a diet to become thin. I'm still a fat girl. I now weigh 86 kg (1401 lbs, 14 st). I wish I could get thinner.

Diets

As we have mentioned, most obese people prescribed a strict diet to lose weight find it to be monotonous and abandon it within a short period of time. However, a strict diet may be useful if the person is very obese, particularly if she is highly motivated and wants to, or is advised to, lose weight quickly. For these motivated people, two diets have proved to be moderately successful. Before embarking on either she should consult a health professional who has experience in treating obesity.

The first diet is 'the milk diet' and the second is 'the very low calorie diet' (VLCD).

The milk diet   The need for a person to be motivated to keep to a diet which achieves a rapid weight loss over a relatively short period of time has led some British physicians to develop a diet which is easy to follow although extremely monotonous. The milk diet, as its name implies, consists of 1800 ml (3 pints) of whole cow's milk or a low-fat milk with supplementary iron, vitamins and, when necessary, an inert bulk laxative such as bran. The diet provides 4900 kJ (1170 kcals) of energy and 59 g of protein. Those who use it claim that the Milk Diet has several advantages over other diets. These are (1) it is cheap; (2) no weighing of foods or making food choices is necessary; (3) the diet is not complicated or troublesome to prepare. The obvious disadvantage of the milk diet is its monotony and that it inhibits the patient's social life, as she is often unwilling to go to social functions where a variety of food is available. A more important criticism is that the Milk Diet does not help to alter the eating behaviour of obese people. The diet can only be used for a short period of time for the reasons given. When the person returns to a more varied diet, she has not learned new eating habits and may rapidly revert to the previous patterns.

In spite of these constraints, the Milk Diet may be of value to some obese people, at least during the initial weeks of dieting. Once some weight loss has been achieved, the person should transfer to the weight-reducing programme, which provides a more varied, palatable diet, and produces a slow but steady weight loss.

The very low calorie diet (VLCD) An alternative to the milk diet, the very low calorie diet (also known as the liquid diet, the Cambridge diet, or the 'protein sparing modified fast') may be tried. This diet, which provides only 1200 to 1800 kilojoules (300 to 430 kcals) a day, must only be started after a full medical check and continued under direct medical supervision, as some people have died whilst eating such a restricted diet. The diet incorporates between 40 and 50 g of protein, and recommended levels of minerals, vitamins, and fatty acids to maintain health. In addition, dietary fibre is added. It is marketed under several trade names.

The VLCD has a place in the treatment of very obese people who are not prepared to lose weight slowly, or who fail to lose weight using the weight-reducing programme, and who wish to try this method of weight reduction rather than having surgery.

The VLCD produces a loss of between 1.5 and 3.5 kilogrammes a week, but only one-third of people are able to keep to it for more than two months. A few very motivated people who are prepared to be under regular medical supervision continue for longer.

As with the milk diet, the VLCD may be used as an initial method for very obese people to lose weight, provided that it is followed by the weight-reducing programme and perhaps the addition of a new drug (dexfenfluramine, see p. 172) which seems to help in weight reduction. Preliminary studies using this strategy have shown that continued weight loss of 0.5 to 1.0 kg a week is achieved over the next 40 weeks.

However, there are several problems with the VLCD. The dieter loses protein from the blood and skin and the mass of the heart is reduced. A parallel reduction in the metabolic rate occurs which tends to reduce the effectiveness of the diet unless an exercise programme is also undertaken. Recent studies show that the VLCD should not be continued for more than 12 weeks as there is an increased risk that the person will develop gallstones.

Table 15. The principles of the Menu Plan

---

1. It must supply *less* than the person's energy requirements.

2. It must provide all nutrient requirements except energy.

3. It must be acceptable to the person.

4. It must be sustained.

5. It must not impair health or well-being (e.g. low-fibre diets may cause constipation).

6. Its effectiveness will depend on the foods the person *refrains* from eating.

The weight-reducing programme People who are content to lose weight slowly without distorting their eating behaviours unduly would be better advised to avoid the strict diets just discussed and to choose a slower, gentler weight-reducing programme. It is termed a 'programme' not a 'diet', as it involves more than dieting; for example, exercise and behavioural change in attitudes to food and eating are equally important. If it is followed, the person will lose weight and be able to maintain her weight at the lower level as long as she wishes.

The menu plan of the programme (Table 16) meets several important criteria. The programme permits a wide variety of food choices, it is well-balanced nutritionally, it reduces the amount of energy, fat, and simple carbohydrate ingested each day, and it enables the person to eat varied, palatable meals so that she does not feel 'different' from family or friends.

Experience has shown that the weight loss in the first four weeks is crucial. At the end of this time three outcomes are possible. First, if the person has lost 4–8 kg (9–18 lbs) and says that she did not find it difficult to keep to the menu plan, future progress is likely to be satisfactory. Second, if the person says that, after four weeks, she has lost less than 3 kg (6½ lbs) and has found it increasingly difficult to keep to the menu plan, or says that she has kept rigidly to it and has lost less than 3 kg, the possible reasons for the poor weight loss should be investigated. The most likely cause is that the person's home or workplace environment is such that the temptation to eat snacks cannot be overcome. In this case cognitive therapy (see page 123) may help the person to keep to the weight-reducing programme. Third, the person may fail to lose significant weight in spite of having kept strictly to the programme. Such people require further investigation, including in some cases an estimate of the person's resting metabolic rate, as described on page 156.

If you choose the menu plan of the weight-reducing programme you have to make some decisions. The first is that you will reduce the amount of fat you eat. This means that you only buy lean mean and trim off the extra fat. You can eat poultry, but not the skin because this is fatty. You should grill the meat rather than fry it. You may eat butter or margarine but you must spread it thinly.

You must avoid eating cakes, chocolates, sauces, pastry, and many kinds of biscuit because these foods contain 'hidden' fat and 'hidden' sugar.

You must restrict the quantity of simple carbohydrates which you eat. That means you stop adding sugar to cereals, tea, or coffee and you avoid sugar-rich foods such as sweets and candies, and you cannot eat honey or jams. In any addiction, withdrawal of your 'drug' may cause upsets. When you stop using sugar you may find that you crave to add it to your tea or coffee or to your breakfast cereal. You can deal with this craving for sugar in one of two ways. Which you choose will depend on your personality. The first way is to stop at once. You stop using sugar in tea or coffee, you avoid using sugar on breakfast foods. You also avoid fruit drinks, including those which claim to have 'no added sugar', because they contain fructose which is in the fruit. The second way is to be more gentle with yourself. If you habitually add three spoons of sugar to your cup of tea, cut it down to two, and then after a few days to one. In other words, wean yourself gradually from your craving for sugar and sweet foods.

You must restrict your intake of alcohol. Although alcohol is not strictly a carbohydrate it provides energy in the same way. And many of us enjoy a drink! Again, you can be very firm with yourself and drink soda water with a slice of lemon and, if you wish, a dash of angostura bitters in place of your favourite drink. Or, if you are less strong, you can if you wish have half a pint (250 ml) of beer, or a nip (30 ml) of whisky, or a glass (125 ml) of a light wine a day. Each of these provides 25 g (a little under an ounce) equivalent of carbohydrate, or about 420 kJ (100 kcals) of energy. But you must not add bitter lemon or ginger ale to your whisky, or drink either of these alone, as they contain a fair amount of sugar, whatever their taste. You can only add water or soda water which contains no calories.

Table 16. The weight-reducing programme: the menu

Daily allowances

Bread, preferably wholemeal: 5 slices of 35 g (1¼ oz)
Rice or pasta or potato: rice (boiled) 60 g; pasta (boiled) 60 g; or 1 large (2 small)
  potato boiled or baked
Milk: skimmed (600 ml or 1 pint) or low fat (400 ml or ⅔ pint)
Butter or margarine: 15 g (½ oz)
Water, mineral water, tea, coffee: unlimited quantities

You should eat three meals a day: breakfast and two main meals

MEALS:

Breakfast: 1 orange, ½ grapefruit, or 100 ml (3½ oz) of fresh orange juice
              Bread from the daily allowance or cereal (½ cup) which equals
                2 slices of bread

Main meals:

  Meat: 60 g of lean beef (minced or steak), lamb or pork; liver, kidney, tripe, or
     or tongue;
  or 60 g of chicken, duck, or turkey (with skin removed), rabbit, hare, or
     pheasant;
  or 60 g of 'fatty fish' e.g. herring, kipper, mackerel, salmon, trout, sardines,
     or pilchards (with oil or tomato sauce discarded) or of shellfish;
  or 90 g of white fish (e.g. cod, flounder, halibut, John Dory, lemon sole, ling,
     plaice, turbot, whiting);

           Meats and fish may only be grilled or boiled NOT fried

  or 50 g cheese (no more than 4 times a week);
  or 2 eggs (no more than 3 times a week)

  Vegetables: As much as you like at each of the two main meals of:
     asparagus, artichokes, cabbage, cauliflower, lettuce, cucumber, beans
       French, runner, or baked), broccoli, brussels sprouts, leeks, spring
       greens, mushrooms, spinach, tomatoes;
  or 50 g (1½ oz) of beans (butter, haricot, red, kidney), carrots, peas, sweet
     potato, swedes, turnips

  Fruit:
     One: orange, tangerine or mandarin, apple, ½ grapefruit, mango, peach,
       pear, or plum;
  or 100 g (3½ oz) of all soft fruit, melon, and ⅓ of an average-sized papaya;
  or 50 g of grapes or ½ a banana

'NO-NO' prohibited foods

Alcohol (if you add a glass of wine or a light beer, you add 80 kcals (340 kJ) to
 your energy intake
Sugar, sweets, chocolate, jam, honey
Canned fruit
Pastries and puddings
Milk shakes, soft drinks, and cordials
Sauces

The suggested weight-reducing programme will provide an average of 1200 kcals
(5040 kJ) a day, and will enable you to lose an average of ½-1 kg (1-2 lbs) a
week

The attraction of this diet is that within certain limits you eat as much
the same foods as the rest of your family, and so you don't feel outcast or
different.

It may well be that while you are on a diet you are invited out to a
dinner party. You don't have to be embarrassed, or embarrass your
hostess, by toying with your food and leaving most of it on the plate. You
just have to be sensible and enjoy yourself. You miss out the bread roll
and pudding unless it is a fresh fruit salad, and you limit the amount of
alcohol you drink. You only take one potato, but you eat everything else.
If you do exceed your daily quota of carbohydrates, well, it is a special
occasion and it won't make much difference in the long run.

The suggested menu, which is low in energy and in carbohydrate and
rich in fibre, has many advantages. It is nutritious; it is relatively easy to
understand and to follow; it doesn't make you feel a freak; it avoids
gimmicks; you can stay on it for a long time, and, most important of all,
it works! These criteria form the basis of a sensible diet for a sensible
person.

The behavioural aspects of weight reduction

A menu, in itself, will not enable a person to lose weight, however carefully it is devised and however many dietary cook-books are made
available. The person has to be motivated to keep to the plan and to
understand it. Unless the person is motivated, she will find it easy to
cheat—just a little! But lots of 'just a littles' equal a considerable amount
of excess energy ingested. Motivation can be encouraged in several ways,

and the woman requires to choose the way which she finds more appropriate for her.

Many people find that their motivation to lose weight is increased if the person can share her experiences with, and obtain support from, other people who are also trying to lose weight. The support needs to extend over a period of weeks or months during the period of weight reduction. Support is also needed when the person has achieved the lower weight, so that she does not regain weight swiftly or insidiously. Many obese women find it helpful if they join an organization such as Weight Watchers or TOPS.

Membership of the organization provides a stimulus to achieve a weight loss (by a system of rewards and demerits) and provides a form of group therapy. The value of such organizations is shown by a study made in Australia in which the weight loss of women attending a hospital-based obesity clinic was compared with that of women who joined Weight Watchers. The women who had joined Weight Watchers lost more weight each week and remained at the lower weight for longer than those women who attended the obesity clinic.

Motivation and knowledge is also required because there is no magical, easy method of losing weight. It is fairly easy to lose 3–6 kg (6½–13 lbs) of weight quickly, but it is difficult to prevent the relentless return of that weight unless the person is sufficiently motivated to continue eating fewer calories than are used up in daily living. Weight reduction is a slow process, but if a person is sufficiently motivated to keep to a diet providing 2100–4200 kJ (500–1000 kcals) less than is needed each day, stored fat will be burned up at a rate of about 0.5–1.0 kg (1–2 lbs) a week. The time that it takes to lose weight may be better understood if we consider as examples two women, both aged 42 and both 162 cm (5ft 4ins) in height. Both work outside the home, part-time. One woman weighs 60 kg and the other 100 kg. The first woman wants to lose weight. The body composition of the two women is shown in Table 17.

It can be seen from this table that the second woman has 40 kg of adipose tissue in her body, 22 kg more than the first woman. If she follows the menu plan (Table 16) of the weight-reducing programme she will ingest 5040 kJ (1200 kcals) of energy a day. As her body needs 9240 kJ (2200 kcals) of energy for its functions, she will have an energy deficit each day of 4200 kJ (1000 kcals). Fat has an energy content of 37 kJ, but about 10 per cent of it is needed for metabolic processes in converting the fat to energy, so that about 33 kJ will be available to reduce the energy deficit. As the daily deficit is 4200 kJ, she will burn

Table 17. The body composition of two women

	Woman A		Woman B	
Age	42		42	
Height	162 cm		162 cm	
Weight	60 kg		100 kg	
BMI	22.8		38.0	
Body composition	*kg*	*%*	*kg*	*%*
Lean body mass				
Water	30.0	50	43	43
Protein	9.0	15	12	12
Minerals	2.4	4	4	4
Glycogen	0.6	1	1	1
Adipose tissue	18.0	30	40	40

off between 115 and 130 g of fat each day (the actual quantity depends on a number of factors). That works out at about three quarters of a kilogram (1½ lbs a week). So that to lose the desired 22 kg she will have to continue her diet for six months to achieve her desired weight.

Another example is given in Beryl's story, which also shows the difficulty of keeping to the 5040 kJ daily intake of energy unless the woman is motivated.

Case history: Beryl

Beryl is an obese, middle-aged woman, whose height is 1.60 m (5 ft 3 in) and who weighs 72 kg (159 lbs, 11 st 5 lbs). Her BMI is 28, so she is overweight. In fact she is about 17 kg (37 lbs, 2 st 9 lbs) more than she would like to be, and most of this excess is due to fat she has made and stored over the years when she has eaten more energy in the form of food than she has used up. Beryl has read articles and is worried about being too fat. She would like to get back to a weight of 55 kg (121 lbs, 8 st 9 lbs). Each day she probably requires to expend about 8400 kJ (2000 kcals) of energy to meet the demands of her body and her work in the house. If she could manage to eat only 4200 kJ (1000 kcals) a day, it would take 125 days—over four months—before she exhausted her stored energy by burning up the fat she had laid down over the years. She talks about losing weight with her doctor, but thinks that she would find it difficult to stick to a

menu plan providing only 4200 kJ (100 kcals) a day, and chooses a menu plan
which provides 6300 kJ (1500 kcals) a day. On this diet, if she sticks to it exactly,
she would burn up 2100 kJ (500 kcal) of stored energy each day and it would
take her 250 days—over eight months—for her weight to fall to the ideal! Beryl
has a real problem, for it is stupid to pretend that it is easy to lose 17 kg (37½ lbs,
2 st 9 lbs) of weight and it is unlikely, whatever diet she decides upon, that she
will manage to do it in less than eight months. As well as this, previously fat
people who have managed to reduce their weight by dieting regain weight very
quickly, compared with untreated fat people, if they start over-eating again. For
this reason, Beryl will have to exert very great will-power to achieve her weight
loss and to keep to her lower weight.

The motivation to keep to the chosen reducing diet is increased if the
person is aware that even when she keeps to her diet rigorously, her
weight may fluctuate within 1–2 kg (2–4 lbs). For this reason she should
avoid weighing herself more frequently than once a week.

It is also important that the diet chosen permits the person to enjoy a
social life. It is pointless and counterproductive to be a thinning, anti-
social, crotchety recluse—it is better to be fat and enjoy life. Becoming
thin should not be made a punishment, nor should an obese person be
filled with guilt as well as fat. The weight-reducing programme recommended in this book (and other sensible programmes) enables a person to
eat with the family and to socialize with friends.

There are other behavioural changes which a person who is trying to
lose weight may choose to adopt. However, if any of them makes the
person think continually about food it may hinder rather than help her
keep to her programme. This applies especially to obese people who
binge-eat. For this reason, care should be taken to choose those changes
which can be adopted comfortably. They can be listed as follows.

● When on the programme take more exercise—if you enjoy it. Don't
exercise and hate it. You will compensate for your dislike by over-eating.
It is helpful if you go for a walk, or do something active, after a meal.
There is evidence that this helps you lose weight rather more quickly
than if you slump down in front of the television set as soon as you have
finished eating. This is because exercise induces heat production and
energy loss.

● Don't go on a 'crash diet' which provides less than 2100 kJ
(500 kcals) a day unless you are under careful medical supervision.
Initially these diets produce a rapid weight loss, but after a while you will
find you cannot keep to the diet, and when you stop you usually over-eat.
If you persist for over a month eating a crash diet and semi-starving

yourself, your body reacts by reducing your basal metabolic rate by up to 40 per cent, so that you burn up less energy than if you eat a sensible weight-reducing diet providing between 4200 and 5000 kJ (1000–1200 kcals).

Crash diets and crazy diets do not really help, despite what the magazines and your friends say. For a short while they seem to succeed. The reason is that most of the weight lost is water (from the glycogen water pool) and not fat. Sooner rather than later, you find that you cannot keep to the crash diet and you overeat. Your weight increases and you become discouraged!

There are two reasons for this. The first is that it is very difficult to keep to an uninteresting diet for long enough for it to be effective, except in the very short term. The second reason is a physiological one. When eating a very low kilojoule diet, the dieter's resting metabolic rate drops rapidly and may decline by 20 per cent within two weeks. This means that although she loses weight fairly rapidly for the first two weeks, after that time the weight refuses to melt away. Also her body adapts to the strict diet by secreting more of an enzyme, lipoprotein lipase, which regulates how much fat is stored in the fat cells. This makes her body more efficient at storing fat, which is precisely what she doesn't want.

To avoid these problems someone who intends to use a weight-reducing programme may be helped if she follows some simple rules.

● Choose a menu plan which is nutritious, and which is sufficiently varied and tasty to enable you to stick to it without getting bored or frustrated. As far as weight loss is concerned it does not matter too much what proportions of carbohydrates, protein and fat you eat in your diet, so long as it is a low-calorie diet, and so long as it contains sufficient vitamins, minerals, and dietary fibre ('roughage') to keep you in good health. But make each meal attractive to look at, pleasant to smell, and good to taste, so that you learn to enjoy what you eat.

● If you limit the dietary fibre in your food you may become constipated and be at an increased risk of developing cancer of the large bowel, coronary heart disease, and haemorrhoids. The remedy is easy: eat wholemeal bread in your ration or one or more of the fibre-rich foods mentioned early. Dietary fibre will not add to your carbohydrate or calorie intake, and it will help you to avoid the side-effects of a 'refined carbohydrate' diet.

● Don't gorge by eating only one large meal a day. You will lose weight more quickly if you eat several small meals spread out over the day—and you will feel more normal if you do this. Do not miss breakfast

Table 18. The principles of a weight reduction regimen

---

* Eat less, aiming for 4200–5000 kJ a day

* Aim for a weight loss of about 2 kg a week for the first 2 or 3 weeks, then 0.5–1.0 kg a week

* Eat three meals a day, choosing from a variety of foods in the four main food groups: cereals and bread; vegetables and fruit; meat, poultry, and fish; dairy products

* Remember that your habits of eating need changing as much as reducing your food intake

* Increase the amount of exercise you take each day. Exercise increases weight loss, and may cause metabolic changes which enhance further weight loss

---

and do not eat your last meal late at night. The reason for eating several small meals rather than a single large meal is that smaller meals eaten at shorter intervals induce a greater production of body heat, which is then dissipated into the surrounding air. Body heat is produced by using energy, and that is what you are trying to do—to use more energy than you ingest.

● Do try and eat your meals approximately the same time each day. This has the psychological effect of helping you to control your feelings of hunger at times other than meal-times.

● When you have a meal, eat slowly. When you have put food in your mouth do not add any more until your mouth is empty. If it helps, put down your knife, fork, or spoon while your mouth has food in it. And chew your food slowly so that you learn to taste and smell the food to the fullest extent. Psychologists believe that eating slowly and chewing meticulously teaches you to be satisfied with less food and to enjoy the smaller quantity more. Additional dietary fibre will also help you to achieve this objective.

● Every fifteen mouthfuls, stop and put down your eating utensils for about half a minute. This strategy helps you to enjoy more the smaller amount of food you are permitted.

● Before you start eating, decide how much of which food you are going to put on your plate, and do not add more. Once you start eating it is too easy to say to yourself, 'I'll just have a little more'. You must not. 'Littles' add up to a lot and you will not control your eating. It often helps if you put your food on a smaller plate, so that the plate looks fuller! This will help you make do with less.

● As soon as you feel full, stop eating, no matter how much is still on your plate. Indeed, it may help you always to leave some food on your plate, and so break the habit of continuing to eat until all the food on your plate has gone, whether you need it or not.

● Once you feel full or finish your meal, leave the table (if you can do so without offending anybody). Staying at the table where there is food may break your resolve not to eat any more.

● Don't keep packets of sweets, biscuits, chocolate, or nuts in the house or office. If you get bored or unhappy you will be tempted to have a nibble. If they are not there you can resist the temptation. If they are, you will be able to resist everything except the temptation.

● Only go shopping for food when you have eaten. If you do your own shopping, or shop for the family, you may be tempted when you see the delicious-looking foods in the shops. You can resist the temptation to buy and eat these foods if you do three simple things. First, only go shopping after you have eaten. People react less to the sight of food when they are not hungry. Second, make out a list of foods you really need before you go shopping. Stick to the list. Do not be tempted by other foods. Third, when possible, only buy foods which need more preparation than just opening the container. This will reduce the risk that you will 'just open a tin or a packet for a little snack'.

● Don't be 'conned' into choosing a complicated or expensive diet. You will not keep to it. Diets which insist that you only eat certain foods on certain days, and other foods only at certain times of the day, should be avoided. They are rubbish. Choose a menu which is no more expensive than your usual food. If you do not, someone will complain and you will become discouraged and start eating more than your menu plan.

Drugs

Although the use of anorectic drugs and of thyroid hormone has been enthusiastically promoted in the treatment of obesity, their value is limited.

Anorectic drugs reduce hunger or increase a feeling of fullness (satiety), but most obese people do not eat because of hunger. Nevertheless, carefully designed studies have shown that patients taking a low energy diet and anorectic medications lose more weight than those on a diet alone, but the effect diminishes or is reversed after about 12 weeks. And when the anorectic drug is stopped, weight is rapidly gained. The place of anorectic drugs in the treatment of obesity is limited, but they may be appropriate if the person's obesity poses a substantial health risk and for those who have to lose weight rapidly, for example, prior to surgery. In most cases, anorectic drugs should only be used in conjunction with diet, exercise, and supportive psychotherapy. Used in this way they help some patients come to terms with the need to lose weight over a long period, by giving them a 'prop' which helps to improve their morale. However, a study of the opinions of 1362 patients about the use of anorectic drugs showed that most preferred diet alone to diet and anorectic drugs. A minority of patients feel that anorectic drugs help. They may take the drugs intermittently over a period of 12 to 14 months, but no course of treatment should exceed 12 weeks. Anorectic drugs may achieve their effect by suggestion rather than by a direct action on the 'satiety' centre in the brain. This is suggested by an investigation which demonstrated and inert injections given to a group of patients produced a greater weight loss than that achieved by most active anti-obesity drugs.

An exception to this statement may be a new drug, dexfenfluramine which is thought to increase the secretion of the brain hormone, serotonin (see page 35). Serotonin appears to play a significant role in the control of the appetite. If the level of serotonin can be raised, the desire for food is reduced and the person may become relaxed and drowsy. If the level of serotonin is lowered, the person may become irritable or anxious and hungry, especially for carbohydrate rich snacks. Early studies using the drug show that dexfenfluramine increases the level of serotonin in the brain and reduces the person's 'snacking' and 'picking' behaviour, as well as reducing the appetite. It is claimed that the weight-losing action of the drug lasts for as long as a year, but in the second six months the loss of weight 'slows down significantly'. At present, the drug has been used in very few double-blind controlled studies. In one multicentre study of nearly 300 people (mainly women), half of whom were eating a restricted diet and took dexfenfluramine and the other half who just ate the restricted diet and were given a placebo pill, it was found that at the end of one year the mean weight loss of the group taking dexfenfluramine was 4 kg more than the people taking the placebo, and 30 per cent of them lost more than 10 kg compared with 16 per cent of the people who took the placebo.

As with other drugs of this nature about one patient in three complains of drowsiness, one in six of diarrhoea, and one in nine of a dry mouth or frequent urination.

Because of this, dexfenfluramine, like other anorectic drugs, should only be tried if non-drug measures have proved inadequate.

Although thyroid extract is still popular among some doctors for the treatment of obesity, there is little evidence that it is of any value. The use of thyroid extract is based on the belief that people who are morbidly obese lack thyroid hormone. The inference from this belief is that thyroid tablets will help weight reduction. Thyroid tablets (available in two forms: thyroxine and triiodothyronine) increase the metabolic rate to some extent in people who have normal thyroid function, but the dose of the thyroid hormone required to produce any significant weight loss causes toxic symptoms in most cases. As well, the weight loss is mainly of lean tissue, not fat. In a careful study of the value of thyroxine in the treatment of obesity, no significant benefit was found over diet alone. Unless the obese person is hypothyroid, thyroid hormones should not be prescribed to increase weight loss.

A number of people complain that when they stop smoking tobacco, because they have been advised that smoking increases their risk of heart attack and lung cancer, they put on weight. There is evidence that most people who stop smoking gain a small amount of weight (2 kg over a few years) and one person in ten (particularly if he or she is aged less than 55 and smokes more than 15 cigarettes a day) puts on more than 10 kg over a ten-year period. If the person is overweight and trying to lose weight this may be a deterrent. However, if the person reduces her or his energy intake still further for a few weeks, the problem usually ceases.

Clearly, if dietary measures and supportive psychotherapy enable the obese person to lose weight and to maintain the body weight at the desirable level, surgical operations to help achieve weight reduction are unnecessary. It seems however that although almost any fat person can lose weight, few can keep it off. Many reports showing that a particular method was successful are methodologically unsound and have too short a follow-up. It has been demonstrated that most people who achieve an initial weight loss fail to maintain the lower weight for longer than 6 to 12 months. If the study terminates before 12 months, an inaccurate success rate will be reported. In longer term studies made over 20 years ago, it was noted that few participants lost as much s 20 kg (44 lbs) and most who did regained weight shortly after treatment ended. A decade later, a large study in Britain showed that between 10 and 40 per cent of participants had lost some weight by the end of the first year of treatment, but fewer than 10 per cent maintained the weight loss for a period of years.

Modern approaches to the problem are first to achieve the weight loss and second to maintain the lower weight by reinforcing the resolve of the person through periodic intervention in the form of supportive psychotherapy. These methods promise a more successful outcome. For example, a study of over 700 women who had reduced their weight over an average period of 30 weeks using the Weight Watchers programme, so that it fell to within the 'desirable range', and who continued to attend group meetings periodically showed that 15 months after the weight loss had been achieved, only 30 per cent weighed more than 10 per cent above their 'desirable' weight.

An obese patient will only achieve and maintain weight reduction if she is motivated, persistent, and prepared to alter her life-style. If she is not prepared to fulfil these conditions, there is little point in persisting with a weight-reducing programme. The psychological assessment of an obese patient is an important diagnostic investigation. Many physicians believe that a full psychological evaluation by a clinical psychologist is necessary, but, from our discussions with our colleagues, and in our own experience, an assessment based on the questions asked in Chapter 5 is usually sufficient. However, if the assessment suggests that the habitual over-eating is a mal-adaptation to an underlying psychological problem, such as boredom, anger, depression, or 'stress', a clinical psychologist or a psychiatrist may help the person to cope with the problem and so cease to over-eat. Some obese patients find it helpful to make a chart of all the food they eat during a week, noting where they were at the time, what they were doing, how they felt, and why they ate the food at that particular time. The therapist is shown the chart and they discuss how the patient can change her eating behaviour. Many of the therapies mentioned in the treatments of the other eating disorders including cognitive and behaviour therapies may be used to help some obese women.

The greater the degree of obesity, the more difficult is it for the person to lose weight permanently. For this reason when medical and behavioural methods of weight loss have failed, the person may wish to consider surgical methods of weight reduction, in spite of their known dangers. Surgical methods may be appropriate for people who are severely obese

(Body Mass Index 40 or more). The three methods to be discussed are jaw-wiring, gastric stapling, and gastric balloons. Suction lipectomy used for cosmetic purposes rather than weight reduction will also be considered, as some obese women having lost weight overall continue to be worried about the size of their abdomen.

Jaw-wiring

Those patients who fail to lose a significant amount of weight in spite of keeping to the 4200–5040 kJ (1000–1200 kcals) diet over a period of weeks or months, or who have an adverse social environment, may choose to have a surgical procedure which may protect them from eating more than their allowance. One such procedure is jaw-wiring. The molar teeth are wired, permitting the jaws to open only about half an inch (1.5 cm) (Fig. 19). This reduces the ability of the person to eat food, unless she removes the wire, homogenizes the food, or 'stuffs' food through the teeth. The person who has had her jaws wired is able to talk easily, but it will be obvious to her friends and relations that her mouth is relatively rigid when she speaks.

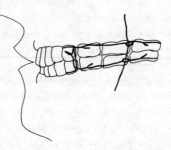

Fig. 19. The technique of jaw-wiring.

Before the molar teeth are wired, the patient has to agree (1) to attend her doctor at four-week intervals for evaluation; (2) to keep the jaws wired until the weight loss is such that no further medical reason for weight loss persists; and (3) to continue dieting when the wires are removed. The reason for the last condition is that binge-eating is likely to occur after removal of the wires with consequent rapid weight gain. The Nutritional Research Group in Britain suggest a device to help the patient conform to the third condition. On the day the wires are removed, a nylon cord is tied around the person's waist! If weight loss is maintained the cord is comfortable, but, if more than 6 kg (13 lbs) of weight is regained, it becomes uncomfortably tight.

Jaw-wiring can only be done if the person has no psychiatric illness, has healthy teeth and gums, and has a resting metabolic rate which is normal or high: a resting oxygen consumption of less than 240 ml/minute is a contra-indication to jaw-wiring.

Jaw-wiring is relatively painless, although some discomfort may be felt in the 24 hours after the procedure. This occurs from spasm of the jaw muscles, from bruising of the gums, or from toothache due to the sideways force on the teeth. Pain killers or sedatives may be required. A few patients develop ulceration of the inside of the cheek or the tongue from movement of the ends of the wires in the first few days after its application. This is easily corrected.

The jaws should not be wired for more than nine months as periodontal problems increase after this time. During the period the jaws are wired, the patient should be seen regularly by a dentist.

It may have become clear from this description that the purpose of jaw-wiring is similar to that of admission to hospital in anorexia nervosa. It is to control the person's eating and other weight-related behaviour until she has learned and can accept a new pattern of eating. From this it follows that although the procedure of jaw-wiring is simple, and physical complications are few, psychological problems may occur. The knowledge that the mouth cannot be opened may cause the person to feel a 'prisoner of her weight', and be attended by depression, or by a lack of ability to relate to her partner or family, particularly during the initial weeks after jaw-wiring. To cope with problems during this period, the patient needs moral and physical support from her partner and/or her family, and may be helped further with supportive psychotherapy.

As a steady, relentless weight gain seems inevitable after the wires have been removed, psychotherapy during this period may be helpful, as may the use of the waist-cord, but some people with morbid obesity may instead choose a major surgical operation to enable them to alter their disordered eating behaviour.

Major surgical procedures for the treatment of morbid obesity

The majority of people with morbid obesity will lose weight on a strict low energy diet, supplemented if necessary by jaw-wiring. Many find it difficult to maintain their lower weight once the psychological support they received during weight loss is withdrawn, and within four to eight months many will have regained 50 per cent more of the weight they lost. These rather discouraging results induced physicians interested in treating obesity to review the physiology of digestion and to talk with their surgical colleagues.

The physiology of digestion (*Fig. 20*)   The primary function of the digestive tract is to provide the body with a continual supply of water, electrolytes, and nutrients. This is achieved by the movement of the food through the oesophagus, stomach, and intestines; by the secretion of digestive juices; and by the absorption of the digested foods, water, and electrolytes from the intestines.

The movement and mixing of foods occurs because slowly moving peristaltic waves of contractions pass regularly along the alimentary tract in response to its distension by food or water. These contractions squeeze the food onwards, mixing it at the same time.

In the mouth, food is masticated and mixed with saliva. It is then swallowed and passes through the oesophagus to enter the stomach. The stomach can store large quantities of food until it can be accommodated in the intestine. During its period in the stomach the food is mixed with gastric digestive juices and dilute hydrochloric acid to form a semi-fluid mixture and is partially broken down. As space becomes available in the intestines, the mixture, called chyme, is moved from the stomach by peristaltic waves of contractions.

Most of the absorption of food takes place in the small intestine, where the chyme is acted on by secretions from the pancreas and by intestinal digestive juices. Carbohydrates are further broken down by the pancreatic secretions, and are absorbed, mainly in the jejunum. Fats are emulsified by the action of bile salts and digested by secretions from the pancreas and intestines to form free fatty acids, monoglycerides, and glycerol. In this state they are absorbed by the intestines, and the greater the distension of the intestines, the greater is the absorption. Protein is further broken down in the intestines into its constituent amino acids and absorbed. It is clear from these observations that most of the absorption of food takes place in the small intestine.

Understanding of these physiological concepts led to the idea that if most of the jejunum was bypassed by cutting it near its junction with the duodenum and anastomosing the cut end to the lower part of the ileum, the patient would be able to eat what she liked but would lose weight

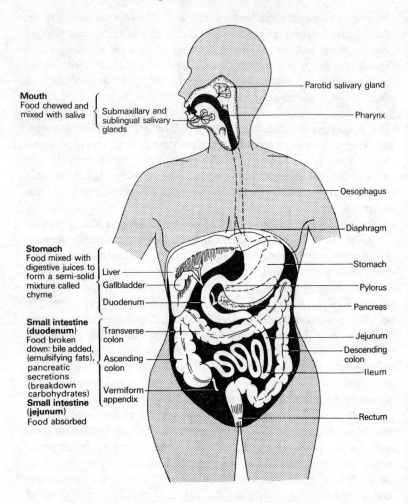

Mouth
Food chewed and
mixed with saliva

Submaxillary and
sublingual salivary
glands

Stomach
Food mixed with
digestive juices to
form a semi-solid
mixture called
chyme

Liver
Gallbladder
Duodenum

**Small intestine
(duodenum)**
Food broken
down: bile added,
(emulsifying fats),
pancreatic
secretions
(breakdown
carbohydrates)
**Small intestine
(jejunum)**
Food absorbed

Transverse
colon

Ascending
colon

Vermiform
appendix

Parotid salivary gland

Pharynx

Oesophagus

Diaphragm

Stomach

Pylorus

Pancreas

Jejunum

Descending
colon

Ileum

Rectum

Fig. 20. The intestinal tract.

because the food would be neither digested nor absorbed. A second idea, which was developed somewhat later, as the complications following jejuno–ileal bypass surgery became apparent, was to reduce the size of the stomach. It was argued that if the size of the stomach was reduced by two-thirds, or more, the patient would be prevented from eating large meals because a feeling of fullness (or satiety) would rapidly come over her when she ate.

The effect of jejuno–ileal bypass (and similar operations) is to reduce considerably the amount of food absorbed from the gut, no matter how much food the patient eats. The principle of gastric reduction or partitioning is to increase the patient's reluctance to eat because she feels 'full' after eating a small amount of food. As it is the quantity of food which produces the feeling of satiation, an unmotivated person can cheat by eating or drinking small amounts of energy-dense liquids or food, most of which is absorbed. If a patient who has had gastric reduction does not cheat, this procedure (and jejuno–ileal bypass) will reduce considerably the amount of energy absorbed, and her weight will decrease steadily to reach her 'desirable' weight range after 6–15 months. It is also expected that the limited amount of food eaten, or energy absorbed, will enable the person to maintain her desired weight, once she had achieved it, and her weight will not increase.

The available operations have considerable disadvantages and some dangers. They should only be suggested to patients who are given full information about the surgical procedure and its effect and who have been carefully selected. The process of selection often involves a careful psychological evaluation to exclude severe emotional problems and to establish that the individual is properly motivated. The operations should not be seen as a 'quick fix' for gross obesity. They should only be offered by a team of doctors who manage obesity and who can provide the necessary follow-up.

Jejuno-ileal bypass This operation was first introduced over 40 years ago, and in the 1970s became popular, particularly in the USA. As mentioned, the concept behind the operation was that if the duodenum and most of the jejunum were bypassed, foods (particularly fats) would not be absorbed. Heralded as very successful (as have been other operations for the treatment of obesity), experience showed that it had serious side-effects. The fat which was not absorbed remained in the bowel where it broke down and prevented the absorption of the fat-soluble vitamins A and D. The breakdown products of fat formed insoluble soaps with calcium and magnesium, which increased the retention of water in the bowel leading to diarrhoea and to steatorrhoea. The frequency of bowel movements, and the chemical nature of the faeces, caused inflammation of the rectum in about one-third to one-half of patients, and to an increased incidence of haemorrhoids. In the normal gut, calcium is bound to oxalate, but after jejuno–ileal bypass the oxalate becomes free and may be absorbed, leading to oxalate stones in the kidneys. Further, as other high energy substances in the diet, particularly carbohydrate, are also poorly absorbed, they are fermented by the bacteria in the gut leading to bloating and the formation of gas which is expelled either by belching or as flatus.

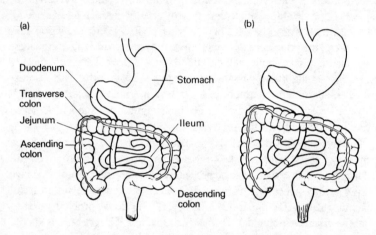

Fig. 21. (a) The end-to-side jejuno–ileal shunt of Payne; (b) the end-to-end jejuno–ileal shunt of Scott.

The long-term complications of jejuno–ileal bypass have been shown to be so severe, with a death rate of about 25 per cent in the five to ten years after surgery, and so common (Table 19) that a committee of experts developed and published a consensus statement in the *Journal of the American Medical Association* in 1981. The Consensus Statement said bluntly: 'In a current assessment of obesity management, one is compelled to reject jejuno–ileal bypass as a metabolically and physiologically unsafe procedure'.

The operation has been abandoned, except for a few highly selected patients who have failed to reduce their weight or to maintain a lower weight following gastric reduction, and who are prepared to accept the possible side-effects of jejuno–ileal surgery.

However many people who had the operation in the 1960s and 1970s are still alive.

Table 19. Complications and undesirable side-effects after jejuno–ileal bypass surgery

	Per cent of patients developing complications
Wound complications	15–25
Severe metabolic (mineral) disturbances	20–30
Ano–rectal pain/discomfort	35–50
Haemorrhoids	14–20
Severe (offensive) diarrhoea	15–20
Bloating, wind, flatus	10–15
Arthritis	8–12
Kidney stones	8–12
Gall-stones	3–7
Psychiatric problems	6–10
Liver failure	3–5
Death	0.5–4
Re-operation required	10–20

Follow-up 1 to 3 years

Case history: Ken

I often sit and think back, was it worth all the problems I have been through.

It all started in 1969 when I asked for a new uniform as I was too fat for the old one, and I was told that I would have to lose weight, because there was not a wardsman's uniform in any larger size than what I already had.

So the next step was to see the staff doctor for a referral to a physician, who suggested that I attend a psychiatrist for hypnosis. I talked to my wife about this, and she suggested that I see a dietitian rather than a psychiatrist.

I did this but had no will-power to stick to a diet, because the slightest upset would make me eat and eat. So eventually I went along to the psychiatrist. But after a couple of visits, I was not too impressed and decided to go and try something else.

My physician was involved with jejuno–ileal bypass operation to lose weight and thought that this might be the answer to my problems, but I should first try dieting.

He weighed me in at 130 kg (287 lbs, 20½ st) and took pulse, blood pressure and temperature readings and all the normal things, and then asked the questions about my past. I explained that at a young age I was not overweight; it was in my mid-teens that the weight started to build up. I took his advice and tried different diets but could not stick to them, and then I had a nasty experience.

I was walking up the hallway of my house and I collapsed, I was taken to the hospital and the doctor there said that I had had a blood pressure attack, and that either I took the weight off within 6 months or I would have 6 months to live. At that stage I was 140 kg (309 lbs, 22 st 1 lb). I went on a 2100 kJ (500 kcal) a day diet, and I was taking Duramine M40 tablets. I was also going to a doctor every second day and having female hormone injections, called chorionic gonado-trophin, which he said would guarantee I would lose weight.

In 5 months I lost 57 kg (126 lbs, 9 st). I kept this off for four years until late 1973, and then with my wife expecting our youngest son, and I was in threat of being retrenched from my job, I put all the weight back on again in 7 months, up again to 109 kg (240 lbs, 17st 2 lbs).

After I had explained all this to my doctor, he told me about the operation in detail. He explained that the surgeon would bypass the small intestine leaving about 50 cm (20 in) but the remainder of the intestine would stay inside me.

Then he proceeded to tell me the side-effects such as diarrhoea, which would mean opening my bowels about five times a day, and that I might have wind pains and also a strict diet to stick to.

This sounded too good to be true; it was like waving a lollipop in front of a baby. So I agreed to the operation, and things went into action.

A date was arranged, and I went into hospital ten days before the operation was due to be performed. I underwent a lot of tests, such as: one day they would make me go without food, and the next day they would take core samples of fatty tissues from my buttocks. Then the next day they would give me really fatty foods such as milk-shakes made of cream and radioactive fatty oil or something like that, and the next day the core tests would be done again.

Then came the operation. About 4 hours later I was back in bed, my wife was there and so were my doctors. I was, of course, very dopey.

In the next few days I went through a lot of pain, I was suffering a lot of cramps and wind pains, I also had a lot of vomiting, and as a result I was only allowed to drink a litre of fluid per day. Then the diarrhoea started, and after about 5 days the nurses sat me on the side of the bed, they walked out and left me there. Five minutes later the bed tipped up, and I ended up on the floor wrapped around tubes and things, I could not move until they came back to help me. A doctor came to examine me to see if there was any damage done, and it was discovered that I had busted a tension stitch.

For the next 13 weeks I had a lot of diet and blood problems which were treated in various ways. I was released from hospital when these things were thought to be sorted out.

I was at home for about three weeks and was opening my bowels about 20 times a day, and I was very weak. My wife was suffering because of this, and was run off her feet with looking after me and running after the 3 chldren, as I could not do anything for her or myself.

I went back to see the physician and he had blood tests done and it was found that I had a low blood potassium. This was treated by admitting me to hospital and using a drip.

About 3 months after that, I was suffering a lot of abdominal pain, so I went back to him and he said I had an incisional hernia. I was admitted to hospital again and I had it repaired. I watched the operation as I had an epidural block, because I had such a bad reaction to anaesthetics.

Both of these problems (blood and hernia) repeated themselves; the hernia twice and different sorts of blood problems repeated themselves on numerous occasions, and were treated the same way, by admission to hospital. It seemed never-ending the weeks in hospital away from my wife and kids over a period of about four years.

I then started to go to a new family doctor, and after a period of time he discovered that I had a magnesium deficiency, so this was also treated. I went back again to the physician, and he noticed that I had a lot of muscle wastage on my left side, and I had practically no strength and was extremely weak. He said it was congenital, but my father said that I was a normal child. It was proved later that I had spinal nerve damage. I have a lot of muscle wastage on my left side and sometimes my leg collapses from under me. This happened on one occasion and I fell and broke my right hip, which meant another operation to put a pin and plate in my hip; this was removed in September of this year 1982, three years after it happened.

From the constant diarrhoea, I have had about 5 fissure operations on my back passage; this happens about every 12 to 18 months.

All this has caused me to be off work for, so far, 8 years, and as far as I can see, no end to it all.

My weight now fluctuates between 76 and 79 kg (168 and 174 lbs, 12-12½ st). In the mornings I have a pretty normal flat tummy, but as the day goes on I blow up in the tummy like a balloon; as a result of this I have to have two sets of clothes, one set for the morning and another set for the afternoon to night time.

I have a blood test once a month and two injections once a month as well as a vitamin B_{12} injection and a vitamin K injection. If I happen to be a few days overdue for these injections my muscles ache and I become pale and weak.

The operation has been successful as far as my losing weight is concerned, but if I had my way again, I would try something else as the emotional strain on myself and my family has left a lot of scars.

Gastric bypass and gastric reduction   Gastric bypass and gastric reduction as methods of reducing energy intake were less popular than jejuno-ileal bypass as earlier researchers found that the loss of weight was less.

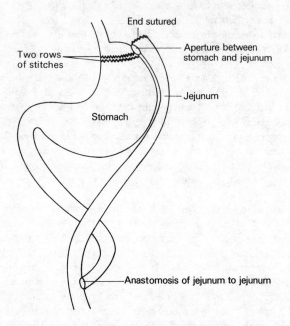

Fig. 22. Gastric bypass.

The initial suggestion was to reduce the size of the stomach by cutting it and to anastomize its upper portion with jejunum (Fig. 22). In recent years this operation has been replaced by vertical gastric stapling (Fig. 23) which effectively reduces the size of the stomach, 'partitioning' it. A small aperture is left between the upper portion (the volume of which is made about 50 ml, and the lower larger portion. The size of the aperture is maintained by using a 'hemstich' of unabsorbable material. The size of the aperture appears to be crucial to the long-term success of the operation. The effect of gastric 'partitioning' is that the person feels 'full' and uncomfortable after eating a small amount of food, because the small pouch is stretched and messages are sent to the 'satiety centre' in the brain. Unless the patient eats slowly and keeps the amount small, the pouch will fill and additional food will remain in the oesophagus, leading to heartburn or vomiting. As both are uncomfortable, as is the feeling of 'fullness', the patient learns to reduce her food intake and consequently loses weight.

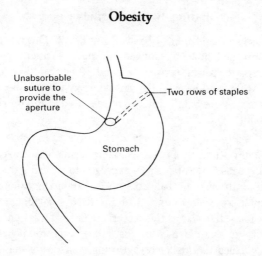

Fig. 23. Gastric reduction by vertical stapling (banding).

Before an operation the person requires counselling and education in nutrition, as she will have to adopt to new eating behaviour. She will be taught the essentials of good nutrition, that is, the need to eat a balanced diet, with a high protein, a moderate carbohydrate and low-fat content, and with adequate amounts of dietary fibre, minerals, and vitamins; the patient is also taught how to cope with a greatly diminished gastric reservoir, the need to chew the food slowly and thoroughly, and the consequences which will occur (mainly vomiting) if she does not.

Gastric bypass and gastric stapling may also be followed by complications. Gall-stones occur as frequently after gastric bypass as after jejunoileal bypass, vitamin deficiencies are frequent, and a few patients develop a stomach ulcer. Gastric stapling seems to be followed by fewer sideeffects, particularly the metabolic upsets, than gastric bypass, but the follow-up period is short.

Gastric stapling must still be considered a potentially dangerous operation. The staples may separate, leading to leakage in the first days to a week after operation; the size of the pouch may increase, as may the opening between the upper and lower pouches. These changes enable a person to eat more without feeling satiated, or vomiting, and as soon as she can eat more she does, with the result that her weight increases. There is no doubt that following gastric stapling (or gastric bypass) a 200 kg (441 lbs, 31 st 7 lbs) patient will lose 12–20 kg (26–44 lbs) in the first month, and the weight loss will continue for some months until the weight is less than 80 kg (176 lbs, 12 st 8 lbs). This is reported as a success, but if the follow-up is longer a number of patients gain weight. In several reported series, between 20 and 30 per cent of patients were lost to follow-up, and have to be considered as failures, because those who were traced were found either to have ceased losing weight or to be gaining weight.

Gastric balloons   The complications that may follow gastric partitioning led some surgeons to develop a new approach to reducing the size of the stomach, by introducing a balloon into it. When the balloon (called a 'gastric bubble') was blown up, it had the effect of reducing the effective size of the stomach (as far as the processing of food was concerned) to a degree similar to that obtained by gastric stapling. Initially the 'gastric bubble' was hailed as a major breakthrough (shades of the jejuno–ileal bypass!) but soon severe side-effects were being reported. It was found that some patients developed gastric ulcers and some stomach perforations occurred. Occasionally the bubble collapsed spontaneously in the stomach requiring major surgery, or it led to intestinal blockage.

Unfortunately the early experience with the gastric bubble was not made in a scientific way, but as scientifically evaluable reports appeared in the medical literature, confirmation was obtained that the method was not an effective method of weight control and that it produced too many severe side-effects. By 1988, the gastric bubble had been deflated!

At present, vertical gastric stapling is the preferred surgical method of inducing weight loss, as it seems to be as effective as other methods and has few long-term complications, either physical or psychological.

The patient must clearly understand, before operation, that the creation of a smaller stomach during an operation which may last 1½ to 2 hours will not cure a lifetime's addiction to food or alter disordered eating habits. The patient must also be aware that, following operation, vitamin and mineral supplements are necessary, pain may occur, as may episodes of diarrhoea, and appropriate follow-up, including blood-tests, is essential.

Case history: Gareth

I was always pretty big and when I was 16 I played Rugby League. Then I weighed about 89 kg (196 lbs, 14 st), but it was all muscle—no fat. That's when I started working in the blast furnace. I drank like a fish and ate like a horse but worked it out and sweated it out so I didn't put on any weight in that job. I didn't like the job much and so I got this job with the railways. The problem was that in the new job I just sat down for 8-10 hours a day and mostly did nothing, but I still had the same eating and drinking habits. So I started putting on weight and got up to 153 kg (337 lbs, 24 st 11 lb). I was so fat I found it hard to do my job. The railways doctor said I'd have to lose weight or he'd take me off driving. I tried diets, Weight Watchers, and all the rest, but it didn't do any good. When you work shifts there's no way you can keep to a diet. I drank a lot of coffee and when you have coffee you have to have biscuits or a sandwich. Then I tried exercise. That didn't work either. I'd play football and then go to the pub. Playing made me hungry. So I ate more. And here I was, 153 kg (337 lbs, 24 st 11 lb) and getting fatter.

About this time I read about some operations and experiments they were doing in the States. Someone was telling me about it where they put a plastic tube inside your intestines so that the wall couldn't absorb the food as it was blocked off. So I went and saw my doctor about it and straight out he said 'I don't agree with it. You are overweight but you have a big frame. You are a big boned boy and you can carry that weight with no trouble. As far as I am concerned, if you can't lose weight on a diet you're going to have to put up with it.' Then I was over at another doctor and she started asking me about my weight. I told her I had asked my doctor about it and she said 'Oh, go and see this bloke' and sent me off to my surgeon.

He told me about the two types of operations he was doing at the time, one that he was doing before where he stitched across the stomach and took a piece of the bowel out and rerouted it into the top of the stomach. He also told me about his other one that he eventually did on me. And that was to make my stomach smaller by stapling across it. He called it gastric partitioning.

He did the operation one Wednesday. I didn't feel too bad after it, I was doped up to my ears the first couple of days with pain-killers and felt nothing. Bill—that's my surgeon—is one of these blokes who are sticklers for exercise and I was up walking around the second day though the walk was more like a slow crawl. He told me I wouldn't want to eat much because I would feel full quickly. When I was in hospital and did start eating again it was on a puree diet, everything blended and only in very small amounts. When I came home I stayed on the puree for a while then gradually started experimenting around with what I could take and what I couldn't. Before I had the operation I would eat a 2 lb rump steak and have a couple of beers and a bottle of wine. But I couldn't do that after the operation. I felt full quickly and if I didn't chew the food into small pieces, up it would come. It couldn't get through the hole or something. Bill had told me that before the operation. He told me what I would be able to eat but that everything would have to be chewed thoroughly until it was pulp because it had to go through the hole of about ⅛ or ¼ of an inch. If you don't chew it enough to let it go through there it comes back. So I adjusted my eating habits. I ate less and chewed well. I still get some regurgitation but not much. I think I'm a hell of a lot fitter than I was before and I think that because I carried the weight for so long

I'm a lot fitter than many other blokes. For example, I suppose about 12 months after the operation I went along to the beach to do a bit of jogging to see how far I could go. I used to be able to jog a mile, no worries, when I was overweight. Well, I went from one end of the beach to the other and back and three-quarters of the way back again, which would probably be nearer 4 or 5 miles and I wasn't even puffing at the end of it, no strain, no nothing, just felt like a walk across the road.

The operation made me change how much I ate and how I ate. It also stopped me drinking beer. Wine is OK, but the gas in beer blows your stomach up and it hurts.

I had a problem about two years after the operation. It seems the hole had got narrower and I couldn't keep anything down—even water. So I saw Bill, and he said 'Back to hospital, over you go'. They put a gastric tube down and pumped my stomach out, put a drip in to feed me and I stayed there for 3 days. They put a thing down to have a look, couldn't see anything and Bill said 'We'll have to open you up and find out what is wrong'. So he opened it up, fixed it and found I had a few gallstones so he took the gall bladder while he was there, and since that I've been well. I'm down to 70 kg (154 lbs, 11 st). I can go out and eat a meal. I don't eat much red meat and I'm off steaks because by the time you've cut it up small and chewed it, the rest is cold. I'm enjoying life. But it is good to know that I can contact Bill if anything goes wrong.

Would I have had the operation if I'd known what it meant? Thinking back I would, but when I came out of surgery and for a couple of weeks after that and the two lots of surgery I've had, up until 6 months ago, I doubted whether I would. One of the blokes at work has just been recommended to have it done and he asked me if I would recommend it. I said 'No, I wouldn't recommend it, but if you want it, have it, it helped me.'

Suction lipectomy   Rather than being generally obese, some individuals tend to deposit fat on their hips and thighs. This is probably an inherited characteristic. There is a belief that the fat cells (adipocytes) in these areas multiply when faced with the need to store fat, whilst the adipocytes of the abdomen, the back, and the upper arms tend to expand considerably before they multiply. The appearance of the thighs has given rise to the name of 'cellulite'.

Suction lipectomy, which is a method of removing localized fat deposits, has been used to remove fat from below the chin, from the sides of the chest, from the fat over the lower abdomen, the hips, and the thighs.

The technique is simple but problems may occur. A small incision is made in the skin over the area and a hollow tube, called a cannula, is introduced through this incision to make radiating tunnels in the fatty tissues under the skin. The fatty tissue is sucked through the cannula. Following the surgery, a compression bandage has to be wrapped firmly around the area for about ten days, and support garments have to be worn for a further six weeks.

Many people suffer from bruising under the skin after suction lipectomy, and often the area becomes swollen. This leads to an uneven skin which may last for two or three months. Most people feel pain and discomfort following suction lipectomy.

Suction lipectomy is not a treatment for generalized obesity, but it may be useful to remove unsightly fatty deposits, particularly in people of normal weight. The best results occur if an experienced surgeon performs the procedure.

The physical and psychological benefits of weight reduction in gross obesity

In spite of the dangers of operations for gross obesity, in spite of complications which may follow surgery, in spite of the need for careful attention to diet, in spite of the need for vitamin and mineral supplements, and the need for frequent visits for 'follow-up', the choice must ultimately be that of the patient. There is no doubt of the physical benefits of weight reduction. Cardiac function improves and the level of

Table 20. The appropriate management of morbid obesity

Appropriate	Inappropriate
Low energy, nutritionally balanced diet for more than 6 months	Complex crazy fad diets
Moderate regular exercise	Excessive exercise with dieting
	Sauna baths
	Electric treatment
Supportive psychotherapy	
? Anorectic drugs (short-term: less than 4 months)	Diuretics
	Thyroid hormones
Surgery	
? Jaw-wiring	Jejuno–ileal bypass
Gastric reduction	Gastric balloon (bubble)

the blood pressure is reduced, which reduces the risk of a stroke. The blood circulation to the legs improves with reduction in thrombophlebitis. There is an improvement in pulmonary ventilation, with a reduction in shortness of breath. If the person has osteoarthritis, or low back pain, the severity of the pain is reduced. Following a significant reduction in weight there is an increase in energy and a reduction in fatigue.

The psychological benefits of surgical measures to achieve weight reduction have been less clearly delineated. As weight loss progresses, patients perceive their bodies more favourably and become more self-confident about their personality. The majority of women see themselves as more feminine and more sexually attractive; however, there is no change in the frequency of sexual activity or in sexual pleasure. They experience fewer mood changes and see themselves as more self-assured, outgoing, and comfortable. They become more sociable, less preoccupied by weight, and less likely to eat more than they intended at meals or between meals. In spite of these positive findings, many others still feel that they are large, and in psychological tests tend to over-estimate their body size.

These findings suggest that grossly obese people who have failed to reduce their weight significantly by dieting or perhaps jaw-wiring, or fail to maintain the lower weight, may benefit physically and psychologically from surgery, but must weigh up the advantages and disadvantages of the operations.

Summary of treatment of morbid obesity

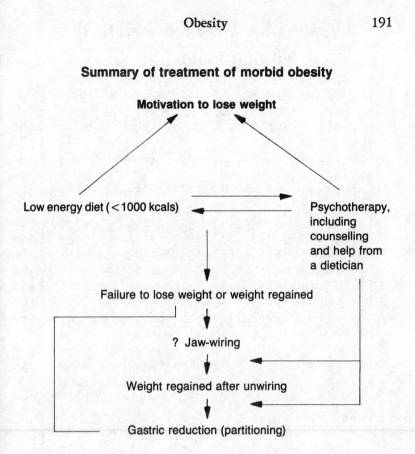

Motivation to lose weight

Low energy diet (<1000 kcals)

Psychotherapy, including counselling and help from a dietician

Failure to lose weight or weight regained

? Jaw-wiring

Weight regained after unwiring

Gastric reduction (partitioning)

Appendix: average weight of women aged 15–69

Average weight of women aged 15–69 (standard body weight)

Average weights in pounds and kilograms (in indoor clothing)

Women

Height (in shoes)		15–16 years		17–19 years		20–24 years		25–29 years		30–39 years		40–49 years		50–59 years		60–69 years	
ft in	cm	lb	kg	lb	kg	lb	kg	lb	kg	lb	kg	lb	kg	lb	kg	lb	kg
4 10	147.3	97	44	99	44.9	102	46.3	107	48.5	115	52.2	122	55.3	125	56.7	127	57.6
4 10½	148.6	98.5	44.7	100.5	45.6	103.5	46.9	108.5	49.2	116	52.6	123	55.8	126	57.2	128	58.1
4 11	149.9	100	45.4	102	46.3	105	47.6	110	49.9	117	53.1	124	56.2	127	57.6	129	58.5
4 11½	151.1	101.5	46	103.5	46.9	106.5	48.3	111.5	50.6	118.5	53.8	125.5	56.9	128.5	58.3	130	59
5 0	152.4	103	46.7	105	47.6	108	49	113	51.3	120	54.4	127	57.6	130	59	131	59.4
5 0½	153.7	105	47.6	107	48.5	110	49.9	114.5	51.9	121.5	55.1	128.5	58.3	131.5	59.6	132.5	60.1
5 1	154.9	107	48.5	109	49.4	112	50.8	116	52.6	123	55.8	130	59	133	60.3	134	60.8
5 1½	156.2	109	49.4	111	50.3	113.5	51.5	117.5	53.3	124.5	56.5	131.5	59.6	134.5	61	135.5	61.5
5 2	157.5	111	50.3	113	51.3	115	52.2	119	54	126	57.2	133	60.3	136	61.7	137	62.1
5 2½	158.8	112.5	51	114.5	51.9	116.5	52.8	120.5	54.7	127.5	57.8	134.5	61	138	62.6	139	63
5 3	160	114	51.7	116	52.6	118	53.5	122	55.3	129	58.5	136	61.7	140	63.5	141	64
5 3½	161.3	115.5	52.4	118	53.5	119.5	54.2	123.5	56	130.5	59.2	138	62.6	142	64.4	143	64.9
5 4	162.6	117	53.1	120	54.4	121	54.9	125	56.7	132	60	140	63.5	144	65.3	145	65.8
5 4½	163.8	119	54	122	55.3	123	55.8	127	57.6	133.5	60.6	141.5	64.2	146	66.2	147	66.7
5 5	165.1	121	54.9	124	56.2	125	56.7	129	58.5	135	61.2	143	64.9	148	67.1	149	67.6
5 5½	166.4	123	55.8	125.5	56.9	127	57.6	131	59.4	137	62.1	145	65.8	150	68	151	68.5
5 6	167.6	125	56.7	127	57.6	129	58.5	133	60.3	139	63	147	66.7	152	68.9	153	69.4
5 6½	168.9	126.5	57.4	128.5	58.3	130.5	59.2	134.5	61	140.5	63.7	149	67.6	154	69.9	155	70.3
5 7	170.2	128	58.1	130	59	132	59.9	136	61.7	142	64.4	151	68.5	156	70.8	157	71.2
5 7½	171.5	130	59	132	59.9	134	60.8	138	62.6	144	65.3	153	69.4	158	71.7	159	72.1
5 8	172.7	132	59.9	134	60.8	136	61.7	140	63.5	146	66.2	155	70.3	160	72.6	161	73
5 8½	174	134	60.8	136	61.7	138	62.6	142	64.4	148	67.1	157	71.2	162	73.5	163	73.9
5 9	175.3	136	61.7	138	62.6	140	63.5	144	65.3	150	68	159	72.1	164	74.4	165	74.8
5 9½	176.5	—	—	140	63.5	142	64.4	146	66.2	152	68.9	161.5	73.3	166.5	75.5	—	—
5 10	177.8	—	—	142	64.4	144	65.3	148	67.1	154	69.9	164	74.4	169	76.7	—	—
5 10½	179.1	—	—	144.5	65.5	146.5	66.5	150.5	68.3	156.5	71	166.5	75.5	171.5	77.8	—	—
5 11	180.3	—	—	147	66.7	149	67.6	153	69.4	159	72.1	169	76.7	174	78.9	—	—
5 11½	181.6	—	—	149.5	67.8	151.5	68.7	155.5	70.5	161.5	73.3	171.5	77.8	177	80.3	—	—
6 0	182.9	—	—	152	68.9	154	69.9	158	71.7	164	74.4	174	78.9	180	81.6	—	—

1) Insured persons in the United States. From Society of Actuaries, Build and Blood Pressure Study, vol. I, Chicago, 1959, page 16, with interpolations by the editors of these Scientific Tables. The average body weight and percentage deviations used in this book were derived from the above table. Recently the average body weight for height and age has been increased both in Great Britain and the USA and new tables are expected. The change does not alter the arguments made here, and further emphasizes that, to look fashionably slim, most young women diet.

Further reading

Bruch, Hilda. *Eating disorders, obesity, anorexia nervosa and the person within.* Routledge Kegan Paul, London (1974) and *The golden cage.* Open Books, Somerset (1978).

Before writing this book Hilda Bruch had been involved in treatment of people with eating disorders for 40 years. She believes that people develop an eating disorder to avoid having to cope with an aspect of their life. She stresses that treatment must be individual and that the aim is not only to restore normal eating behaviour but to ensure the happiness of the 'person within'.

Crisp, A. *Anorexia nervosa—Let me be.* Academic Press, London (1980).

Crisp's theory is that young women develop anorexia nervosa because they seek to return to being a child biologically and, in many ways, socially and psychologically. They fear the challenges of adolescence, with its maturative and sexual connotations.

Dally, P. and Gomez, J. *Obesity and anorexia nervosa—A question of shape.* Faber, London (1990).

This book gives an outline of the problem of eating disorders, and describes the ways in which treatment is undertaken. Written for the general reader it gives much information in a clear concise way.

Palmer, R.L. *Anorexia nervosa—A guide for sufferers and their families.* Penguin, Harmondsworth (1989).

Trained at St. George' Medical School, Palmer supports Crisp's view that anorexia nervosa is due to a psychobiological regression to childhood. Written for the general reader, the book acquaints sufferers from anorexia nervosa and their families of the possibilities for treatment and of the probable outcomes.

Garfinkle, P.E. and Garner, D.M. *Anorexia nervosa, a multidimensional perspective.* Brunner Mazel, New York (1983).

This is an excellent book, written for health professionals. The extensive literature about anorexia nervosa, and anorexia nervosa with bulimia nervosa episodes, is critically evaluated. The many studies made by the Toronto group are reported and placed in perspective. The book is written in lucid English and integrates the physiological, psychological, and clinical aspects of a complex, multi-dimensional eating disorder.

Garrow, J.S. *Treat obesity seriously*. Churchill-Livingstone, Edinburgh (1988).

Dr Garrow has headed a research group into nutritional problems for some years and has written extensively about obesity. This book is designed to help general practitioners and general (fat?) readers understand the biological problems associated with obesity. A personal account, it gives an excellent review of the problems and of treatment strategies.

Glossary

Adipose tissue

The tissues of the body which contain numbers of fat cells. Adipose tissue is 80 per cent fat, 2 per cent protein, and 18 per cent water. Because of the large proportion of fat, adipose tissue is often called fatty tissue.

Alkalosis

An increase in the alkalinity of the blood, which normally is slightly acid. It is usually due to an increase in the level of bicarbonate in the blood.

Amenorrhoea

The cessation or absence of menstruation for more than 3 months.

Anastomose

To join together two hollow tubes; in this case to join the stomach to the intestine.

Anorexia nervosa

See p. 18 for definition.

Anovulation

Lack of ovulation over a period of months.

Average Body Weight (ABW)

The average body weight for age, height, and weight. (The tables are shown in the Appendix p. 192.).

Bariatric physician

A doctor who specializes in treating obesity.

Behaviour therapy

A psychological therapy based on experimental psychology, intended to change symptoms and behaviour by various techniques, for example, anxiety management training, assertiveness training, aversion therapy, biofeedback, and desensitization.

Biceps

The muscle extending from the shoulder to the elbow joint, on the front surface of the arm.

Body Mass Index (BMI)

A measure devised over 100 years ago to determine whether a person is of normal weight, underweight, or obese. The calculation is made in the following way:

$$\frac{\text{Weight in kilograms}}{\text{Height in metres} \times \text{Height in metres}};$$

for example, a woman aged 24 weighs 46 kg and is 1.57 metres tall:

$$46 \div 1.57 \times 1.57 = 18.6$$

The index of 18.6 indicates that she is underweight.

Bulimia nervosa

See p. 22 for definition.

Calories

A lay term for kilocalories (see entry for kilocalories).

Carbohydrates

The class of nutrients made up of starches and sugars. Carbohydrates provide the main source of energy needed for the human body to function. Starches are the most common form of dietary carbohydrate, and are found in cereal grains, roots, and tubers. In the human gut starches are broken down to sugars, finally to glucose, which is absorbed into the blood.

Chorionic gonadotrophin

A hormone derived from the placenta which was used to treat obesity. Also known as human chorionic gonadotrophin, or HCG.

Cognitive behaviour therapy

Psychological therapy intended to change maladaptive ways of thinking and thereby bring about improvement in psychological disorders. In other words, a technique used to help people think differently so that they will behave differently.

Diuretics

Drugs which act on the kidney to increase the flow of urine.

Electrolytes

A substance which, dissolved in water, separates into electrically charged particles (ions) capable of conducting an electrical current.

Flatus

'Wind' or gas accumulated in the bowel and expelled through the anus (back passage).

Follicle-stimulating hormone (FSH)

A hormone secreted by the pituitary gland that stimulates the growth of the egg follicles in the ovary and the development of sperm in the testis.

Gastroplasty

An operation on the stomach in which a small section is 'partitioned', so that the size of the stomach is effectively reduced.

Glycogen

The form in which sugars and starches are stored in animals. Sucrose and starches from plants are converted into glucose before being absorbed into the human body from the gut, and the glucose is converted into glycogen for storage in the liver and in muscle.

Gonadotrophin
A substance, usually a hormone, capable of stimulating the ovaries or the testicles (trophin means growth).

Gonadotrophic releasing hormone (GnRH)
A substance secreted by the hypothalamus which is carried by blood-vessels to the pituitary gland to stimulate the production and release of the gonadotrophic hormones.

Haematemesis
Bloody vomit.

Hypertension
High blood pressure.

Hypothalamus
The part of the brain just above the brain-stem which controls the activity of the pituitary gland.

Ketosis
An accumulation of excessive amounts of chemical compounds in the tissues, which produces acidity in the body tissues and fluids.

Kilojoule
Measure of energy, which has replaced the kilocalorie. One kilojoule = 0.24 kilocalories.

Kilocalorie
A kilocalorie (also called Kcalories, Kcals, or calories) is a measure of the energy in foods. It is defined as the amount of heat required to raise the temperature of a litre of water from 15 °C to 16 °C. Each food contains a different amount of energy, which is absorbed into the body after eating and expended to keep the body functioning. Recently kcals have been replaced by a new energy measurement called a kilojoule 1 kcal = 4.19 kJ.

Lanugo
Soft, downy hair, similar to that found in small babies.

Laxatives
Drugs which act on the bowel to increase the speed of the passage of food and of the stools through the gut. They cause soft and frequent motions.

Libido
A person's sexual desire, arousal, and awareness.

Luteinizing hormone (LH)
A hormone secreted by and released from the pituitary gland which leads to the release of a mature egg (or ovum) from an ovarian follicle and

converts the follicle into a corpus luteum (or yellow body).

Megajoule   This is a measure of energy in foods, or expended by the body. 1 megajoule (MJ) = 1000 kilojoule (kJ) = 239 kcals.

Menarche   The onset of menstruation.

Millilitre (ml)   Equivalent to 0.035 fluid ounces.

Obesity   See p. 26 for definition.

Osteomalacia   Thinning of the bones.

Peristalsis   The wave-like progressive, sequential movement of the wall of the intestines which churns up food and moves it on towards the anus.

Picking behaviour   Moving from food in cupboard, to pantry, to fridge, to pick and eat small quantities of various foods.

Pituitary gland   The gland located at the base of the brain that affects the function of other glands by releasing special hormones.

Placebo   A harmless substance administered to test the effectiveness of an active substance in a scientific study.

Quetelet Index   See Body Mass Index.

Resistance behaviour   Behaviour used as methods of stopping abnormal eating patterns.

Satiety (Satiation)   The feeling of 'fullness' after eating food.

Steatorrhoea   Offensive, loose, 'fatty' stools.

Suprailiac   The region of the body just above the pelvic bones which identifies a person's waist.

Triceps   The muscle on the back of the upper arm.

Venous thrombosis   A clot in a vein.

Index